D0583915

MERCHANTS OF THE RIGHT

MERCHANTS OF THE RIGHT

GUN SELLERS AND THE CRISIS OF AMERICAN DEMOCRACY

JENNIFER CARLSON

PRINCETON UNIVERSITY PRESS

PRINCETON AND OXFORD

Published by Princeton University Press
41 William Street, Princeton, New Jersey 08540
99 Banbury Road, Oxford OX2 6JX

press.princeton.edu

All Rights Reserved

Library of Congress Cataloging-in-Publication Data

Names: Carlson, Jennifer, author.
Title: Merchants of the right : gun sellers and the crisis of American democracy / Jennifer Carlson.
Description: Princeton, New Jersey : Princeton University Press, [2023] | Includes bibliographical references and index.
Identifiers: LCCN 2022029527 (print) | LCCN 2022029528 (ebook) | ISBN 9780691230399 (hardback ; alk. paper) | ISBN 9780691230382 (ebook)
Subjects: LCSH: Firearms ownership—Political aspects—United States. | Democracy—United States. | Conservatism—United States. | Right-wing extremists—United States. | Polarization (Social sciences)—United States. | BISAC: SOCIAL SCIENCE / Violence in Society | SOCIAL SCIENCE / Sociology / General
Classification: LCC HV8059 .C3727 2023 (print) | LCC HV8059 (ebook) | DDC 363.330973—dc23/eng/20221011
LC record available at https://lccn.loc.gov/2022029527
LC ebook record available at https://lccn.loc.gov/2022029528

British Library Cataloging-in-Publication Data is available

Editorial: Meagan Levinson and Erik Beranek
Production Editorial: Terri O'Prey
Text Design: Karl Spurzem
Jacket and Cover Design: Karl Spurzem
Production: Erin Suydam
Publicity: Kate Hensley and Kathryn Stevens
Copyeditor: Karen Verde

Jacket image: Brandon Bourdages / Shutterstock

This book has been composed in Arno Pro

Printed on acid-free paper. ∞

Printed in the United States of America

10 9 8 7 6 5 4 3 2 1

For those looking to shatter the looking glass.
And for my father, Steven Carlson.

CONTENTS

PREFACE

Born in 1951, my father grew up with the contemporary conservative movement, and in many ways, he's been the implicit driver of my own interest in US conservative politics. My dad took the rightward path throughout his life—to the point of cliché. With a letter of endorsement from Donald Rumsfeld, my father matriculated at West Point Military Academy. After completing his military service, he attended the University of Chicago and earned an MBA in the 1980s, just as the school became known for its global export of libertarian economic theories (hence the term "Chicago Boys" to describe Latin American economists who rose to prominence in Pinochet's neoliberal regime). He would spend the rest of his life rising to the top of corporate America and eventually retiring as a chief officer of a multibillion-dollar, multinational corporation. As a young husband and father, he eagerly followed Reagan's rise, writing letters to the editor and posing with Republican campaign signs for photographs that would populate our family albums. A devout Catholic, my dad's traditionalist politics aligned more and more with the party that was capturing Evangelicals dismayed at the moral disintegration they saw in sexual promiscuity, gay marriage, and legal abortion—all troubling developments, as they saw it, endorsed by liberals.

I came along in 1982, as the Reagan Revolution roared. My dad raised me to think of the "Democrats" as "Democraps" and told me that one "votes for the party, not for the person." As a young child, I remember asking my dad about the difference between the political parties—it seemed so important to him, after all, that I thought I should know. He replied with a logic appropriate for my age, but not his: "the Republicans are the good guys, the Democrats are the bad guys." My mother was not amused. As I developed my own political ideas, our political conversations rarely made it beyond that level of analysis—and often ended in screaming matches if I pushed too far. One of my last memories of talking politics with my dad took place when I was home from my liberal arts college on the East Coast; Bush had been elected, the War on Terror had been declared, and as I remember it, I was trying to get my dad to acknowledge that civilian casualties were part of air strikes and other acts of martial violence—surely, as I grasped for an example, Israelis had killed innocent Palestinians even if their intent wasn't so. With that comment, I had pushed too far; my dad called me a "terrorist."

That was the last time I attempted to deliberately and directly engage him in a conversation about politics. I knew at that point that there would always be a part of my father that was inscrutable for reasons I didn't, and at the time couldn't, understand. After all, I wasn't yet a sociologist; I failed to grasp how my personal challenges—my inability to communicate "civilly" with my father about politics—reflected not just the idiosyncrasies of my dad's style of politics or my own poor handling of sensitive topics or even our sometimes-explosive interpersonal dynamic but rather a more profound division in politics that would fester, and then erupt, over the years. The divide left me with a twofold loss: I lost the opportunity to understand my dad's politics, and I also lost the expectation that he would ever care to understand mine, as tentative and naïve as my politics might have been.

The Obama years felt newly divisive, introducing a brash brand of political incivility that worked its way from the halls of Congress to American dinner tables and back again. Going home to my conservative Midwestern family, traveling now from the other coast where I was attending graduate school at UC Berkeley, felt like an ethnographic encounter every time I stepped into my parents' home, with FoxNews dependably clamoring as background noise and my dad occasionally ranting about this or that political injury inflicted by Democrats onto Republicans. Though my dad cared deeply about education (he was the one, after all, who encouraged me to pursue the very education that would put us at loggerheads), and though he himself was a student of history, of economics, and of military strategy, he seemed less and less driven by the intellectual side of politics and more driven by its emotional tenor. Despite Trump's makeshift intellectual aptitude, his cowardly military background, his crass sexism, his flagrant disregard for the Republican Party as an institution—all things that I thought that conservatives like my dad would have found disqualifying—my dad gravitated to Trump's bravado. He had recently been diagnosed with ALS, abruptly retiring from the top of the corporate ladder he had spent his whole life climbing and moving to Arizona to live out the last three years of his life, yet my dad still managed to vote absentee one last time in Michigan, where his vote counted much more than it would had he cast it in Arizona: indeed, it helped ensure the razor-thin margin that edged Michigan Republican Red for Trump's presidential victory in 2016.

On the day that Trump was elected, I was angry that my father couldn't see the consequences of his vote. But at the same time, neither could I—because I still hadn't quite comprehended my dad, much less the political territory he inhabited. His ALS diagnosis was the final barrier to ever really understanding him. The urgency of impending death made talk of politics inane, and as his days diminished under the weight of disease, my father showed more interest in baseball scores and stock prices than keeping up with Trump. Had he not been sick, though, would he have rallied alongside Trump and all he came to stand for since his election in 2016? Would I have become a "socialist" in his eyes for pointing out that children were being separated from their families on the US–Mexico border? Would he have cheered on Trump's undiplomatic behavior with foreign officials—and embraced Trump's chummy relationship with Vladimir Putin? Would he have entertained the damning accounts of Democrats as murderers, Satanists, and pedophiles—and maybe even become a follower of Q? As 2020 unfolded a year after my dad left us, I found myself wondering relentlessly: Would my dad think coronavirus was a hoax, and public health measures a sham? Would he see the Black Lives Matter rallies as paid-off protesters, duped into believing that rioting and looting could change the world? Would he have rallied around efforts to delegitimize democratic elections in the hopes of securing a win for the Republicans—and eventually even believe that Biden stole the election?

Whether or not he *would have*, plenty of conservatives in the United States *did*. I write this book to understand—from the perspective of conservatives—the politics of 2020 and their consequences. It focuses on gun sellers as merchants of conservative thought to make sense of how right-wing values were pursued in 2020 through a tying together of armed individualism, conspiracism, and partisanship. By examining the politics of gun rights as a microcosm of the US Right, this book reminds us why arguing about specific political points feels so futile—because often it is. Our interest in unbiased evaluation of policy-related evidence is meaningless when our basic political coordinates—how we find and hold onto a sense of security, how we know what we know, and how we relate to the different people with whom we share this society, whether or not they agree with us—are so vastly at odds. I learned that the last time I talked politics with my dad years ago, and I learned it again in 2020.

July 2022
Tucson, Arizona

MERCHANTS OF THE RIGHT

Introduction: Democracy Disarmed

In late May 2020, I placed a call to Robert (a pseudonym),[1] a thirty-something white Florida gun store owner still reeling from the surge in gun sales amid the outbreak of the coronavirus pandemic. The surge had started some time in March, and it started suddenly. One day it was business as usual, and the next day sales were on fire, lines were out the door, shelves were cleared, and phone lines were ringing with people desperately looking for any gun—any *handgun or shotgun*—that they could get their hands on. As Robert saw it, the surge was different from previous panic buys: more first-time gun owners, more women, more couples, more elderly people, more people of color, more LGBTQ-identified people. Enthusiastic about ever-more gun buyers, Robert was also apprehensive about the "liberal" gun buyers now in his store: "We've had a lot of people openly expressing the fact that they are in disbelief that they'd ever be purchasing a firearm, and here they are! . . . I've had people say 'I've been voting against these things [guns] for my entire life' . . . [Or they'll say] 'What do you mean a three-day wait?' I tell them [sarcastically], 'this is common sense gun control, isn't it?'"

Coronavirus—and the social, economic, and political precarity that followed in 2020—opened up the floodgates of American firearm demand. Many found that they suddenly needed a gun, but few—at least when I talked to Robert—really knew how to make sense of it all. For his part, Robert fit coronavirus into his broader skepticism surrounding American politics. He blithely moved from questioning whether 9/11 was an "inside job" to wondering whether coronavirus came from a "Wuhan lab" with "an American scientist, American backers, American funding." In a show of profound skepticism, his statements were phrased as questions ("Did the virus come from the Wuhan lab? Did they release the virus intentionally in China? Did they let it spread and keep misinformation, and keep this quiet, and that way they could use it as an opportunity to quash the protests in their country?"). And his answers were equally equivocating ("That's something that you will never know the answer to 100 percent . . . Who the hell knows?"). Robert seemed sure about only one thing: "The possibility for a conspiracy is extremely large. The thing is, people who were conspiracy theorists five, ten years ago are now right."

Perhaps Robert wasn't all that interested in the answers, though. While he waxed on about the media's misreporting of not just COVID-19 deaths but also crime and civil unrest, not once did he mention wanting to know the concrete numbers or express a desire to firm up the facts. He didn't grope and grasp for truth. Instead, he saw that distinguishing truth from fiction was a fool's errand. Coronavirus had turned truth-seekers into dupes: Robert ridiculed the people following mask ordinances or relying on contactless delivery to keep them safe because no one really knew whether any of it mattered: "you are [just] putting a trash bag on a nuclear reactor . . . it's all pointless." Though I interviewed him before Black Lives Matter protests seized the nation to demand accountability for police violence and racial injustice, the skepticism he voiced about coronavirus echoed how other gun sellers talked about the uprisings for racial justice in the summer of 2020. They wagered that the Black Lives Matter protests might be a political hoax, they could be a terrorist element, but they most definitely were an opening for power-hungry elites—after all, they wondered, what else could explain their sudden spread? To Robert and other gun sellers, clinging to facts was political infantilism; in contrast to what they saw as obsequious deference to elites in the media, government, or science, skepticism amid uncertainty was a politically mature stance, an act of courage.

Throughout our conversation, Robert moved nimbly between armed individualism (particularly the eminence of guns in everyday life as instruments of safety and security), conspiracism (in its most skeptical form), and partisanship (not just regarding disagreements about policy or ideology but also regarding basic faith in the integrity and capacities of one's political opponents). But as I listened to him, I realized that these pillars of conservative thinking were more than mere ideologies, worldviews, or frameworks. At this moment of social uncertainty, these themes served as *tools* for Robert and other gun sellers I met during 2020, who *used* them to build conservative culture from the ground up. Armed individualism, conspiracism, and partisanship allowed Robert and others to locate a sense of control amid chaos, tame the cacophony of divergent opinions and divisive rhetoric, and ultimately provide them with a sense of their own standing as good citizens amid a country they believed had gone astray. As Robert told me, "I've been using the words 'fake news' for a while now, for both sides of the aisle. And I think that [fake news] has caused the uncertainty, and when you have uncertainty, you have to have a guarantee, and the only guarantee in this country is the right to protect yourself." In a world of hidden agendas, of abridged rights, of chaos, panic, and uncertainty, no one—in Robert's view, at least—could argue with the barrel of a gun.

The Spirit of January 6th

A half-year later, I couldn't help but think back to my conversation with Robert. It was January 6, 2021, the day that a violent right-wing mob rushed the Capitol Building as the US Congress met to certify the election results that confirmed Joe Biden as 46th president of the United States and Donald Trump the loser. Throughout his 2016 election campaign and subsequent term as president, Trump had relentlessly pushed the envelope on democratic norms: rampant attacks on free speech, the endorsement of violence as legitimate political expression, interference with the judiciary, and open praise for anti-democratic leaders like Vladimir Putin—to name just a few examples. And then came January 6th. In the weeks before that day, Trump and his supporters had orchestrated a multipronged, desperate, and largely failed attempt to overturn the election results. They filed countless lawsuits. They pressured state officials to fraudulently change election results. They engaged in a disinformation campaign that sowed distrust not just in the electoral results but also in the electoral process itself.[2] Various organized factions of the Right—from the Republican Party to the Oath Keepers—undertook proactive roles in spreading the lie that not only had Trump won the election, but that the election had been stolen through the coordinated efforts of election officials working in cahoots with the Democratic Party.

As many as 2,500[3] people entered the US Capitol on January 6, 2021, in opposition to the election results that would be certified that day. In all likelihood, many of those gathered that day may well have believed that they were not democracy's detractors but rather its last line of defense—and that their patriotic actions were necessary to save America. Unable to fathom the more than 81 million people[4] who cast their vote for Joe Biden, they were convinced that the election had been stolen from them and that it was their patriotic duty to "stop the steal." To wit, a rioter, facing federal charges in the aftermath of January 6th, tearfully explained his decision to come to Washington, DC: "He [Trump] was the commander-in-chief and the leader of our country . . . And he was calling for help! I thought he was calling for help! . . . I thought I was doing the right thing."[5] They were die-hard Trump supporters; many were taken in by QAnon, Pizzagate, and other loosely coherent "big tent conspiracy" theories that encouraged skepticism at all costs. Others were confederate flag-carrying white supremacists who saw in Trump an ally who was in the top office of American political power, and they were committed by any means necessary to keep him there. And then there were those who wanted—perhaps as part of the "Boogaloo movement"—to cause chaos and undermine law and order on principle. One participant, who eventually pled guilty to two federal crimes, posted that morning on social media: "What [do] patriots do? We f—n' disarm them and then we storm the f—n' Capitol."[6]

Outside the US Capitol that day, the rioters espoused slogans like "Come and Take It" and "Don't Tread on Me." They taunted members of the Democratic Party with a noose. They called for an end to the impending communist state that they believed Joe Biden would enact. They yelled racial epithets at law enforcement officers of color, revealing the limits of the strong support among conservatives for Blue Lives Matter. But some police and rioters posed for selfies together; in one video, one officer appeared to open the gate that would allow a flood of rioters into the Capitol Building; and one officer on the scene of the invaded Capitol Building explained the seemingly relaxed approach of law enforcement by saying, "We just got to let them do their thing for now."[7]

But violent expression soon begat physical violence. The rioters joined a long, if too often forgotten, history of white Americans justifying violence in the name of patriotism and democracy. They smashed windows and broke in doors as politicians fled from harm's way. While the quick thinking of Capitol police officer Eugene Goodman, who directed the mob away from the Senate Chamber, likely prevented untold casualties, others were not so fortunate. Protesters beat Officer Brian D. Sicknick, who died as a result;[8] roughly 140 officers were injured in what the *New York Times* called "one of the worst days of injuries for law enforcement in the United States since the Sept. 11, 2001, terrorist attacks."[9] Ransacking, defacing, and destroying the Capitol Building, more than 800 rioters were charged with federal crimes by May 2022.[10]

As I watched the insurrection unfold through the live YouTube broadcasts posted by the rioters themselves, and as I listened to the frightened voices of reporters on the major broadcast networks, I wondered whether Robert or the other gun sellers I had talked to during 2020 were there. They had certainly raised the specter of a stolen election. They had been open with their conspiracist views (even as they predicated them with the disclaimer that "I'm not a conspiracy theorist, but . . ."). They talked about the possibility of another civil war—or knew people who did. They could have been there, even if they weren't; indeed, many more millions of Americans—judging from the 74 million votes Trump received—shared some sympathies with the rioters.[11] And in a sense the gun sellers already *were* there; as merchants of guns, gun culture, and gun politics, they helped build conservative culture from the ground up, reinforcing and at times reworking the top-down rhetoric promulgated by conservative pundits and politicians.

Within days of the insurrection, public debate across the political spectrum converged on a few explanations of what had happened: many (largely on the Left) saw the work of a dedicated cadre of right-wing and white supremacist extremists; some (largely on the Right) saw the machinations of an infiltrating cell of left-wing and Black Lives Matter extremists; and still many others (across the political spectrum, though less so on the Right) saw the expected outcome of Trump's conspiracist lies and distortions that had emboldened people over the last four years to engage in anti-democratic action. But as the dust settled over the course of 2021 and into 2022, the Republican Party and conservative Americans at large have generally agreed that the event represented legitimate, even patriotic, political expression.[12] Chalking up the riot as a one-off instance of extremism, or believing that it was entirely Trump's fault (and addressed by simply removing Trump from the office of the presidency), misreads the message of the January 6th insurrection and the underlying politics it reflects. The rioters represented not an isolated, tiny fringe, but a broader political spirit—an embittered remixing of the Spirit of '76, a term that captures the nostalgic romanticizing of patriotism and self-determination in the wake of the American Revolutionary War. Watching January 6th and its aftermath unfold, I found it was too easy to dismiss it as a reflection of the brazen lawlessness of fringe individuals instigated by Trump. The Spirit of January 6th reflected deep attachments to gun rights, conspiracist thinking, and extreme partisanship, and listening to gun sellers navigate 2020, I knew that the insurrection was a culmination of an everyday politics, shared by many conservatives, that would persist with or without Trump in office.

The Great Run on Guns

Amid a once-in-a-century pandemic, civil unrest, and a teetering democracy, American life felt on the brink of breakdown. This feeling was very evident in the surging appeal of guns—and their seeming capacity to serve, as Robert said, as a "guarantee." In 2020, millions of people in the United States—including up to 8.4 million new gun owners[13]—bought nearly 23 million guns.[14] Strikingly, these purchasers didn't fit the mold of the "typical" gun owner: a conservative, white, straight male who already owned guns. In their shops, gun sellers noticed different clientele breaking this mold in one way or another. Some saw an increase in new African American and Asian American gun owners. Others remarked on the women and families. Some gun sellers noted members of the LGBTQ community coming to buy guns. And then there were the liberals, who never thought they "really needed" a gun—until 2020. They, collectively, appeared to adjudicate a long-standing mantra of radical equality, premised on the firearm, within American gun culture: "God created people, but Samuel Colt [the gun manufacturer] made them equal." But just as sales data were demonstrating the mass appeal of guns well beyond the NRA-stylized gun owner, sectors of American gun culture—and American conservative politics more generally— became more acrimonious and insular, and more divisive and defensive, than ever. As a precarious moment for US democracy, did the surge in gun sales represent a new, democratizing moment for gun rights—or a retrenchment of a decades-long campaign to position gun rights as a key element of American conservative politics? What might the politics of gun rights in 2020 tell us—about conservative politics and about American democracy more generally?

In *Firepower*, political scientist Matthew Lacombe argues that the forging of a "social identity built around gun ownership" and a "political ideology that connects gun rights with a range of other issue stances and beliefs"[15] on the Right has been one of the most consequential achievements of the National Rifle Association. In large part because of the NRA's efforts in shaping American gun culture as a conservative phenomenon, to be a gun owner has come to mean something above and beyond simply owning a gun.[16] Gun ownership has come to represent the embrace of a particular ethic of security (i.e., guns as a bulwark against victimization), a particular understanding of freedom (i.e., guns as a vehicle of individual rights), and a particular stance against the state (i.e., guns as a defense against government control and liberal indoctrination).[17] The millions of new gun owners threatened that gun owner identity and the gun-centric worldview it fostered—as did the very uncertainties that overtook 2020. This book examines how American gun culture was defended as conservative terrain in that tumultuous context—and how novel, and at times illiberal, understandings of democracy were forged in the process.

Rather than looking to the NRA, the Republican Party, or other macro-level actors, I take a bottom-up perspective by centering people positioned on the front lines of one key arena of conservative politics: gun sellers. Gun sellers are merchants not just of guns but also of conservative gun culture. They are uniquely positioned to understand shifts in who is buying guns and why; they are acutely attuned to how gun rights are articulated on the ground through their conservative politics—and vice versa; and they are themselves invested in promoting gun rights as both a personal and professional matter. And, in my sample of interviewees, they are overwhelmingly and committedly conservative. Reflecting and reproducing gun rights as an economic enterprise, a political agenda, and a cultural practice, gun sellers are ideal interlocutors to make better sense of conservative politics during 2020.

In what follows, I listen closely to gun sellers to understand, at the level of everyday politics, how gun rights have been mobilized as conservative firepower (to borrow Lacombe's phrasing) and with what consequences for American democracy. I focus on three civic tools to illuminate how the foundations of conservative politics are built through everyday politics and practices. *Armed individualism* tames the messiness of American democracy (and all that it entails) into individualized problems of safety and security, and it situates the gun not just as a primary means of personal protection but also as a key vehicle of political empowerment. *Conspiracism* cultivates an ethic of skepticism to speak to the gulf—always wide, even in democratic societies— between the rulers and the ruled, but in the process, it pulverizes the possibilities for shared truths necessary for democratic consensus. *Partisanship* sequesters the potential for political disagreement to generate a more engaged citizenry and a more responsive government; instead, partisanship justifies the denigration and even dehumanization of political opponents, casting doubt on their worthiness to engage in politics at all. This civic toolkit—armed individualism, conspiracism, and partisanship—carves out a distinctive brand of conservative political culture, deepening the fault lines that run through American democracy. The result is not just a retrenchment of one of the gun lobby's most valuable resources—gun owners—as champions of conservative politics, but also a hollowing out of liberal democracy as a consensus-based, justice-oriented, and equality-driven mode of politics. By exploring the puzzle of not *why* but rather *how* many gun rights proponents remained deeply wedded to a conservative agenda, it helps illuminate the underlying processes by which many conservative Americans have retreated from liberal democracy, and with what consequences.

How Guns Turned Right

Gun rights are not inherently a cause célèbre of the conservative Right.[18] Up until the mid-twentieth century, gun policy positions were not intrinsically divided by party lines or between liberal and conservative ideologies, and there was no such thing as "the gun lobby" as we understand it today. Guns were not a broad-based political issue in themselves, nor a potent political "dog whistle" that could signal, for example, a political candidate's broader agenda regarding race.[19] But since the 1960s, gun politics has become a more and more divisive issue in American politics, as people—particularly on the gun rights side—have increasingly centered their political identities on gun politics.[20] Today gun rights are overwhelmingly associated with conservative politics and the Republican Party, and pro-gun rights Americans are disproportionately likely to be white men living in rural and suburban America, and they are also disproportionately likely to embrace conservative ideologies, such as Christian nationalism.[21] No matter a person's views on women's rights, civil rights, the economy, welfare, crime policy, or any other issue, their stance on gun regulations has increasingly defined party allegiance, sorting strident gun rights advocates—politicians and voters—into the Republican Party.[22] To understand this shift, we must first understand how the NRA transformed itself into a partisan organization—and gun rights into a conservative issue—in the second half of the twentieth century.

We can start the story in the 1960s. In that decade, crime spikes, high-profile assassinations, mass protests, riots, and surges in armed groups across the political spectrum galvanized a profound turn in the racial politics of the United States. Americans broadly responded to the social unrest of the 1960s with calls for law and order that would pathologize urban African Americans as the progenitors of subversive politics and criminal activity.[23] Jim Crow might have been crumbling in the South under the pressure of the Civil Rights movement, but what would replace it—the system of mass incarceration that legal scholar Michelle Alexander[24] would call the "New Jim Crow"—was already beginning to take shape. Whether explicitly aimed at disarming Black Power groups (such as California's Mulford Act of 1967) or galvanized by the problem of urban crime that framed Black boys and men as violent criminals (such as the 1968 Gun Control Act), the embrace of gun regulation in the 1960s was intertwined with the broader criminalization of Blackness. But so was the turn to guns as objects of self-defense in that decade.[25] In the mid-1960s, the percentage of Americans who thought that handguns—the weapons of choice for both gun crime and self-defense *against* that gun crime—should be banned dropped below 50 percent for the first time and only dropped further in the decades to come.[26] While marginalized peoples—most famously, the Black Panthers—turned to guns as a means of self-defense and community protection from white supremacy, guns became an appealing solution to the problem of crime,[27] a problem that was increasingly imagined through the threat of what legal scholar Katheryn Russell-Brown[28] captures with the term "criminalblackman." The NRA colluded with these racial politics from both sides: not only did it infamously use, for example, images of rioting African Americans in its print materials to galvanize support for gun rights in the 1960s,[29] but it also supported gun laws—specifically, California's Mulford Act of 1967—clearly aimed at disarming politically organized African Americans while leaving well-armed their white counterparts in the Ku Klux Klan and other white supremacist and nativist groups.[30]

However, in contrast to its bombastic and self-assured rhetoric today, the NRA also wavered as it navigated the changing gun politics of the 1960s. Consider the 1968 Gun Control Act, which would restrict mail-order guns, ban felons from gun possession, and further empower the federal government to regulate firearms. The so-called sportsmen faction of the NRA, which included those gun owners who loved hunting and saw gun rights as compatible with some gun restrictions, had small but underwhelming grievances with the law. The law eventually passed without much opposition by the NRA[31]—much to the chagrin of the "hard-line" faction within the organization who viewed the law as a dangerous first step down a road to total gun confiscation.

In contrast to the sportsmen faction, this hard-line faction saw guns not merely as an all-American pastime but also as integral to the social, political, and moral well-being of the United States. Gun control was not an inconvenience but an anti-American, even conspiratorial, threat to undermine the United States from within. As longtime gun rights activist and former NRA lobbyist Neal Knox later reflected on the violent turmoil of the 1960s, "Is it possible that some of those incidents could have been created for the purpose of disarming the people of the free world? With drugs and evil intent, it's possible. Rampant paranoia on my part? Maybe. But there have been far too many coincidences to ignore."[32] Rather than negotiate "disarmament," Harlon Carter, another hard-line gun rights proponent, forged the stance that would characterize the NRA's platform for decades to come: "a simple concept—*no compromise. No gun legislation.*"[33]

By the late 1970s, the hard-line faction had ascended to NRA leadership. Carter was elected in 1977 to the NRA's Executive Vice Presidency, transforming the organization into the formidable leader of the gun lobby. Carter's NRA popularized the notion of the "slippery slope"—the argument that one small concession to gun regulations could lead, like the trickle that becomes a river, to a torrent of gun control that would eventually culminate in gun confiscation. Hard-line gun rights advocates saw conspiracy where others might have just seen compromise: the tyranny of gun control could be lurking around the corner of any gun-restrictive policy. Rather than compromise with gun control, the NRA rallied gun rights advocates to resist it by buying guns, voting for pro-gun politicians, supporting pro-gun judges and justices, and voicing their opposition to gun restrictions through petition and protest.

By the late twentieth century and into the twenty-first, the rhetoric continued to escalate. For its part, the NRA's leaders called federal agents "jack-booted thugs,"[34] and they argued that gun control advocacy represented "[a] hateful and bigoted war" and even a "cultural cleansing."[35] In doing so, the organization repeatedly emphasized the threats that everyday American gun owners (themselves disproportionately white men) faced from below (in the form of criminals) and from above (in the form of government control)—two threats that, as Angela Stroud notes in *Good Guys with Guns*, articulate white masculinity as precious, precarious, and persecuted. Reminding gun rights advocates that the Second Amendment was about securing gun rights but also about laying claim to American freedom more generally (after all, the NRA's magazine dedicated to the Second Amendment is titled *America's 1st Freedom*), NRA spokespeople decried the "violence of lies" promulgated by the Left as an existential threat to American freedom.[36] With liberal, leftist, and progressive politics framed as unwarranted attacks, vicious lies, and manipulative distortions, this divisive rhetoric undermined any chance of genuine engagement with one's political opponents or even with inconvenient facts. As political scientist Matthew Lacombe notes, "the NRA's identity-based appeals tend to rely on fear in a way that encourages polarization, discourages compromise, and—in some cases—advances conspiratorial views that are misleading and offensive."[37] Armed individualism, conspiracism, and partisanship animated the NRA's political reasoning, and as it turned out, this style of politics would inflect not just conservative gun rights politics but contemporary conservative politics more broadly.

Headed Right

Rather than being alone at sea, the National Rifle Association gained momentum from the rising tide of conservative politics in the second half of the twentieth century. The NRA's "no compromise" stance on gun rights resonated with the broad smattering of right-leaning Americans who would make up the various strands of contemporary conservative politics: evangelical Christians,[38] John Birch Society adherents, anticommunists, segregationists, free market libertarians, states rights activists, culture warriors with an aversion to feminism and gay rights, tax revolters, and so forth. Policy stances aside, these various factions were united by a shared "bunker mentality" that many mid-twentieth-century Americans adopted as they experienced the efforts to expand the rights and freedoms of racial minorities, sexual minorities, women, and other vulnerable groups within American society as a curtailment on their own rights and freedoms. Evangelicals rallied against the threat of communism by promoting "family values";[39] anti-integrationists shrouded their racism in a language of "rights, freedoms, and individualism";[40] free market libertarians advocated for union busting by celebrating free enterprise; gun rights advocates opposed the liberal establishment by railing against gun confiscation.

The histories of these different flanks of contemporary conservative politics reveal uncanny commonalities in how they understood the social threats they confronted and how they improvised responses. But perhaps this was not so uncanny: despite their apparent differences, each of these factions was galvanized by similar fears of displacement and drew upon widespread and deep-seated American tropes such as populism and producerism, which often validated traditional social arrangements, in response to those fears. Starting as early as the 1950s, conservative media activists and right-wing politicians reinforced[41] these sensibilities across different[42] segments of conservative politics by converging on a common enemy: the liberal elites who "coddle nonwhites, women, gay, criminals, and atheists."[43] The conviction that the liberal establishment had destroyed a once-great country injected contemporary conservative politics with a nostalgic "vision of the country's founding as a moment of perfection that they must attempt to restore," as sociologist Ruth Braunstein[44] describes the group of conservatives she studied. This conviction made it easy to reject bipartisanship[45] in favor of an all-or-nothing politics that celebrated conservatives as the only "real Americans"—an illiberal[46] move that broke with the pluralistic vision of the public sphere that had dominated politics in the post–World War II era.[47]

By the time Ronald Reagan was elected president in a landslide victory in 1980, the conservative movement had cohered into a national phenomenon united by disdain for liberal elites and their policies.

Government—and the liberal establishment that presumably controlled it—was framed as the primary problem facing middle-class Americans,[48] and whites (white women and especially white men) flocked to the Republican Party.[49] By the time Barack Obama was elected for his first presidential term in 2008, the Republican Party had largely abandoned attempts to grow the party's appeal beyond its base of white men. Instead, movements like the Tea Party and its supporters within the Republican Party attacked social welfare and entitlements for the "undeserving"—a pejorative category largely comprised of immigrants, racial minorities, and young people—in favor of political, social, and economic supports for the "hardworking" Americans who had earned their place in society and were being unduly harmed by liberal policies.[50] As religion scholar Anthea Butler[51] notes, the backlash to Obama's two-term presidency galvanized elements that had already long defined conservative politics: "a higher tolerance for conspiracy theories, hucksterism (Trump), and out-and-out grievances." By the time Trump became a successful candidate for the US presidency, the Republican Party had become the party of, by, and for white Americans.[52]

And yet, that story—while illuminating—is also too simplistic. At the level of everyday politics, the significance of race and racism in politics is often as slippery as it seems straightforward.[53] As legal scholar Ian Haney-Lopez[54] notes of conservative voters, "The overwhelming majority are decent folks quick to condemn naked racism. But this is a far cry from saying that racial fears do not motivate them." While Trump's bigotry was not a deal-breaker for Americans voting for him in 2016, neither is it clear that it was the primary driver for most voters—at least as they saw it. Rather, decades after the Civil Rights movement, white Americans too often remained "confused and conflicted"[55] regarding the politics of race. Further, while Trump himself welcomed his popularity among white supremacist groups and also supported policies that have targeted racial minorities, curtailed reproductive rights, and criminalized immigrants,[56] his failed 2020 bid for the presidency revealed not losses but small gains among racial minorities as compared to four years earlier. Trump's 2020 share fell short of several Republican candidates who proceeded him, but his platform nevertheless appealed to just under

a third of Asian and Asian American as well as Latinx voters.[57] This is a
sizable minority that likely reflects a mix of many factors: the appeal of
populism, the rejection of liberalism, growing dissatisfaction with socioeconomic decline, a widespread investment in nostalgia for a bygone
era of America, and perhaps also the fungibility of whiteness—or, at
least, honorary whiteness.[58]

Regardless of its Asian and Latinx supporters, the Republican Party
has largely bet on demobilizing the vote *outside* of their core base of white
Americans[59] while also galvanizing the vote *within* that base. In concert
with other arms of the contemporary conservative movement, the NRA
has been crucial in mobilizing what has become one of the Republican
Party's most precious assets: American gun owners, who have historically been disproportionately white conservative men.[60] And over the
years, the NRA and the Republican Party have grown closer not just in
substance but also in style—anticipating a populist conservative leader
like Donald Trump. Trump's elite-but-outsider status to the Washington
establishment, his brash bigotry, and his conspiracist thinking made
him an appealing conduit for the rage, frustration, and entitlement of
those beleaguered Americans who felt the country had been led astray
by liberal chicanery. Thus, while Trump's record on gun rights might
have been mixed (he, after all, supported a ban on assault weapons as
recently as 2000[61]), his political style aligned deeply with conservative
politics in general and conservative gun politics in particular. As Lacombe observes, "Trump's attacks on the media closely echoed decades
of NRA appeals in which the organization has derided the so-called
mainstream media for being phony, biased, and dishonest."[62]

Contemporary conservative politics should not be reduced to the
conservatives who support gun rights. But conservative gun politics are
an illuminating place to start if we want to understand contemporary
conservative politics and how these politics come to matter for the
people who embrace them. Accordingly, this book draws on in-depth
interviews with a particularly revealing group of conservative Americans:
gun sellers, who experienced 2020 as a year of record gun sales amid a
global pandemic, anti-racist uprisings and civil unrest, and democratic instability. Listening to gun sellers helps illuminate the broader conservative

movement that has shaped their political sensibilities by providing the civic tools they used to navigate their political realities. And in doing so, we can understand just how, and with what consequences, defending gun rights has become a means of doing democracy.

Defending Gun Rights, Doing Democracy

In the middle of 2021, I received a distressed email from Everytown for Gun Safety, an advocacy group for gun regulation, stating that the "NRA's cynical, divisive, and frightening vision for guns in America is making our country more dangerous." I read on: "they're spending millions to block *any* progress on gun safety in Congress." As with much academic scholarship and popular commentary about gun rights, the focus of this call to action was on the tip-top of the gun rights pyramid: the NRA. To many advocates for greater gun restrictions, the NRA's "danger" was in its capacity to mobilize the American political system to block, or pass, laws that would increase gun access within the United States. As political scientist Kristin Goss[63] shows, the relative power of gun control groups versus the gun rights lobby can be traced in part to how the latter has managed to harness American political institutions to its benefit. From the US Constitution to the system of federalism, the odds are stacked in favor of the NRA and other gun lobby groups in expanding gun access and stalling gun regulations.

By and large, political scientists, political psychologists, and sociologists have focused on explaining how and why the politics of gun rights have become ascendant, but less attention has been focused on the consequences of this ascendance on the threads of American democracy. For example, political scientists such as Kristin Goss and Matthew Lacombe have traced how the political environment has favored expanded gun rights, focusing on formal political processes (like electoral politics and congressional proceedings), as well as the organizations (such as the NRA) and legal apparatuses (including the US Constitution) that shape political possibilities, political behavior, and political identity. Political psychologists have located the appeal of conservative politics, including gun politics, into particular personality structures that predispose them to embrace a "strict father" metaphor—to use George Lakoff's terminology—to make sense of the world around them. Finally, sociologists of guns, including my own work, have unearthed how concerns surrounding safety and security, socioeconomic shifts, anxieties surrounding the declining power of white masculinity, and major shifts in governmentality, such as the War on Crime and the dismantling of the social safety net, continue to press the appeal of guns for their largely, though far from exclusively, white, male owners. Gun scholars across disciplines have revealed much about why so many Americans own guns, and why the policy apparatus continues to support them in doing so.

But for the many conservatives who embrace gun rights, gun politics is about far more than influencing political institutions; gun politics offer to right-leaning Americans one way of "doing" conservative politics in everyday life—a social practice aimed at navigating the tensions that are inherent to any democratic society but take particular shape in the US context. Understanding the *how* of gun politics is at least as important as *why*—especially if we wager that understanding conservative gun politics might help illuminate the politics of democracy among US conservatives. With these stakes, this book flips the question usually asked of gun politics and democracy.[64] Instead of focusing on how democratic institutions and social arrangements within the United States have shaped—and largely facilitated—a vibrant, robust, and unapologetically conservative gun politics, this book focuses on how conservative gun politics in turn shapes the culture of democracy within the United States.

Before beginning my analysis, I must call the reader's attention to an unavoidable frustration in terminology. Throughout this book, I will use the word "liberal" in a variety of ways: to discuss a particular form of democracy; to examine partisanship; to label the political boogeymen that gun sellers saw in their political opponents; to recognize the self-labeling of people opposed to conservative politics. Unfortunately, creating new terms for each of these usages doesn't quite work. It matters that even as political philosophers define liberal democracy as an idealized political project, everyday conservatives have transformed "liberal" into the ultimate political insult. Meanwhile, even though "liberal" describes an end of the political spectrum that has increasingly ossified into a set of sensibilities that "spill over"[65] beyond politics proper, it is also useful to remember that this ossification contradicts the dictionary definition of "liberal" as eclectic, open, and unencumbered by ideological rigidity.

For clarity, this book uses "liberal" in the following contexts:

- *Liberal Democracy*: I use "liberal" here to refer to a system of government legitimated by appeals to popular sovereignty, or "rule by the people," that is characterized by due process, electoral representation, consensus-based decision-making, civic inclusion (particularly with regard to the definition of "the people"), and political values of equality, freedom, and justice—especially vis-à-vis one's political rivals.[66]

- *Liberal as Conservative Insult*: I use "liberal" here to capture how conservatives understood "liberals" and "liberalism" as a political insult to capture what they saw as a loathsome blend of entitlement, dependency, and victimization that prevents independent thought and self-reliant action—a political insult that effectively effeminized, dehumanized, and/or pathologized their political opponents. Though race-neutral on its face, this "liberal" insult can be used as a racial code word[67] to discount the political voices advocating for racial justice and to resist advancements in racial equality, particularly with respect to political power.

- *Liberal as Political Identification*: I use "liberal" here to capture people's own partisan self-identification as liberal, progressive, or left-leaning; this labeling typically captures affiliation with the Democratic Party as well as allegiance to state- or collective-orchestrated solutions to social problems.

- *Illiberal*: For the sake of parsimony, let me also define what I mean by the term "illiberal," which I use throughout this book to describe political desires, sensibilities, and imaginations. "Illiberal" refers to an impulse that (1) centers on a narrow understanding of "the people"; (2) draws on an exclusionary understanding of rights as privileges accrued to those deemed politically worthy; and (3) often endorses non-representative and/or

non-consensus-based styles of decision-making, including
the endorsement of strongmen political leaders like Donald
Trump and the appreciation—if not outright approval—of
political violence.

- *The Contemporary Conservative Movement*: Finally, while this
term does not explicitly include the word "liberal," it would not
exist without its implicit orientation against liberals, the liberal
establishment, and liberal ideology. Throughout this book, I will
refer to the "contemporary conservative movement" as well
as "contemporary conservative politics" and "conservatives." As
already noted in the brief historical review above and as unraveled throughout this book, there is no monolithic or coherent
"conservative movement" (or even a coherent "conservative gun
rights movement," as chapter 4 shows) but rather a resonant set
of orientations and organizations—from evangelical Christians
to free market libertarians—that converge on their disdain for
liberal ideology.[68] I use the term "contemporary conservative
movement" as shorthand for capturing this political junction
among right-leaning Americans.

Attending to how liberals, liberal ideology, and liberalism animate conservative gun politics is crucial for understanding how, in turn, the politics of gun rights shapes American democracy. But to do so, we must
look beyond the power center of the gun lobby (as Everytown's missive
emphasized). Instead, I focus attention on the everyday politics of conservatives who find in gun politics an appealing set of tools—armed
individualism, conspiracism, and partisanship—for navigating their
political realities and reimagining democracy in the process.

Civic Toolkits and Democratic Imaginations

To understand how gun sellers build conservative culture from the
ground up, I draw on insights from political sociology and the sociology
of culture. Within sociology, there is a long tradition of understanding politics as experienced by Americans as political *culture*: a set of narratives,

practices, and norms used to make sense of political life. As sociologists of culture remind us, culture is not merely a set of values or meanings; culture shapes people's actions. This approach, developed by the sociologist Ann Swidler, is known as "toolkit theory" because it assumes that people don't just *have* culture, they *use* it—like a tool—to solve problems. Those problems may be concrete and task-oriented (how do I cast a ballot in the upcoming election?), or they may be abstract and oriented toward meaning-making (how do I make sense of others with whom I deeply disagree?). Culture gives us tools—from the formal regulations set by institutions (e.g., voter qualifications) to the informal rules that govern social interaction (e.g., political civility)—that allow us to navigate those problems, but in doing so, culture fundamentally shapes the terrain of imaginable actions as well as puts limits on what's possible. Culture is always at work—we use it all the time—but usually, it hides behind the scenes, unremarkably greasing the wheels of social initiative and social institutions. But that's not the case when tensions are high, when people are faced with problems they experience as novel and urgent, and when hitherto effective initiatives and institutions break down or prove futile. In these "unsettled" times (as Swidler calls it), people rely more explicitly on culture to help them solve the problems they face in their daily lives.

American politics represents one terrain where tensions beckon us to more explicitly think through the toolkits—in this case, the *civic* toolkits—that people take up to navigate their everyday political realities. Taking up the concerns of Alexis de Tocqueville[69] flagged a century and a half earlier, the sociologists Robert Bellah, Richard Madsen, William Sullivan, Ann Swidler, and Steven Tipton remind us in *Habits of the Heart* that in their everyday lives, Americans confront a contradictory politics—one that emphasizes the cult of the individual while simultaneously embracing ideals of equality, justice, and freedom that challenge the eminence of personal choice and individual prerogative. Political tensions, we should remember, are core to *any* democratic regime, and they take many forms: between government underreach and government overreach, between the ideal of popular sovereignty and the reality of representation (and the expertise that representation necessarily entails), between the tolerance for conflict and the embrace of universal commonalities among citizens. These tensions, however, take specific shape amid US democracy's historical—and continued—significance as a battleground for racial equality, inclusion, and power. As Bellah and his co-authors note, "our society has tried to establish a floor below which no one will be allowed to fall, but we have not thought effectively about how to include the deprived more actively in occupational and civil life."[70] Indeed, as the events of 2020 instruct us, the questions of civic inclusion, substantive equality, and democratic participation remain open terrains of political struggle.

From the Left to the Right, Americans engage in this struggle not just as they engage in formal practices of democratic engagement—such as voting—but also as they struggle to make sense of, and make decisions within, their everyday lives. In other words, thinking, talking, and doing—the stuff of everyday life—are citizenship acts in and of themselves.[71] These acts can be understood as the practical pillars of what political sociologist Andrew Perrin calls a "democratic imagination." A broad concept that transcends specific political parties and ideologies, democratic imagination describes the cultural repertoires that everyday people draw upon to make sense of "what is possible, important, right, and feasible"[72] within democratic political systems.[73] Democratic imaginations vary because, as political sociologist Ruth Braunstein notes, "American democracy . . . means profoundly different things to different people."[74] Democratic imaginations may be creative and capacious, or they may be apathetic and anemic. They may entitle some with dreams of action and efficacy, but may rebuff those same inclinations in others by shrinking the sphere of imaginable action, discounting certain perspectives as personal rather than political, and defining the public entitled to fully participate in governance in narrow, exclusionary terms. They may encourage people to see certain places and spaces as appropriate, urgent venues for politics[75] or to avoid politics in public altogether.[76] There is no single democratic imagination, but many imaginations forged as everyday people harness the culture at their disposal—ideas, narratives, stories, rituals—to make sense of, navigate, and ultimately enact their personal preferences, civic experiences, and political observations.

Democratic imaginations thus depend on civic initiative; they don't come about in any automatic or straightforward way from the mere fact of living in a democracy. They require work. And that work, it turns out, is crucial for maintaining democracy as a robust and responsive political apparatus. This is because democracy is a system fundamentally animated by irresolvable (but, in the ideal configuration, deeply productive) tensions—between the obligations to the collective and the rights of the individual; between the ideal of popular sovereignty and the reality of representation; between the singularity of policy and the multiplicity of publics.

In the American context, these tensions are inextricably bound up with the violent founding of the United States as a political order by and for white, property-owning men despite an expressed allegiance to liberal democracy as defined by due process, electoral representation, consensus-based decision-making, civic inclusion, and political values of equality, freedom, and justice. The United States' founding documents celebrated the inherent equality of individuals, while rendering enslaved peoples just three-fifths of a person and indigenous people outside the purview of the public sphere altogether. They promised prosperity to all through the pursuit of private property, obliterating the collective entitlement to land by indigenous peoples while also denigrating racialized peoples *as* private property. They set up an enviable system of justice centered on due process—for white, property-owning men. For everyone else, parallel systems of slave law, mob rule, and vigilante justice rendered law and order not an exemplar of democratic process but a manservant to white supremacy. And that was just the beginning. American history is a history of the narrow breadth of American democracy: the Trail of Tears, lynch mobs, racial cleansings, internment camps, the exoneration of murderers—police and civilian—under the mantra of self-defense; the systematic exclusion of people of color from government benefits; racist redlining; the Chinese Exclusion Act; the Dred Scott Decision; de jure and de facto segregation; McCarthyism; bloody strike-busting and white rioting; wanton police killings of people of color, especially African Americans and indigenous peoples . . . the list not only goes on, but is still being written. Alongside the violent repression of dissenting voices, a powerful source of US democracy's continued legitimacy lies in the capacity of those Americans invested in the white, middle-class status quo to justify the systematic anti-liberal features of the American political structure while still holding onto the belief that they live in a free, equal, and just society notwithstanding overwhelming evidence to the contrary.

Despite the violence that mars American past and present, the work required to keep democracy running is often unremarkable, if not invisible, whether taking the form of apathy[77] or ideology.[78] Perhaps people in the United States make small talk about politics[79] with their friends, neighbors, and colleagues without much of a fuss about differences of opinion, instead building civic ties through voluntary associations— political scientist Robert Putnam's bowling leagues of yesteryear,[80] perhaps—that transcend political differences. Or maybe they recognize that while they can't be sure that everything heard on the news is true, they can still try to stay informed, trusting that experts, journalists and politicians are at least trying to get the facts right. They might even vote assuming that their ballots will be counted and counted fairly, and that whoever wins office will work on behalf of Americans at large rather than on behalf of one political party. The wheels of civic engagement, in short, are oiled by this mutual understanding (some would say, illusion) that at least to a minimal degree, people in the US can trust one another, their leaders, and their political system to function.

But in times of crisis, this trust breaks down, and the everyday work that undergirds democracy suddenly becomes visible and contentious. The populist turn in US politics during the 2016 presidential election cycle intimated such a crisis in political authority.[81] Americans across the political spectrum turned to two anti-establishment figures—Bernie Sanders and Donald Trump—who railed against global capitalism and political elites, while championing—albeit in strikingly different ways—everyday working people. Advocating a populist brand of law and order, a protectionist foreign policy, a return to America's manufacturing heydays, and a disdain for inconvenient facts, Trump and his adherents retooled core conservative sentiments into an America First doctrine that gave voice to surging resentment, growing alienation, and sheer rage that was directed up at journalists, politicians, and academics, as well as down toward immigrants, racial minorities, and women. The crisis, of course, didn't stop with Trump's election in 2016; as president, Trump pursued little of the economic populism he promised. Failing to address the structural problems that helped make possible his rise, he encouraged millions of Americans to join in a rage-fueled, resentful, and reactionary identity politics invested in American whiteness. On the eve of 2020, American politics was embattled over the terms of the racial contract that, as Charles Mills[82] reminds us, shapes civic membership in Western democracies: will the United States be a multiracial and in-clusive democracy in substance or in name only?

And then 2020 happened, spinning the country deeper into political crisis. The coronavirus pandemic revealed a government incapable of concerted effort, exposed the shallowness of Americans' collective ob-ligations to one another, and challenged confidence in scientific analysis and advice. The Black Lives Matter protests turned up the volume on the broken record of white supremacy in the United States for all to hear, exposed the shameful lack of accountability for police who kill, and showcased the frailty of political protest as a sacred act of democ-racy as police harassed, threatened, and assaulted[83] protesters gathered to raise public awareness and demand accountability over the issue of police violence. Meanwhile, the political instability surrounding the 2020 US presidential election demonstrated that despite high rates of voter turnout, many people no longer imagined the United States as a place where they could live alongside, debate with, or—in the case of those who claimed election fraud—concede to their political oppo-nents. For anyone not yet awake, the January 6th riot—triggered by what should have been the mundane certification of Joe Biden's presi-dential electoral win—was a blaring alarm bell. Democracy in America is now far from unremarkable.

As I learned in my conversations with gun sellers, though, 2020 did not just challenge American democracy. It also challenged the demo-cratic imaginations of Americans. Gun sellers, for their part, turned to the civic tools at their disposal—armed individualism, conspiracism, and partisanship—to navigate the political impasses around them.

Armed individualism simplified complex dilemmas of collective insecurity and social vulnerability into problems of personal security, reframing intractable social problems into more straightforward problems that people can more readily imagine solving with guns. *Conspiracism* promoted a stance of skepticism toward elites—whether political or scientific elites—and encouraged adherents to impute dark motivations even to seemingly benign policy maneuvers or scientific questions. And finally, *partisanship* justified outright hostility, instead of deliberative engagement or consensus-driven decision-making, as an appropriate response to political opponents and denigrated compromise with one's political opponents as a dangerous show of weakness. Together, these tools formed a civic toolkit that "provide[d] individual social actors with solutions to various problems they encounter in everyday life,"[84] as sociologists Andrew Perrin, J. Micah Roos, and Gordon Gauchat describe with regard to the diverse political orientations within conservative politics. As recent history reveals, this civic toolkit did not suddenly emerge in 2020; for quite some time now, armed individualism, conspiracism, and partisanship have animated conservative politics in general and conservative gun politics in particular. But by tracing the everyday utility of these civic tools for gun sellers who navigated the chaos, insecurity, and uncertainty of 2020, we can better understand not just the challenges facing American democracy but also the factors shaping the democratic imaginations of Americans. By examining conservative gun politics, this book examines how people's political imaginations narrow the linchpin of governance to the individual and their firearm (armed individualism), cultivate an ethic of skepticism that vastly restricts the terrain of shared knowledge (conspiracism), and ultimately render one's political opponents as unworthy of political engagement (partisanship).

Beyond Liberal Democracy

Many readers might pause here and ask whether the term "democratic imagination" is appropriate for describing the inner political lives of people who have, for example, insisted that coronavirus is an elaborate hoax, embraced QAnon as a voice of resistance against the so-called Deep State, and supported the January 6th insurrection to interrupt the certification of Democrat Joe Biden as the 46th president of the United States. After all, popular banter and academic discourse—including voices from the Right like David French[85] and David Frum[86]—have increasingly framed the Trump administration and its supporters as a threat to American democracy in terms such as "authoritarian," "autocratic," or even "fascist." To seriously consider such "democratic imagination," amid continued support for Trump and Trumpist politics, may seem deeply misguided at a moment that appears to demand the strength of principled action rather than the meekness of conciliation. "Democracy" is, many would wager, not simply an analytical term; it is a moral ground that should not be ceded without due consideration.

Despite this urge, this book attempts to suspend—at least temporarily—this moral politics of democracy because doing so opens the door for a more analytically honest approach to the contemporary political moment. It also makes possible a more robust defense of democracy beyond merely "defending existing institutions"[87] that have been antithetical, in the past and present, to the values of equality, freedom, and justice often conflated with US democracy. That is, American democracy has often been equated with *liberal* democracy: a system of political decision-making characterized by electoral representation, consensus, due process, and civic inclusion. Liberal democracy aims at maximizing the political values of equality, freedom, and justice, even or *especially* with respect to one's political opponents. Liberal democracy guards politics as an uncertain, unpredictable, and dynamic terrain where any particular political party or coalition sometimes wins, sometimes loses—but always gets a chance to try again.[88]

Yet democracy need not take on these classically liberal values. As Dylan Riley[89] and Michael Mann[90] each argue in separate studies on "the dark side of democracy" (to use Mann's formulation), democracy at its core is simply an argument for the legitimacy of a system of governance: whereas governments might be justified by the notion of divine rule (such as the French monarchy) or through sheer coercion (such as the rule by terror in Stalinist Russia), democracies look to "the will of the people" for their legitimacy. Illiberal democracy, like liberal democracy, would still celebrate governance as a mechanism for channeling the "will of the people." But unlike liberal democracy, illiberal democracy might stipulate "the people" in narrow, exclusionary terms. It would likely treat rights not as universal attributes of the citizenry but as privileges reserved for those fully included in "the people." And it would eschew consensus-based processes in favor of despotic tactics— such as executive orders or political violence—in order to transform the "will of the people" into political decisions and outcomes.

The concept of illiberal democracy helps clarify the politics of Trump, who has often presented himself as a crusader for popular rule of an exclusionary kind. Fueled by racist tropes and xenophobic banter, Trump's populist promises to "drain the swamp" and build America as "Great Again" are also calls to reclaim a lost American democracy—one that re-asserts an anachronistic version of "the people" who presumably have been abandoned by the Democratic Party and its progressive, multiracial politics. While Trump's attempts to overturn the 2020 election results can be chalked up to sheer self-interest, many of his supporters were genuinely baffled that roughly half the country's voters could have cast votes for Biden—as much as Biden supporters found themselves baffled that nearly half could have voted for Trump. As much as an authoritarian power grab, their insistence and effort to "stop the steal" can *also* be read as disclosing a peculiarly "democratic" conviction among those conservatives supporting Trump's presidency: a conviction that Trump represents the will of ("real") Americans—and that if the electoral process failed to produce him as a winner, then there must be something wrong with how that process was executed.

Even explicit conservative rejections of US democracy—the quip, for example, that the United States is better off as a republic than a democracy because a democracy, as the saying goes, "is two wolves voting on what to do with a sheep"[91]—reveal not a straightforward call to authoritarianism but rather a clear, if contrived, allegiance to "the will of the people." As Braunstein[92] notes in her comparison of conservative and liberal civic organizations, Americans across the political spectrum express "a profound faith in the American democratic project itself and a conviction that ordinary citizens have played a crucial role in propelling this project forward." Whether these are opportunistic rhetorical moves rather than sincere investments in democracy is beside the point; approaching democracy as simply a system of governance based on the will of the people opens the door for exactly this kind of impasse because democracy, crucially and frustratingly, leaves open the questions of *who*, precisely, counts as the "people" and *how*, exactly, their "will" is to be represented.[93] Though *liberal* democracies have inclusive answers to these questions, there is no a priori reason that illiberal understandings of "the people" and illiberal forms of enacting their "will" might not also be incorporated into a governing apparatus that—by virtue of seeding its legitimacy in the will of the people—would earn the moniker of "democracy." No reason, that is, other than our own investment in democracy *as* a liberal institution.

Rather than a benchmark of liberal institutions and norms, American democracy has historically been a struggle over *which* people are included in government's legitimating "will" and *how* that will is "represented." Moving through their everyday political lives, people help to constitute those realities by forging who is included in "the people," which aspects of their "will" rise to the occasion of governance, and how that "will" should best be championed. Democratic imagination is not just about levels of civic engagement or enthusiasm about liberal norms; the very heart of democracy—that is, what democracy means as a system that celebrates the "will of the people"—is at stake. Opening up the terrain of democracy beyond the presumption of liberalism allows us to analyze a much more contested struggle over democracy—one that takes shape not just in high-level political machinations but also through the everyday practices and meanings forged by people on the ground.

Evidence

Recognizing the contemporary conservative movement as a multifaceted phenomenon, this book focuses on gun politics as one window into conservative politics, and it primarily relies on in-depth interviews with gun retailers and analysis of contemporary pro-gun media, as well as historical and legal accounts that help put the 2020 crisis into context. Situated at the intersection of gun markets, gun politics, and gun culture, gun sellers are in the business, quite obviously, of selling guns. Gun sellers are certainly the financial beneficiaries of strident efforts by the gun lobby to protect their industry as a matter of rights. No doubt, they gain from the deregulation of firearms and the protection of gun rights, which have translated into new markets and surging profits for those in the gun industry. But expansive gun laws are *simultaneously* about championing rights, safeguarding a culture practice, *and* protecting a market.[94] Chalking up the incentives of gun sellers to mere profit motives, however, vastly simplifies the cultural work that happens within, around, and through the marketization of gun rights. As they sell the firearms central to the Second Amendment right to keep and bear arms, gun sellers also shape how those rights are engaged and exercised.

To put this into sociological perspective, recall that deliberative spaces are crucial building blocks for what Jürgen Habermas[95] theorized as the "public sphere"—that arena where citizens can discuss public issues, exchange ideas, and eventually form public opinion that reflects mutual understandings. The public sphere paved the way, in Habermas's[96] view, for the rise of Western democracy by providing a means of organizing people—and their multitudes of attitudes, ideas, and opinions—into a public with coherent political objectives and cohesive expectations about how to reach those objectives. Refracted into our contemporary context of raging partisanship, gun stores are not entirely unlike the nineteenth-century coffeehouses and salons that, as Habermas[97] saw it, provided the infrastructure for the public sphere. Gun stores are *not* spaces of yawning political discourse that can traverse the spectrum of views (nor were the coffeehouses and salons of the past, although many have idealized them as such). Rather, gun stores are vibrant arenas for debates *within* conservative politics.

From the conservative, pro-Trump signage some hung on their walls to the political banter many encouraged among their customers and employees, almost every gun seller I interviewed intimated that political engagement was inextricable from the business they ran. Customers hoping to simply buy a gun might instead find themselves in the middle of a lecture on gun laws, the ethics of self-defense, and perhaps chastised for not voting for Trump. Employees might spend their downtime wondering about the likeliest cause of the Apocalypse or bemoaning the latest anti-gun power grab by Democrats. During one interview, a gun seller suddenly put me on speaker phone with a crew of his customers and employees; I didn't realize until they started energetically responding to what I thought were questions he was posing rhetorically—in fact, he had an audience! Apparently, he just couldn't pass up the opportunity to turn our one-on-one interview into a communal ritual of political banter.

Gun sellers sell guns, but they also build political culture. While this everyday politics, as this book will show, largely operated within quite conservative parameters, the active engagement of gun sellers in building conservative culture from the ground up upends the presumption that conservatives are political dupes "clinging to guns and religion."[98] Rather, gun stores (alongside shooting ranges, gun training, gun shows, and even other pro-gun businesses adjacent to the gun industry—like the coffee brand Black Rifle Coffee) provide space for conservative gun rights proponents to share and sharpen their views. Politics appears as part of the "package deal" of running a gun store—something that gun sellers provide and gun buyers expect, too. Indeed, the only real exception[99] to this was one of the few self-identified left-leaning gun sellers I interviewed: citing the "us versus them" mentality, "blatant racism," and "crazy antics" she observed in her store and the broader gun culture, she took advantage of the lockdown orders of 2020 to permanently close the public-facing portion of her gun store, putting some distance between herself and the customers who came there looking not just to buy a gun but also to talk gun politics.

The 50 gun sellers interviewed for this book span four states in order to maximize variation in state-level gun cultures, gun laws, and—crucially—responses to the multilayered crises of 2020: fourteen gun sellers in Arizona, twelve in California, fourteen in Florida, and ten in Michigan. Rather than big-box gun retailers like Cabela's or Walmart, the gun sellers I interviewed ran independent "mom-and-pop" shops that were not beholden to the kinds of business guidelines that might shape more corporate gun retailers. As compared to big-box employees, these kinds of gun stores were more likely to be overtly political and more likely to exercise discretion in business operations. Reflecting the dominance of conservative sentiment within gun culture as well as the diversity of thought within conservative politics, the vast majority of interviewees—42 out of the 50—were on the conservative end of the political spectrum, but they described themselves with a mix-and-match of right-signaling labels: conservative (as 52% of right-leaning gun sellers described themselves), Republican (36%), libertarian (17%), Constitutionalist (12%), and Christian conservative (2%).[100]

Crucial to the methods of the book is both who was interviewed as well as when. Rather than asking interviewees to present their reconstruction of "historical" events, interviews with gun sellers were conducted as the multiple crises of 2020 unfolded, starting in April 2020. This unique timing allowed me to trace how the multilayered crises of 2020 sparked distinctive responses in gun sellers; how gun sellers struggled to make sense of still-unfolding events (crucial for understanding political culture in "unsettled" times[101]); and, thanks to the frankness of my interviewees, how gun sellers made sense of their own changing attitudes as the events of 2020 developed. I interviewed gun sellers remotely to comply with pandemic restrictions on research, travel, and social distancing. (Remote interviews, it turned out, not only were quite accommodating for conducting interviews with gun sellers, who were now managing fast-paced and unpredictable gun counters, but also helped advance my own thinking on qualitative research methods, especially regarding the "gold standard" of in-person interviews that I had long endorsed.) To understand gun sellers' accounts in terms of the broader political, social, and cultural context, I also draw on a dataset of stories on coronavirus, Black Lives Matter, and the 2020 US elections produced by the top two most-visited online gun news outlets, *The Truth About Guns* and *Ammoland*, and by the leader of the gun lobby, the National Rifle Association. These data cover "the long 2020," as sociologist Sarah Quinn put it,[102] spanning from the first mentions of coronavirus in early 2020 through the thirteenth month of 2020—January 2021. Interested readers should look to the Reflections on Methodology appendix, which provides a fuller description of the methods used for this book and offers some lessons gleaned from conducting qualitative research during a pandemic.

In mobilizing gun markets as a window into the dynamism of everyday conservative politics over the course of 2020, two key disclaimers must be emphasized. First, I focus on a conservative corner of American gun culture and American gun politics, but the reality is that there is a great deal of diversity among gun owners and gun rights advocates that this book does not engage nor attempt to capture. Though gun owners are disproportionately white conservative men, many gun-owning Americans do not fit that profile. Many gun-owning Americans, furthermore, stand in strident opposition to the practices, attitudes, and values[103] that will be unraveled in this book, and many of them are organized—either informally or formally, as political organizations or cultural groups—accordingly. Rather, this book *does* make an argument about *dominant strains* of gun rights politics as part of conservative political culture. Second, this book focuses on dominant strains of gun rights politics as a window into the conservative mobilization of armed individualism, conspiracism, and partisanship. However, as illuminating as conservative gun rights politics are for understanding contemporary conservativism, this cannot capture the whole of conservative thought—whether from the bottom up or top down. Accordingly, the goal of this book is not to convince readers that all gun owners are conservative adherents to the blend of armed individualism, conspiracism, and polarization that arrested broad swaths of the American public in 2020, nor is it aimed at arguing that all adherents to this conservative culture are gun owners. Rather, the goal is to draw on interviews with gun sellers to examine *how* this civic toolkit becomes useful to those conservatives who embrace it, and with what consequences for the politics of democracy.

Organization of the Book

This book is not about what democracy is, but about what people define democracy to be. It unravels how gun sellers of 2020 made sense of the surge in demand for guns; how they struggled to find certainty amid incertitude; and how they reimagined and at times even rejected liberal democracy in the process.

The book begins with a frontline view into 2020's busy gun counters. Fielding lockdown orders and dramatic surges in gun sales, gun sellers understood themselves as *both* the defenders of gun rights amid the threat of government tyranny *and* the marketers of gun rights amid the danger of government abandonment. Armed individualism—which positions guns as the solution to both government overreach *and* government underreach—allowed gun sellers to navigate this tension and, in the process, transform their gun stores into political arenas in their own right. From their unique position as merchants of rights, gun sellers did not just sell firearms in 2020 but also provided a political education in gun rights, steering new gun buyers to understand the right to keep and bear arms from the perspective of its predominantly conservative adherents.

In chapter 2, the book addresses how gun sellers embraced conspiracist thinking as they weighed reports from government officials and scientific elites against their first- and second-hand experiences and their own personal "research." This chapter challenges the urge to dismiss conspiracist thinking as the stuff of far-right fringe. Instead, it considers that conspiracist thinking communicates a democratic desire to shrink the gap between the people and their rulers by championing the former as the source of political truth. But this desire—especially as embraced by many of the gun sellers I interviewed—comes with a cost: conspiracist thinking stood to undermine liberal democracy by stigmatizing collective action as either too spontaneous to take seriously or so well-organized as to be suspicious. This, in turn, paved the way for dismissing alternative viewpoints out of hand and for elevating rugged individualism as the most cherished expression of popular sovereignty.

The book dives into partisanship in chapter 3. Though they bemoaned their *own* treatment by their political opponents, gun sellers were often riled by liberals—whether the liberal gun buyers they met in their stores, the mask-wearers they assumed were liberal, or the advocates for racial justice they presumed to also be liberal in mindset. Forgoing the productive democratic tension between tolerance for disagreement alongside an embrace of universal rights, they chastised their political opponents as irresponsible, ignorant, and even unworthy of civic engagement or political voice. As one of the few arenas in which bigotry (indeed, across the political spectrum) remains largely acceptable, partisanship took shape *not* as principled disagreement among political equals *but rather* as an impulse to stigmatize, pathologize, and even dehumanize political adversaries, shrinking the horizon of "the people" that democracy purports to represent.

The book culminates in the question of democracy by examining the political imaginations that animate conservative gun politics. Chapter 4 lays out three distinct political imaginations among gun sellers—including the handful of liberal gun sellers I interviewed alongside the majority of gun sellers who were conservative. It details the libertarian imagination (and its celebration of individual rights), the illiberal imagination (and its construction of an exclusionary vision of "the people"), and the eclectic imagination (and its cobbling together of stances typically associated with *either* liberal *or* conservative politics). In doing so, it reveals how—in different ways—gun sellers reworked and, at times, rejected liberal democracy as an inclusive political project rooted in popular representation.

Rather than see the conservative-dominated arena of gun sellers (and conservative gun culture, for that matter) as an aberration or fringe element within American politics, the book concludes by encouraging readers to view contemporary gun politics as the canary in the coal mine of American democracy: a harbinger of the kinds of thinking, engagement, and desire that may not simply destabilize but also increasingly dominate the American political scene as the United States continues to become both more racially diverse and more socioeconomically unequal. Amid the ongoing fallout of the January 6th riot on Capitol Hill and widespread—and widening—distrust among conservatives regarding the results of the 2020 presidential election, this book yields some important, but difficult, lessons: that democracy is a troublingly amenable discourse, acquiescent to political projects ranging from liberal to illiberal; that merely working to reinforce seemingly quintessential democratic practices and institutions—such as the vote or the election—cannot fortify liberal democracy all on its own; and that, therefore, attending to the political dilemmas we face today requires that we look not just upward toward the strength of our political institutions but also inward toward the robustness of the political culture we embrace as part of "doing democracy"[104] in the United States. We must forge a different civic toolkit—one that includes political equanimity, civic grace, and social vulnerability, which I describe in the conclusion—if we are to repair and rebuild not just the democracy in which we live but also the democratic imagination that lives within us.

Armed Individualism

Guns—and the security they carry with them—mark our starting point. This is because mainstream gun rights discourse is an illuminating example of the kinds of political engagement that had ascended within conservative circles by 2020. It is also because guns themselves serve as powerful linchpins linking up everyday action, political beliefs, and historical narratives. As Jonathan Obert and Elias Schultz observe in their analysis of militia activists, "guns are tangible artifacts that uniquely align existing social practices with an important historical tradition, enhance agency, and provide interpretive finality."[1] Not every gun carrier is a militia activist—very far from it—but every gun carries symbolic, material, and political potential embedded not only in its owner's intentions but in the broader social constellation that makes guns appealing, even urgent, to their owners.

Part of the social constellation that makes guns appealing and urgent is their significance as vehicles of safety and security. Guns have increasingly taken on this role in the minds of Americans and in the structure of our collective security apparatuses. Over the past 20 years, Americans have increasingly come to see guns as making their homes and their streets safer—a striking reversal[2] that signals a deep shift in the social place of guns in American society. Over that same period, American society has reaped the grim harvest of emaciated social bonds and a fallow government hollowed out by neoliberal defunding of education, welfare, mental health care, and other social safety nets.[3] The availability of guns combined with their felt necessity amid social precarity has fostered a culture of armed individualism:[4] people in the United States, seeing themselves as the only ones ultimately responsible for their own safety, have turned the vice of neoliberal disinvestment into the virtue of gun rights as an everyday ethic of civic engagement. Overwhelmingly, protection has become the primary reason for gun ownership in the United States: as of 2021, some 21.5 million-plus Americans have concealed carry licenses,[5] and over three-quarters of Americans agree that handguns—the preferred self-defense gun—should not be banned.[6] Those caught in the cross fires of neoliberalism's fallout have caught on to the appeal of guns as a means to address felt insecurities ranging from violent crime to socioeconomic precarity to the declining social status of white, heterosexual men amid real, if ultimately underwhelming (and now eroding), gains of women, racial minorities, and sexual minorities since the 1960s.[7]

Armed individualism captures a long-standing gun-centric sensibility within the gun-rich US context, one that has roots in settler colonialism and chattel slavery but has been updated throughout American history to cast the armed individual as a key protagonist of safety, security, and sovereignty.[8] Not merely an ideological discourse to believe in, armed individualism comprises a practical politics to enact in daily life. And if guns were already a central way to do something about elements of life's insecurities that are ultimately out of our control—whether seemingly "random" instances of criminal victimization or the bewildering threat of economic, political, and social breakdown[9]—then the multilayered crises of 2020 put that impulse into overdrive. As early as March 2020, politicians, pundits, and public health officials climbed aboard a jolting ride of lockdowns and shutdowns, on the one hand, and inaction and equivocation, on the other, in their response to coronavirus. By June 2020, yet another series of brutal killings of Black people[10] by private civilians and police sparked a summer of protests pressing for racial justice. Largely peaceful, though sometimes not, the sheer number of cities in turmoil raised the specter of civil unrest. Some, like the armed 17-year-old Kyle Rittenhouse, brought firearms as a counterprotest; Rittenhouse killed and maimed protesters, but his actions were deemed acts of self-defense by a Wisconsin court a year later. And by the confirmation of Joe Biden as the Democratic nominee in August, many were already anticipating political instability in the upcoming elections amid heightened racial tensions, upheavals in protocols at polling locations, and surging distrust. Millions of Americans responded to these threats—and the threatening uncertainties they entailed—by purchasing a gun. As they did so, they fell into lockstep with a long-standing American tradition:[11] when the going gets tough, the tough get guns.

CHAPTER 1

Viral Gun Rights

In 2020, the firearms industry was one of the largest and most resilient industries in the United States,[1] with its overall economic impact swelling to $63 billion that year.[2] This has translated into many jobs (342,330 by the National Shooting Sports Foundation's count in 2021[3]) and many firearms. According to the most recent ATF figures for 2019, roughly 6.7 million guns manufactured in the United States stayed in the country—alongside another 4 million imports.[4] Without a national tracking system, we can't know for sure where these guns ultimately go (the US military, for example, "acquires virtually all its small arms from domestic commercial firearm manufacturers"),[5] but the FBI has reported more than 20 million background checks every year since 2013—a figure that swelled to nearly 40 million in 2020.[6] Though there are flaws with using background checks as a proxy for gun purchases,[7] the NSSF estimates that the 2020 January–July background check figures indicated a firearm purchasing surge that was up roughly 72 percent from the 2019 figures.[8] While other industries and economic sectors collapsed over the course of 2020 under the weight of lockdown orders and vanishing consumer demand, the firearms industry—buttressed by demand from private civilians for firearms—boomed.

To those buying and selling guns, the multilayered crises of the long 2020—first coronavirus, then anti-Black police violence and anti-racist civil unrest, and finally democratic instability—provided a vindication of gun rights as an ultimate safety net in a country rocked by uncertainty, insecurity, and chaos. Struck with an uncomfortable and extraordinary dread, millions of people—including many who fell outside the profile of gun owners as white, conservative men—found themselves drawn to guns as a matter of practical necessity. The headlines confirmed the onslaught, from hipster news outlets to the voice of the gun lobby itself: "Gun Lovers Are Claiming a Huge 'I Told You So' Moment with the Coronavirus Outbreak" (Vice)[9] and "Pandemic Engenders Appreciation for Second Amendment Rights" (NRA-ILA).[10] Gun sellers indeed experienced this period as an adjudication on the mass appeal of guns in times of uncertainty, recognizing that the acute and amorphous fears that circulated in American society throughout 2020 pushed a markedly massive, and absolutely distinctive, clientele their way. Armed individualism was not simply an ideology; it was a way to navigate seemingly unprecedented insecurity that millions of Americans suddenly found useful.

Armed individualism captures the widespread sensibility among gun rights proponents that people's everyday security rests ultimately in their own hands. This sensibility is heightened during times of emergency—times when gun rights advocates view their rights as *most necessary* due to the apparent collapse of safety and security and *most vulnerable* due to the opening that emergency presents for tyrannical overreach. Alongside the growing appeal of gun rights in 2020, then, there was an acute reckoning—one that seemed a long time coming among gun rights proponents. Amid lockdown orders from above and panic buying from below, gun sellers in 2020 saw a renewed necessity for gun rights—and they ensured that new gun buyers saw this necessity, too. Whether through the sheer act of refusing to close their stores or their insistence on explaining gun laws to newbie gun owners, gun sellers navigated this felt fragility as political vanguards, mobilizing and proselytizing armed individualism to confront the uncertainty of 2020.

Through armed individualism, gun sellers defended—from their vantage—democracy in a double sense. On the one hand, they understood gun rights as a shield against democracy's biggest threat—tyranny in the form of gun control. On the other hand, they celebrated how gun rights "democratize" security into the hands and holsters of everyday

Americans as they searched for certainty and control amid insecurity and government inefficacy. In contrast to voting or petitioning, the gun provided direct access to popular sovereignty. And as compared to voting or petitioning, gun ownership provided an immediate and satisfying relief from political tensions that had become increasingly acute in 2020, such as the core democratic tension between "protecting lives and preserving freedom."[11] If coronavirus precautions ignited the tension between "protecting lives and preserving freedom,"[12] guns could cunningly resolve it by at once being objects for protecting oneself and for flaunting one's freedom.

Centered on the tension between government *underreach* and government *overreach*, this chapter starts with how gun sellers understood themselves as political vanguards at the front lines of resisting government overreach. It examines how gun sellers made sense of the deluge of new gun buyers as a response to government underreach: faced with the felt breakdown of security, guns were the only "guarantee" that could provide a semblance of self-protection and restore a sense of safety. This emphasis on government underreach helped gun sellers frame the appeal of guns in democratic terms—great equalizers erasing the messy politics of race, gender, and other lines of difference to assuage a basic human need for security. And if the purchase of a gun equalized security amid government underreach, gun sellers also believed that that same act exposed new gun owners to government overreach—perhaps for the first time—as buyers navigated the rules and regulations that purchasing a gun entailed. With its unruly cacophony of government directive and government retreat, the year 2020 provided an acute opportunity for gun sellers to preach their politics—not just to long-standing gun owners but also to a new constituency of first-time gun buyers.

The Tyranny in Emergency

In March 2020, the National Rifle Association released an ominous video warning about impending societal collapse and the politicians who would exploit the pandemic to "enact strict gun control measures in the name of safety." The video's narrator, Carletta Whiting—an African American woman with a disability and a breast cancer survivor—explained:

> I hope I survive the coronavirus. That's up to God. What's in my control is how I defend myself if things go from bad to worse. You might be wondering why I'm holding this [referring to her AR-style firearm]. I know from history how quickly society breaks down during crisis, and we've never faced anything like this before. And never is a Second Amendment more important than during public unrest . . . even liberals in California are lining up because they know the government will not be able to protect them . . . you may not have heard of what happened during Hurricane Katrina, but police actually went door to door stripping our society's most vulnerable people of their guns . . . make no mistake, anti-gun politicians will seek to use the current pandemic to enact strict gun control measures in the name of safety.[13]

More than just championing self-defense, her words establish an American ethic of self-reliance robust enough to rise to the occasion of all-out social collapse and protect even the most vulnerable in society, such as an African American woman with a disability. The threat was more than just a virus; it was total social breakdown. In recognizing the prospect of social breakdown, Whiting describes an eviscerating lack of faith in government, government capacities, and government decision-makers—including elected politicians. Admitting she can do little about surviving a virus, she sees her rifle as the necessary control in the face of a government "not able to protect," a "society that breaks down during crisis," and "anti-gun politicians . . . seek[ing] to use the current pandemic" for their own agenda.

The video represented a 2020 version of a narrative that, as legal scholar Susan Liebell notes, has been "developed over decades and promoted by the National Rifle Association (NRA), constitutional scholars of the Second Amendment, public officials, and the conservative press."[14] As Liebell describes it, by placing outsized emphasis on "the individual opinion of gun owners as 'citizen protectors,'" "this narrative insists that guns uphold freedom and rights, maintain order, and prevent tyranny."[15]

As the history of the modern conservative movement reveals,[16] this narrative gained traction in the mid-twentieth century from the anger and anxiety of whites, particularly white men, who found themselves facing fundamental transformation in racial and gender relations amid declining socioeconomic opportunities. But Whiting's standing as an African American woman with a disability works to acquit this narrative of its social origins (or at least push these origins below the surface). This opens up space for her to pivot long-standing arguments from the other side of history—that government, including police, has historically harmed people of color while upholding the rights and freedoms of whites—into a pro-gun stance of individual empowerment amid the prospect of total social breakdown.

A similar narrative circulated throughout pro-gun media in 2020. *The Truth About Guns* sarcastically quipped, "with no supplies, there's always government assistance. Just like at the Superdome in New Orleans during Hurricane Katrina, right? Failing to prepare translates to preparing to fail" (March 4).[17] The reference to Hurricane Katrina is a requiem to a widespread lament within pro-gun circles: the collapse of New Orleans's political and physical infrastructure in the aftermath of Hurricane Katrina at the time demonstrated the acute need for guns in times of catastrophic social failure, but the existing government structure managed to execute enough gun confiscations—how many is disputed—to demonstrate that not only *can* emergency gun restrictions happen in the United States; they *did* happen.[18] Many worried that coronavirus could be the next Katrina. An *Ammoland* article surmised, illustrating the decades-old melding by gun rights advocates of fascists, communists, and gun confiscators:[19] "If you're a communist gun-grabber . . . you call for nationalizing industry and letting the same government that failed to protect anybody in this run everything. And 'progressives' call us the fascists." [20]

In the early days of the coronavirus pandemic,[21] however, the central perceived threat to gun access was not government agents going "door to door" looking to seize guns but rather government orders shuttering the doors of gun sellers as part of broader lockdown restrictions. While the world ground to a halt under the weight of the coronavirus pandemic, local, state, and federal officials in the United States had to consider a set of vexing questions: should gun stores be considered an essential business in times of crisis? Were they part of the critical infrastructure—not simply providing an important service but also contributing to the systems foundational to society's rudimentary functioning? In short, could the basic coordinates of American society remain themselves without the gun industry?[22]

Among gun sellers, the answer to this last question was a resolute "No." When I asked Aaron, a California gun seller who identified as "white with a touch of Mexican," about the designation of gun sellers as essential businesses, he peeled off a list of reasons why:

> This is an individual right, and the Supreme Court affirmed that, Number 1. And Number 2 . . . police don't have an inherent duty to protect you. By default, it falls on the individual. [And finally,] I don't believe the government should have the right . . . to just decide at random [which businesses stay open and stay closed].

For Aaron, guns provided the *only* guaranteed source of security amid a government that neither has a duty to protect individuals nor a right to decide who has access to firearms and who does not. To force a gun store to close in the middle of a pandemic? "That couldn't be more wrong—especially in a time like this. You are taking advantage. And I'm not okay with that. It's okay for all of us to crowd into Costco for us to buy toilet paper, but I can't have two people in my gun store at a time by appointment only? Come on."

Kyle, a white gun seller also in California, made a different but equally contemptuous comparison:

> McDonalds is NOT an essential business, I'm sorry! You can get your food somewhere else—you can cook at home. But that's allowed to go [without controversy], whereas the gun store? Hey, maybe there is reduced police presence. Maybe somebody might be desperate. If somebody needs that tool to defend themselves, you know, that may be a little more essential than, say, a Big Mac and fries.

For both Kyle and Aaron, shutdown orders represented an infuriating blend of opportunism and ignorance. They weren't the only ones. As Ben, a 30-something white gun seller in Michigan, noted, "it was 'snap your fingers, and BOOM! Your rights are gone!'" Meanwhile, Sam, a white Hispanic Michigan gun dealer, highlighted the non-negotiable status of gun rights: "people have a fundamental right to defend themselves, and ultimately, at the same time, it's not really up to the government to tell people . . . in most cases, what they can't, should, and shouldn't own." Though they obviously gained monetarily from the surge in gun purchasing, they were more concerned with politics than profits: Aaron, Kyle, Ben, and Sam all framed their insistence on staying open through a political commitment that presented gun rights as a retort to the biggest problem as they saw it—the government.

Aaron, Kyle, Ben, Sam, and other gun sellers from California and Michigan were perhaps particularly vocal about the lockdown orders because in their states, the status of gun stores remained tediously unresolved in the early days of the pandemic. Rather than a theoretical debate about gun rights and self-defense, the lockdown orders forced these gun sellers to make a sudden choice: abide by public health guidance and close down or stand by the right to keep and bear arms and stay open. Michigan's governor declined to delineate gun stores as essential or non-essential,[23] leaving gun stores themselves to try to ascertain their legal status amid a dynamic public health emergency and fluctuating executive orders. Noting that "it's important to exercise those rights that were given to you," Sam took the initiative to "deem myself essential" even as the governor declined to clarify the status of gun sellers.[24] Meanwhile, Paul, a white gun seller also in Michigan, explained, "It was very strange in Michigan. It was a gray area. It's like she [Governor Whitmer] didn't want to get into that. I would say half of the gun stores in Michigan closed on their own for a very short time . . . we went down for just a week to kind of gather . . . our opinion . . . on what we thought was the best for our family and for our store, and kind of see what it's all about." Unlike Sam, Paul chose to close down temporarily, but he quickly recognized the political ramifications of his decision: "I received hate mail . . . We were called communists, unpatriotic for not standing up against the governor, [that] we're not protecting Second Amendment rights . . . people thought we were infringing on their rights. . . . to where they said, I'm never going to step back into [your store] because you stayed shut down and didn't open back up." As Paul's description suggests, gun sellers weren't alone in understanding themselves as uniquely positioned to stand up to government overreach; the broader gun rights community expected them to act out that role as well.

California gun sellers likewise navigated a hostile political environment. California's Governor Gavin Newsom was initially ambiguous about the status of gun sellers in his lockdown orders. Eventually, he deferred the fraught decision to local law enforcement, stipulating that county-level authorities—specifically, county sheriffs—would decide whether to keep their gun stores open or not.[25] Gun sellers were relieved: the county sheriffs, at least as far as most gun sellers saw it, were usually in favor of gun stores staying open.[26] Carl, a California gun seller who told me he grew up as "white trash," noted that his local sheriff had already decided to keep gun stores open the day before Newsom's announcement: "The sheriff basically said, yes we want gun stores . . . [and] No, we don't want to shut down gun shops because we believe that would do nothing but encourage a black market in guns." Richard, another white California gun seller, likewise relied on his good relationships with local law enforcement: "I am actually the primary dealer in my city for the local police department, and so I'm very close with lots of them, and none of them are going to mess with me. . . . the sheriff and chief of police are both extremely pro-gun." Likewise, Oliver, a California gun seller who identified as "not Caucasian," felt protected by his local sheriff's insistence that gun stores stayed open despite his city council voting to shut them down. One noteworthy exception, however, was Los Angeles County's sheriff, who deemed gun sellers inessential and ordered them shut down. Apparently, however, fear of legal reprisals stopped the closures.[27] As Billy, a white California gun seller, explained, "Well the board of supervisors didn't want to get sued for that shit, and they told him—cut it out, you need to make them essential . . . [So] the LA County Board of Supervisors removed the sheriff as the head of the emergency response. That's his freaking job! That's what he does! [laughs] So, California is rowdy! California is rowdy, man! It's one of the most ass-backwards states."

Tangled up at the intersection of gun rights and public health mandates, gun sellers in California and Michigan had to navigate a dynamic, chaotic situation inaugurated by the pandemic's arrival on American shores. From their vantage point, guns were a single, and singular, vehicle of security that felt as fragile as it was precious. They thus understood that to insist one's gun store stays open was not simply a business decision. It was at once a defense of individual rights, a reinforcement of the means of safety and security, and a rejoinder—in their view—that the will of the people fundamentally relies on their ability to protect themselves. As Andrew, a biracial California gun seller, told me, "the Second Amendment—as a fundamental human right, a natural right that is only protected but not granted by the Constitution—does not get suspended for a global pandemic."

In contrast to California and Michigan gun sellers, gun sellers in Arizona and Florida[28] were confident that their respective states would not interfere in their business operations. For example, Arizona gun sellers unanimously agreed that their state's reputation as a staunch supporter of gun rights translated into freedom for their business operations. Bryan, a white gun seller in his sixties, when asked if he ever believed Arizona would shut him down, exclaimed, "No, no, absolutely not!" Appealing to the politics of their state, the vast majority of Florida gun sellers likewise felt secure in their status as essential businesses. Traversing from market prerogatives to rights, Robert, a white thirty-something gun seller, told me confidently, "Florida is the wild west. And we always have been. Um, we've got legal weed, and we have machine guns. So, it's another—a whole freaking animal here . . . I think it's been a beautiful situation for rights."

Gun sellers across Arizona, California, Florida, and Michigan were well aware that their experiences *as gun sellers* varied dramatically across states. But they also saw that their experiences *as everyday citizens* varied across the United States, too. Consider Nathan, a white gun seller in Arizona, who quipped as he observed California's lockdown orders from across state lines: "I watched California lose its damn mind!" Having spent time in California before moving to Arizona, he noted "such a sharp divide" between the two states:

> Look, particularly in a time like now, [at] all of the restrictions that they've got going on in California, versus an essentially open state like Arizona. All the negativity and all the bad things that people in California are talking about gun owners [i.e., gun harms resulting from gun ownership], none of that is happening [in Arizona.] . . . [In California, you have] all these restrictions, all these "hey, we are going to put gun store owners in jail if they open their doors in California." But in Arizona, I've got guys coming left and right buying guns. Where's the truth in that?

Nathan characterizes the threats to California gun dealers in escalated terms: he describes the government's willingness, as he sees it, "to put gun store owners in jail if they open their doors" as evidence of overreach rooted in myths and misunderstandings about guns (e.g., "Where's the truth in that?"). He sees the debate about firearms in terms of a fundamental divide in how people understand guns—as objects of safety and security versus objects of danger and harm. This distinction maps onto the political divisions that some have described as "two Americas": Red America and Blue America; conservative America and liberal America; Bedrock America and Cosmopolitan America; and, for Nathan, free, gun-loving America and unfree, gun-fearing America.

This divide reflects political attitudes and opinions, no doubt, but it also reflects a distinction in what it means to be a citizen. As Nathan told me later on in our conversation, "neutering your citizens because you think that's the right thing to do is *not* right." Guns allowed Nathan not just to feel safe and protected but also self-reliant and self-possessed—a real man, in contrast to the "neutered" citizens of California. This explicitly gendered language declared California-style government overreach (such as gun control) as a threat to citizens—but not just *any* citizens. Overreach particularly threatened those who embraced the civic values of self-reliance and rugged individualism, of individual rights and personal responsibility. Nathan's perspective illuminates that gun bearers' fears over tyranny, as sociologist Angela Stroud examines in her book *Good Guys with Guns*,[29] are often expressed through concerns about gun control, but they are about much more. As Stroud unpacks it, the fear of government control goes as follows: government regulatory and re-distributive regimes aimed at promoting greater inclusion and equality, particularly among historically marginalized groups, threaten to harm people, especially and unduly white men, by stealing their private prop-erty (i.e., the taxes redistributed to social programs), controlling what they can do and say in the workplace and beyond (i.e., civil rights legis-lation), and shaming them just for being . . . white men (i.e., the specter of "political correctness" and its latest incarnation, "cancel culture"). This fear inverts the promise of "the rising tide that lifts all boats": instead of a rising tide, government initiative meant stagnation, torpor, even down-ward mobility—a fundamental default on American democracy's founding promise. Democracy, then, was in the eye of the beholder. In Nathan's view (and other gun sellers who made similar comparisons), California and Arizona were not just divided by a state border; they were political worlds apart with radically different understandings of what rights, freedom, and citizenship mean, how they matter, and why. Rather than submit to government overreach and live out a clipped civic life, Nathan found in the state of Arizona a recognition of his citi-zenship as he understood it—and as illustrated by the state's unwilling-ness to fetter his gun rights.[30]

Though they navigated different political contexts, gun sellers across Arizona, California, Michigan, and Florida put into practice the NRA's proclamation in March 2020 that "the 'essential' character of the right to keep and bear arms was settled in 1791, and no public official has the authority to revisit that decision."[31] The insistence on staying open was an act of armed individualism: an everyday embrace of gun rights, a civic practice of self-reliance. In the uncertain context of the pandemic's unfolding, it represented a political act aimed at defying any act of tyr-anny that would infringe on the core of the American political system's pledge to popular sovereignty: individual rights, particularly the right to keep and bear arms *and* the right to private property. Gun sellers saw themselves not just as sellers of guns, then, but also as defenders of rights—crucially positioned, they soon found out, to address a surging demand for guns. This demand would provide the opportunity for gun sellers not just to let their political colors fly as they refused lockdown orders; it also allowed them to engage new, desperate gun buyers in an education in gun politics.

"One Day It Was Normal, and the Next Day It Was Just Chaos"

In the gun industry, panic buying is part of the business cycle.[32] Every election year, especially a year that Democrats appear poised to take over US Congress or the US presidency, is a good year for gun sales. But 2020's surge didn't quite fit into the usual rhythm of panic buying.[33] Sure, 2020 was an election year, but the surge was too early and too sudden to be chalked up to politics as usual. Likewise, while highly publicized mass shootings often led to sudden and dramatic surges in gun purchasing, there was no mass shooting to point to, and even so, this surge was much, much larger. As Bree Lang and Matthew Lang found,[34] the increase in background checks from February to March 2020 was roughly five- to sevenfold *greater* than the surges following mass shootings. Americans were buying guns, and they were buying them in droves.

But why? Gun sellers found themselves grasping for answers.

As they experienced it, 2020's gun-buying surge—its sheer magnitude, the panic that drove it, and the people it touched—was palpably different than surges that had come before. As Andrew in California told me, "I've been through gun sale surges before . . . gun owners or at least gun enthusiasts saying, 'I better buy these . . . guns before they outlaw them.' This time, it was new buyers [saying], 'I have to buy these because tomorrow my door might get kicked down by someone who is motivated by lockdowns and shortages of supply to feed their family or get what's mine, kill me to take my supplies. Kill me for my food.'" When I asked gun sellers to compare the panic buy of 2020—especially early 2020—to the surges that accompanied high-profile mass shootings and election year fears, I often received this response: "it doesn't even fall in the same *category*. And that's what so crazy," as Brenda, a white gun seller in California, put it. Leonard, a Florida gun seller who had been in the business for decades, had to reach back to the 1960s to find a meaningful comparison: "When Martin Luther King was shot . . . But that was for a relatively short period of time. And that was a long time ago, maybe before you were born." The magnitude of the 2020 surge was record-breaking; the desperation that accompanied it appeared unmatched; and the gun buyers themselves—first-time gun owners, coming from all categories of people outside the profile of the white, conservative men who typically owned guns—were strikingly different from the kinds of buyers worried about a federal cap on magazine capacity or a ban on assault-style weapons.

For gun sellers who tried to pinpoint it, a range of triggers seemed to have opened the floodgates of firearms demand: local school closures; sudden lockdown orders; the unexpected emptiness of grocery store shelves stripped of basic goods; even the viral spread of rumors about martial law on Facebook and other social media. As Brenda joked, "It almost was as if as soon as everybody got the call [that the community was shutting down], the first stop was our shop!" But others admitted that trying to find one specific cause was really just grasping at straws. Brandon, a white Florida gun seller, mused, "there wasn't one specific day or reason or speech that the President gave. It was just: one day it was normal . . . and then the next day it exploded. And it was just nonstop. I can't think of . . . the particular date where it just went nuts. It was just: one day it was normal, and the next day it was just chaos."

And chaos it was: gun sellers arrived at their stores to find jammed parking lots, lines already formed at the doors, and phones ringing off the hook. One unassuming Arizona gun seller named Liam, a white man in his late thirties, found himself fielding a seemingly routine request for ammunition pricing from a customer. As he described it, his store had "several thousands of rounds of that caliber he was looking for—and I looked at my distributor, and they had tens of thousands of rounds." This ample supply was short-lived, as everything changed in only a few hours: "People are running to stores, they are calling [and] asking for this ammo. [I think], 'I'm going to order some more so I have it.' So, we're talking two, three hours later. I log back in, and those tens of thousands of rounds are already gone." The next day, it was on for

Liam and his store: "we sold out of every ammunition we had for ARs or pistols within about three hours."

Some gun sellers put the surge in financial terms, providing staggering figures to illustrate the dramatic enormity of the surge:

> In one day, I believe that [the start of the surge] was a Tuesday, and from a Tuesday to a Wednesday, our daily gun sales went from $3,000 to $45,000. In one day. (California)

> I showed up at 9:45—we open at 10—there was 45 cars in our parking lot. . . . Say we average about $3,000 a day [prior to March 2020]. We were doing $29,000 on average per day [in March]. So that's like, what, a 1,000% increase? (Michigan)

> I'm gonna just use simple numbers for ease of use. Let's say I made $1,000 a month on average. Well, that day [the surge started], I made say $1,000 or $1,200. The next I may make $800 or $900, then $700, then $1,000, then $900. And it just kept going and going and going. (Arizona)

Even as they represent back-of-the-napkin calculations, these are remarkable sums, definitively shaking the firearms industry out of what some gun sellers called the "Trump Slump."[35] And this was just the beginning: gun sales wouldn't plummet until early 2022—when sales would drop roughly 42 percent from their year-to-year figures.[36]

The abruptness and size of the 2020 surge, combined with the unsuitability of the ready-made explanations for surges in gun purchasing, left gun sellers perplexed and overwhelmed by the general sense of uncertainty and unpredictability that the early days of the pandemic had unleashed. A white Arizona gun seller named Ian zeroed in on how the unprecedented experience of quarantine rocked people's sense of safety:

> We all like to have that common sense of "we're always safe," especially in our homes. And I think [with] this coronavirus . . . everybody's at home. They are going to be stuck at home, and suddenly it becomes, "well, now, what if someone tries to break in? Because now I'm home. What if this happens? What if that happens?"

As Ian notes, and others suggested as well, the home had become a microcosm of the new texture of insecurity that many Americans were experiencing as the pandemic rolled on. Since the 1950s, homes—especially the suburban home—have paradoxically figured in the American imagination as both sanctuaries of idyllic safety and sites of inherent vulnerability,[37] animating real-life and fictionalized horror from the Charles Manson murders[38] to the movie *Scream*.[39] The lockdown orders of early 2020 put this paradox into overdrive. Many Americans secured their homes like small fortresses fit for a one-person (or one-household) army, buying guns as well as hoarding toilet paper, sanitizers, food, and other essentials.[40] This, in turn, increased the likelihood that the lockdown orders meant to safeguard them from the virus would expose them to new threats (such as surging domestic gun violence, as discussed below).

Gun sellers cited pandemic-related fears, rather than specific fears regarding local crime for example, as driving a meaningful portion of gun sales in early 2020.[41] Aaron watched the coronavirus pandemic unfold from his California gun store. When I interviewed him in April, he admitted, "we are all kind of flying blind . . . [the pandemic] has the potential to be very dangerous to us as a society: economically, socially, everything." He could already see how the pandemic was changing the people who were coming to his gun store: fear, desperation, panic. It was palpable to him: "there is panic, and I see it, and I feel it   I see it and feel it in people's emails and their messages. Their phone calls. In person." The new buyers that came to his store may not have known much about guns, but they knew they had to have one, any gun. Aaron explained,

> I couldn't express it as a percentage, but enough [people] to make a marker in my head, asking "Hey, I've got $900 on my credit card. What will that get me? Tell me what I can buy. I want a pistol, and I want it to be 9 mm. What do you have?" And generally speaking, they'll buy the first thing you suggest.

Aaron wasn't the only one fielding this kind of request. Buyers often reached out to gun sellers not knowing exactly what they wanted, or how they could get it, just that they desperately needed to acquire a gun.

A few gun sellers even told me about calls they receive from hours away and even out of state, from people in places where gun stores had been emptied. One California gun seller in a rural area, far from the metropolises of San Francisco and Los Angeles, conveyed just how motivated buyers had become: "People are making calls on a massive radius from where they are located . . . saying, "Oh, I'll be there in about three hours. I'm leaving here in about 15 minutes!'"

By June 2020, gun sellers were already talking of a second surge, "even bigger than the first." This surge was sparked by a more familiar terrain of racial unrest and rebellion—specifically, the Black Lives Matter and Defund the Police uprisings in the aftermath of George Floyd's murder by Minneapolis police. Unlike their lack of experience with pandemics, Americans alive today have not only experienced waves of racial unrest but have also inherited powerful, historically rooted narratives that frame Black protest and uprising as riotous acts of criminal disorder.[42] Even though the vast majority—96.3 percent, according to one study[43]— were peaceful by any definition, many gun sellers associated the protests of 2020 with criminality, disorder, and violence, viewing racial unrest as a clear warning sign that people had to take their safety and security into their own hands—or, for that matter, holsters.[44] In this regard, the insecurities upon which panicked buyers acted in response to the unrest were similar to the feelings of abandonment activated with the unfolding of the pandemic. Consider how Gabe, Nathan, and Carl made sense of the unrest:

> You are on your own. The riots proved to *everyone*, regardless of political agenda or political affiliation, that they cannot protect you. People were getting drug out of their cars, places of business were being burnt to the ground, people were being killed, people were being attacked, and the police could not do anything. And the general theme was: *I always just thought I was safe. I didn't realize that when it hits the fan, there's no one to protect you but yourself.* (Gabe, white, Michigan)

> When, pardon the language, the shit hits the fan, and you watch it keep hitting the fan. Eventually, you are going to look at your own

views and go—*even though I'm anti-gun, watching these riots, watching these people's houses get broken into, watching, you know, people get murdered. Maybe I should go get a gun just to protect myself* . . . like, oh now Atlanta is in riots. Portland's going crazy! (Nathan, white, Arizona)

Whether it's for providing for your own physical security after the government murders a man [George Floyd], or whether it's for your own financial security when you see your business being destroyed and toilet paper running off the shelves . . . what they are seeing in real-life is that, yes, they are their own first responder. What they are seeing in real life is that police will make a great effort to defend their precinct while literally watching on the same block rioters rifle through businesses and set them on fire . . . all the while not making any effort to stop them whatsoever. Cops [laughs] and the government will protect themselves before they will protect you. (Carl, white, California)

Discussing the events that led to mass protests as well as the protests themselves, these gun sellers focused less on the messages of anti-racism that protesters had tried to convey and more on the general threat they could pose to individual security. The main lesson to be learned from the protests, unrests, and riots, then, was not that life chances are deeply unequal in America (although some gun sellers, like Carl, recognized this); it was that *when* (and not *if*) society collapses around you, you have no one to protect yourself but you. Accordingly, individual vulnerability overwhelmed the racial politics that bred protests in the first place—reframing, for example, police not as perpetrators of violence (as in George Floyd's murder) but rather as negligent protectors against violence (i.e., "the police could not do anything"). This reframing galvanized the need for gun ownership.

Armed individualism could be gleaned from how gun sellers understood the uprisings: in the face of crushing insecurity, guns are the only source of freedom, and the only vessel of equality, that can carry people through. Indeed, the people who gun sellers found flooding their stores seemed to bear out exactly this: the broad appeal of the gun. As first-time gun buyers, women, racial minorities, members of the LBGTQ community, and even liberals came to their stores to buy guns, gun sellers found themselves reassured that they were not merely selling guns to the gun-converted but promoting a right to the gun-curious,[45] a right fundamental to the political order they believed in.

The Freedom in Fear

Because the United States has no national mechanism for tracking gun buyers, we can't be sure exactly how many people bought guns in 2020 or what kind of people they were. We know that in 2020, gun sales most definitely surged from the number of national background checks, even though gun sales hardly match up to background checks in any one-to-one fashion. We can surmise based on aggregated data that gun sales may well have crossed party lines and included a sizeable chunk of first-time buyers: economists Bree Lang and Matthew Lang found that the surge was indistinguishably large in Republican-leaning versus Democrat-leaning states.[46] Survey data, however, provide a conflicting picture with regard to the question of new gun owners: public health scholars Jagdish Khubchandani and James Price[47] found that previously owning a gun was a predictor of pandemic gun purchases, based on a survey conducted via mTurk and social media, as did public health scholars Michael Anestis and Craig Bryan[48] in their census-matched survey of 3,500 Americans. In contrast, political scientists Abigail Vegter and Donald Haider-Markel conducted a nationally representative survey in October 2020 and estimated that 8 percent of US adults purchased a gun between March and August of 2020—a staggering half of whom were first-time gun owners;[49] other scholars put the gun buyers of 2020 closer to 6.5 percent, of whom one-fifth were first-time firearms purchasers.[50] Meanwhile, the National Shooting Sports Foundation,[51] which often relies on gun sellers to gain a picture of gun purchasing in the United States, reported that a striking 40 percent of sales were to first-time gun buyers in the first half of 2020, roughly equating to 5 million new gun owners, with significant leaps in purchases among African Americans and women. Surges in the membership rolls of the National African American Gun Association (NAAGA) since 2019 also vindicate

a leap among purchasers who break with the stereotype of white conservative gun owners;[52] according to NAAGA's founder Philip Smith,
in just 36 hours after George Floyd was murdered by police, 2,000
people joined the organization.[53] By year's end, the NSSF estimated
that 2020's sales resulted in 8.4 million[54] new gun owners across the
United States—a figure close to the number extrapolated in the analysis
from Vegter and Haider-Markel.

As scholars waited (and still wait) for data on how many guns were
sold in 2020 and to whom they were sold, gun sellers were already fielding these would-be buyers. Pausing to articulate what felt so different
about the people coming into his store Aaron told me, "I just feel like
there's this change in attitude, and I tell you . . . the demographic of people
coming in the store is radically different." Noting that this new clientele
was noticeably not "hardcore conservative," he estimated that "upwards
of 75% or more are first-time gun buyers. And of those 75%, I would
argue that at least 50% of them were people that were probably never in
their life planning on buying a gun."[55] The long 2020 had taken people's
differences and pulverized them into a sheer and basic demand for guns.
With a glint of enthusiasm in his voice, Aaron, who identified as libertarian, described the gun buyers of 2020 as a point of pride: "For the first
time, regardless of your demographic, regardless of your background . . .
everybody is . . . looking at the future and realizing, 'Shit. I'm not necessarily guaranteed anything tomorrow.'"

Based on exisiting survey data, the gun buyers of 2020 *did* fit into
many of the categories that struck gun sellers as noteworthy: as compared to their usual clientele, they were less likely to be white men and
more likely to be first-time gun buyers[56] (and thus more likely, as discussed in chapter 3, to be liberal).[57] But Aaron's emphasis on the note-
worthiness of these categories is *itself* revealing. No doubt, his enthusiasm reflected an expanded market—and thus, expanded profits—for
the gun industry. But this isn't the only interpretation. His enthusiasm
for gun buyers across demographics and backgrounds shows just how
ideals of diversity, inclusion, and equality—terms typically associated
with liberal efforts to increase representation in educational and corporate organizations—are viewed through the lens of armed individualism

and enter the democratic imaginations of gun sellers.[58] To gun sellers, the surge of 2020 seemed to vindicate the universal promise of security and defense that guns made. Indeed, Aaron's sentiments intimated an emancipatory flash within gun culture, with gun sellers as its vanguards: an impulse to see guns as universal instruments of empowerment, leveling any disadvantage or difference no matter its form. Guns could stand as vehicles of defense not just for the generic everyman often defaulted as a white, working-class guy, but also for women, for racial and ethnic minorities, for members of the LGBTQ community, even for immigrants and perhaps religious minorities, too. As one *Bearing Arms* headline gleefully noted of the surging gun sales, "there's more diversity at a gun range than a university faculty lounge."[59] No matter who you were, the demographics that gun sellers reported seemed to suggest, you could find a reason to need a gun.

The demographic details varied by shop—some gun sellers were taken aback by the number of women, of Asian Americans, of LGBTQ people, of elderly people. One gun seller described his new clientele as "all 31 flavors," referring to the famous Baskin-Robbins tagline. Another gun seller explained, "All walks of life . . . it's like, huh, this is affecting everybody." A self-described "white guy" in his fifties, Peter in Arizona estimated, like Aaron, that roughly 70 percent of his gun buyers were first-time owners. To illustrate just how much they broke the mold of the typical gun owner, he offered this anecdote of an older gay man: "I had a sixty-year-old man [in the gun store] . . . he'd never seen a gun in his life. A real gun. And he got it on the counter, and for 10 minutes he stared at it, and then he asked me if it was going to go off. And then he wanted to know if it was loaded. And I said, 'You mean like a Pez dispenser?' And you know, we kind of laughed, and he actually became a client—he and his husband came out [to train]. So, an atypical population."

Several gun sellers highlighted the increase in women gun buyers. Perhaps this rise seemed particularly palpable to gun sellers because it followed decades of efforts by gun rights advocates to court women[60] as gun owners, as well as the increasing space for conservative women to adopt a hardened femininity (think: Sarah Palin's Mama Grizzly[61]).

As Nathan described: "I had a big uptick in women who were either single or, you know, were in a partnership but didn't have kids." Paul highlighted women as well: "The women demographic was . . . maybe the highest—they were ones that were kind of on the fence before. They all crossed over during that time." One California gun seller simply noted, "I've never seen so many women." Gun sellers often had gendered explanations for why. Robert, appealing to the gendered division of labor that relegated grocery shopping to women, noted, "When they see that they cannot get the toilet paper, they cannot get the meat, we have lines and rationing,[62] they are the ones seeing the stuff on TV, people getting their carts knocked over, raided, fighting in the parking lot. And they are thinking, well heck! 'My husband doesn't come with me grocery shopping—I need to be self-empowered.'" A gun, it seemed, could be a stand-in for a missing male protector.[63] Rebecca, a white gun seller in Michigan, also emphasized the vulnerability of women, especially single women. When asked to characterize what was distinctive about her new clientele, she described: "Single women. Specifically, that live alone. Don't have a dog at the house or something like that. People that are more apartment-dwellers. I'm seeing a lot more people from the city directly than the rural areas that our shop typically services: 'I want to be able to protect myself and my home if something were to happen.'"

Several gun sellers also noted a surge in racial minorities, particularly Asian Americans. Hate crimes against Asian Americans would rise dramatically and disproportionately in 2020 and into 2021,[64] revealing both acutely heightened vulnerability as well as an appalling lack of government protection. But even before the statistics were clear, in early 2020, some gun sellers could already anticipate the rising violence from the Asian American buyers that came to their stores. Dave, a fifty-something white gun seller from Florida, characterized the surge in purchasing in his shop by noting,

> A lot of Asian Americans that we normally don't have. They would come in typically in big groups of people. Yeah, they were buying guns like crazy. Which, I mean they were just—they would come in

and they'd all want guns and um—and they were really afraid of re-taliation [due to the coronavirus] . . . They were really afraid . . . that people were going to attack them.

Similarly, Andrew, the biracial gun seller from California, sold a gun after a high-profile attack against a Chinese American in San Francisco had rocked the Asian American community. He explained,

> I had previously read about an attack on an old Chinese American in San Francisco by a gang of people on the street. There were racial slurs, and corona insults thrown as the guy was senselessly beaten and kicked on the curb. A week and a half later, I sold a gun to a man who told me that his [relative] in San Francisco had been beaten by a street gang over being Chinese during coronavirus. That's how he said it—he said, "during coronavirus."[65]

Andrew connected this sale and others to an ethic of empowerment: "I tell you I delight when I put a gun in the hands of any marginalized or discriminated minority group. I believe that is *exactly* what the gun is for. So that they can defend themselves and stand as an *individual* even against oppression."

Robert, from Florida, also connected the appeal of guns to Asian Americans to a surge in anti-Asian hate crimes. As he described,

> We've had . . . anybody who identifies as Asian, for two reasons. One, they are typically business owners in lower income areas and two, they are being targeted due to the "Chinese virus" or the nature of where we believe this has been originated from. Chinese restaurants, for example, closed before restaurants were required to close because they were afraid that people would be blaming them. There could be racism . . . since the '90s, they saw it can go bad really, really fast.

Like Andrew, Robert recognizes the appeal of guns as tools of empow-erment and, indeed, asserts guns as a solution to systematic oppression, like racism. And Robert concludes with a loaded statement: "since the '90s, they saw it can go bad really, really fast." As he made clear during the interview, Robert's statement referred to the 1992 Los Angeles riots and the meme-inspiring images of armed Korean Americans on the rooftops of their businesses (who, importantly, never killed anyone— only firing warning shots).[66] The reference surely asserts gun acquisition as a response to civil unrest and criminal insecurity, but it also intimates the complicated racial politics at play in the celebration of armed people of color. Though Korean Americans were marginalized politically, socially, and economically in Los Angeles leading up to the riots,[67] they became celebrated heroes, particularly among conservatives, once they found themselves on the front lines of the 1992 LA riots in part because their actions—small business owners defending themselves with guns against riotous African Americans—resonated profoundly with both the myth of the American Dream and anti-Black racism.[68]

If the historical specter of Black protest, civil unrest, and rioting haunted the Asian American politics of gun ownership, the contemporary appearance of the Black Lives Matter uprisings shaped how gun sellers understood African American gun buyers. For example, Ben in Michigan referenced the Black Lives Matter protests ongoing at the time of our interview—and the fears of civil unrest that they instigated—to explain an uptick in racial minorities buying guns:

> From minorities, and from Black women actually . . . [I hear] that a large number do not support the Black Lives Matter protests or rioting or any of that . . . And that's the greatest thing about gun ownership! Everyone can connect in it—it's a primal thing and a big jump in personal responsibility that carries over into everyday life.

In this excerpt, Ben salutes a respectable faction of African Americans who embrace armed individualism: those who "do not support the Black Lives Matter protests or rioting or any of that" and can see the value of empowerment—that is, personal protection—that guns can provide. He situates guns as vehicles of protection that transcend demographics—what he called at one point a "connecting theme among the demographics"— for those willing to take the personal responsibility to own and bear them. In doing so, Ben, like Robert, intimates the complicated politics of gun ownership and race. As Ben's words make clear, African Americans were not denied entrance to gun culture but, at least in Ben's shop, enthusiastically welcomed. At the same time, they seemed to pay a distinct "price" for their admission "ticket" rooted in the racial politics of respectability:[69] they had to not only embrace guns as instruments of personal empowerment but also refuse the collective modes of redress, such as mass protests like the Black Lives Matter movement, that have historically characterized Black politics in America.

The sudden diversity in gun buyers activated a long-held understanding among Second Amendment enthusiasts that guns were "great equalizers," along the lines of the gun-famous mantra that "God made man and woman, but [the nineteenth-century gun entrepreneur and subsequent firearms manufacturer namesake] Samuel Colt made them equal." Celebrated as an individualistic approach to the all-too-human vulnerabilities of insecurity and uncertainty, guns figure into the political imaginations of gun rights advocates as a solution that transcends the inequalities of race, gender, sexuality, and other lines of difference.

From another perspective, though, this embrace of guns represented not empowerment but further danger. Increased gun sales interacted with a "perfect storm"—to use public health scholar Daniel Webster's description[70]—of economic distress, pandemic lockdowns, political instability, and overall social disruption.[71] While women and racial minorities were celebrated as the new face of gun ownership, they were also the disproportionate victims of the record-breaking surges in domestic gun violence and street gun violence, reflecting the prevalence of guns as well as the patterned systems of inequality that render vulnerable Americans more likely to be victims.[72] Though they may have also found gun violence intolerable, gun sellers rejected the logic that guns were simply means of violence. Rather, if "power flows from the barrel of a gun,"[73] then many gun sellers—as one Arizona gun seller told me—viewed their work fundamentally in terms of "empower[ing] people." And to gun sellers, a gun empowers its owner not just as a means of personal protection but also as a vehicle of political education.

Common Sense Gun Control

Political vanguards in the business of firearms, gun sellers did not just sell guns to the onslaught of new gun buyers; they engaged their customers, queried their motivations, and alerted them to the gun laws that these would-be gun owners had perhaps only considered in the abstract. In doing so, they provided them—as gun sellers described it—with a reeducation in gun control. As Nathan in Arizona told me, "the best part of it is being able to talk to my customers." Gun sellers told me that first-time gun buyers often owned up to their newfound need for a gun, admitting that "I've never owned a firearm before, but I think maybe now is the time. I want to be able to protect my family," as Leonard from Florida paraphrased. Many proactively engaged their customers simply because that was how they had always run their businesses: Arizona's Frank, a gun seller who described himself as American Indian and white, told me, "I'm not just going to sell somebody a gun [when] they come in and [say] 'I want a gun!' I always talk to people, find out what they want, what do they want the gun for, what's their plan?"

Because all gun sales other than private transactions have to be processed through a licensed firearm dealer, the very act of buying a gun opened up a space for a sort of crash course in gun policy. Gun sellers told me that their own adherence to gun laws exacerbated the desperation in buyers—which they took as an opportunity to school new gun owners in the politics of guns. (Whether they treated different gun buyers differently is another issue; though they often emphasized their embrace of customers of different racial and gender identities, they were very open with their differential treatment of customers they saw as "liberal," as we will explore in chapter 3.) Aaron in California explained how this opportunity for political education presented itself "multiple times a day": "People [come in and say], 'I'm here to pick up my gun!' No, you are here to start the background check. You are here to start your 10-day wait[ing period]." Rather than inspiring confidence in the state's regulatory framework, Aaron found what he considered to be strict gun laws only ramped up the panic of new customers:

> The panic in people, when you tell them, "Hey I'm really sorry, you have to wait 10 days." I think for those people, this is back in late March, mid- to late March when this was just kind of getting going, people were mortified that they couldn't take this gun out with them. And they could not believe—and you could see the panic, and hear it in their voice. Ten days is a long time to wait if I need this tomorrow night. You know? And that was kind of the mentality.

What gun buyers wanted was guns; what they got was a political education. The very gun control laws meant to regulate access to firearms were being used to galvanize would-be gun owners into the pro-gun project.

Billy in California likewise found himself explaining the process of purchasing a gun to "frustrated" buyers: "Just [from] the process alone, people are so frustrated. [And] these are people that like voted for gun control and stuff. And they came in here and they're like 'Oh, I'm clean, I'm a law-abiding citizen!' Well, there's still hoops you got to jump through." Andrew, also in California, likewise conveyed hysteria and anguish that took hold of people in his store in the face of waiting periods: "Many of our anti-gun would-be customers were upset [about having to undergo a waiting period and thus delay taking possession of their guns] to the point of getting red in the face and shaking."

A *The Truth About Guns* headline captured this contempt for gun buyers who didn't want to wait for their guns: "Karen Isn't Happy About Waiting to Get Her First Gun During an Emergency" (March 30).[74] Though "Karen" has provided the Left with "a symbol of racism and white privilege,"[75] this conservative derision for "Karens" seemed more aligned with a disdain for demanding, nagging, "shrill,"[76] or "nasty"[77] women (adjectives associated with women Democrats such as Nancy Pelosi and Hillary Clinton). In response to the "Karens" they might encounter in their stores, gun sellers asserted themselves as responsible to the legal terms of their firearms licenses and committed to the gun rights they espoused—in legal compliance with, but political defiance of, the gun policies they enforced by virtue of their profession.[78]

While gun sellers in California—the state I studied with the most extensive regulations on gun purchasing—were particularly vocal about their frustrated buyers, gun sellers elsewhere also found themselves having to correct misperceptions regarding gun laws, explaining, for example, why buyers could not have guns shipped directly to their homes. A white gun seller in Florida named Jake joked, "Yes you can buy a gun online—you can actually pay for it! [laughs] But you can't take possession of it. And people do not understand that." Frank in Arizona likewise noted, "you can [buy a gun online], but it has to be shipped to a licensed dealer in your state. That was a surprise to a few of those people . . . they were surprised at the fact that, 'Oh! I can't just buy it and have it shipped to me?' No, you can't." Robert also joked: "I've had people calling up—'I need it delivered to my house! Why can't I order it off the Internet? Why can't I do this? What do you mean a three-day wait?' I tell them, 'this is common sense gun control, isn't it?' [laughs]."

As suggested by Robert's sardonic laugh, gun sellers schooled these new gun owners with a satisfied smugness, eager to provide them with a lesson on how gun law really "works." As Brad, a white gun seller in Arizona, told me,

> A person will call and say, "I ordered a gun online, and they're telling me I have to have it transferred to you, and you charge for that? That's not what I understand [to be gun law]." I mean, I've had people argue with me . . . I've said, "That's what you read in your newspaper, and that's what you are listening to [from] the Democrats in Washington, DC, but that's not the way it works."

Attributing misinformation to a person's sheep-like willingness to believe what they've been told (i.e., from "the Democrats in Washington, DC"), the sheer act of purchasing a gun allowed Brad and other gun sellers an inroad to sway first-time gun buyers into the worldview that gun sellers embraced. Similarly, Dylan, another white gun seller in Arizona, bemoaned people's reliance on misleading news as he parodied first-time gun buyers in his store: "Oh, this isn't what the news has been telling me!" Dylan saw that the process of purchasing a gun compelled these new gun buyers to "start thinking about [gun rights] more when they found out the hoops they had to jump through to get the gun." In other words, the experience of purchasing a gun—according to Dylan, Brad, and others—could serve as a kind of political incitement against gun regulations. As Brad noted to me, "Some people were like, 'this is baloney, we shouldn't have to do this!' And I was like, 'I agree! But that's the way it is!' [And] other ones [were] like 'Okay, now I see why this [fighting against gun control] is so important.'"

As Joan Burbick argues in her 2006 book *Gun Show Nation*,[79] the sale of guns is intricately wrapped up in the politics of guns. The people who animated Burbick's book on gun shows were largely white conservative men who embraced guns as a means of resisting government tyranny and defending their standing at the top of America's social, political, and economic hierarchies. Almost 15 years after Burbick's observations, the gun sellers I interviewed described themselves and their stores in ways that echoed her analysis, albeit with one key difference: the clientele they suddenly found themselves serving no longer fit what many called the "traditional" gun owner as white conservative men but instead noticeably included women, racial minorities, sexual minorities and, as will be discussed in more detail in chapter 3, even *liberals*. At turns smug and sympathetic, gun sellers were almost always quite satisfied to remind these new buyers not just *what* "common sense gun control" looked like on the ground, but *how* to make sense of it—as government overreach on a right that perilously delayed its exercise just when that right was most urgently needed.

Gunning for Democracy

Gun sellers weren't the only ones to see the possibility for tyranny in the catastrophes of 2020. Noting an inherent democratic tension between "protecting lives and preserving freedom,"[80] scholars warned that "many western democracies, . . . attempt[ing] to adopt a war-like response to the threat posed by [COVID-19], [are] reacting in remarkably similar ways" as they had to the threat of terrorism.[81] Across the world, institutionalized channels of emergency response were bypassed; expertise became political.[82] In-person elections[83] suddenly seemed an ill-fated luxury in a pandemic driven by human contact, and quarantines and lockdowns became go-to tactics "not so much inspired by benign, 'pure' science, as constituted thorough political strategy."[84] Yet, as cultural critic Alberto Toscano presciently reminds us, "the role of the state . . . is marked by deep ambivalences, we might even say contradictions."[85] David E. Pozen and Kim Lane Scheppele[86] characterize the US response to the coronavirus pandemic, especially at the federal level, as a manifestation not of *overreach* but of *underreach*: "situations where an executive sees a significant threat coming, has access to information about what might mitigate or avert the threat along with the power to set a potentially effective plan in motion, and refuses to pursue such a plan."[87] Pozen and Scheppele note that "underreach may also tend to foster cynicism and distrust of government, diminish state capacity, exacerbate inequality, and stimulate dangerous or inefficient forms of self-help by private actors,"[88] such as defensive gun ownership. Guns serve as powerful symbols of individual sovereignty, personal freedom, and rights—so powerful, in fact, that they stand to crowd out other possible solutions, including collective solutions.[89]

Indeed, underreach helps explain why, by the end of March 2020, guidelines from the Department of Homeland Security declared gun stores—and the broader gun industry—part of the critical infrastructure. The decision, praised by the National Shooting Sports Foundation as "recognizing the vital role our industry fulfills in our nation,"[90] responded to government underreach by presenting an individualized solution—the gun—to the insecurities that could otherwise be addressed through the collective efficacy of the state. But the Department of Homeland Security's decision also represented to gun rights advocates a victory against government overreach, made acute by the coronavirus pandemic. As the NRA noted, "The COVID-19 panic has been used by would-be state and local authoritarians as an excuse to keep Americans from exercising their right to keep and bear arms. Thankfully, American gun owners have a friend in the White House that [sic] has worked to protect their rights on the federal level by declaring the firearms industry to be critical infrastructure."[91]

Critics, like president of Everytown for Gun Safety John Feinblatt, described the DHS advisory decision as "shameful" and "nonsensical"—an example of the "Trump administration . . . caving to the firearm industry by treating gun store workers just like the real frontline responders—police, doctors, nurses."[92] Gun sellers, of course, would take umbrage at the notion that they aren't "frontline workers"; they saw themselves providing a vital good (guns) and protecting a vital right (gun rights)—services that became ever more urgent as threats from above and demand from below increased. No matter that you can't shoot a virus, as even a few gun sellers themselves joked. That wasn't the point: rather, armed individualism provided a means of taking control of uncertainty, and it redrafted from below the meaning of popular sovereignty that positioned gun ownership as an ever more central civic act. Political engagement—certainly for gun sellers, and perhaps also for the new gun buyers they aimed to educate—centered on the celebration of the gun as a vehicle of individual freedom: individual freedom from government overreach, individual freedom amid government underreach, and individual freedom *despite* social difference, such as race or gender. The individual freedom, in short, of *being left alone*.[93] But in forwarding a version of freedom—individualistic, anti-statist, and superseding of social difference—that tends to resonate, though not exclusively so, with the lived experiences of conservative white men, armed individualism passed over alternative ways of understanding freedom, such as freedom *through* collective action as well as freedom *within* social difference, sidelining the hard work of multiracial democracy with an enthusiastic appeal to the gun as the great equalizer.[94]

The politics of guns in 2020 thus brings us back to a paradox at the heart of American democracy, a paradox animated by the tension between government underreach and government overreach and the precarious balance between collective efficacy and private initiative it compels. Guns are potent symbols for negotiating American democracy's contradictions precisely because guns can and do play such divergent roles in the chronicles that mark American history up to the present: chronicles of white supremacist violence, exploitation, and genocide, on the one hand; and on the other hand, self-reliance, resistance, and empowerment for white men and, in important instances, marginalized people as well.[95] Imagined as premiere instruments *both* for resisting government tyranny *and* for filling in the security voids of government underreach,[96] guns are not less powerful because of their ambiguous social import but all the more powerful because this ambiguity speaks to fundamental, and arguably irresolvable, tensions surrounding the relationship between the state and the citizen within democratic orders—tensions that, in the US context, are inextricably bound up with American democracy's long-standing ambivalence toward inclusion as a substantive, rather than merely superficial, political value. Thus, gun sellers did not merely retreat from democracy. Rather, they redrafted and defended it from below, turning their stores into political venues where they could express *and* enact armed individualism. They schooled the first-time gun buyers who flocked to their stores, and they resisted what they saw as government tyranny in the form of lockdown orders and public health restrictions.

And as they did so, they often embraced a politics of knowledge that resonated with, but also transcended, their embrace of gun rights: conspiracism.

Conspiracism

A style of knowledge-seeking, conspiracism doubts the "official story" and places stock in a network of hidden power brokers to explain events and trends. Conspiracism is an epistemological style, a way of relating to reality. It is also a historically rooted, and commonplace, way of thinking in the United States.[1] As the late historian Bernard Bailyn[2] noted, those who led efforts to overthrow British rule in the United States believed "that they were faced with a deliberate conspiracy to destroy the balance of the constitution and eliminate their freedom"[3]; the Declaration of Independence was not just a white propertied man's defense of liberty but also "the enumeration of conspiratorial efforts"[4] undertaken by the British Crown. Conspiracist thinking can be traced through the mistrust toward centralized government in the early years of the American Republic—mistrust that framed said government as an encroachment on the self-rule of white, property-owning men as well as a threat to the system of slavery that advantaged them. Historian Carol Anderson[5] and legal scholar Carl Bogus[6] have both examined how conspiracist fears regarding federal infringement on slavery—and the institutions, like the militia, that protected it—facilitated the inclusion of the Second Amendment in the Bill of Rights. Into the nineteenth and twentieth centuries, conspiracist thinking allowed whites to frame the systematic repression, brutalization, and terrorization of African Americans— whether under slavery, Jim Crow, or the War on Crime—as a reasonable response to an unseen but sinister threat of Black uprising. Into the twentieth century, conspiracist thinking was responsible for government-coordinated campaigns against African American activists in the 1960s (COINTEL-PRO[7]), sexual minorities in the federal government in the 1940s and beyond (the Lavender Scare[8]), and Jewish members of the Hollywood elite in the same period (the Hollywood Blacklist[9]), bolstering white supremacy, homophobia, and xenophobia. Themselves motivated by conspiracy theories fueled by bigotry, these initiatives in turn gave rise to their *own* conspiracy theories among the marginalized peoples that these campaigns targeted[10]—attempts by everyday people to make sense of the systematic disadvantage they experience—and many of *those* conspiracy theories have turned out nothing short of true, including the Watergate scandal, the Tuskegee Study of Untreated Syphilis, Operation Paperclip, Project Mkultra, and more.

Conspiracism has thus long crossed ideological divides and appealed across demographic categories in the United States. Yet, there is a predilection for conspiracism that characterizes contemporary American conservativism. For decades, conservative and right-leaning Americans have been more likely to distrust scientific elites[11] and the mainstream media;[12] one recent Pew survey found that 52 percent of Republican-identified respondents had "not too much" or "no confidence at all" in "college professors to act in the public interest" (in contrast, 83 percent of Democrat-identified respondents had a fair amount or great amount of confidence).[13] Leading up to 2020, nearly two-thirds of all Americans reported that they found it "very hard" or "somewhat hard" to distinguish fact from fiction when listening to elected officials and 61 percent believed that mass media ignores important issues, but Republicans were more worried than their Democrat counterparts about bias in news media, especially one-sided coverage involving Trump.[14] If conspiracism emerges at the intersection of "declining public trust in institutions and a legitimacy crisis around expert knowledge,"[15] then contemporary conservatives seemed primed for conspiracist thinking as 2020 began to unfold.

As political scientist Matthew Lacombe suggests, the NRA has anticipated, if not helped facilitate, this conspiracist turn in conservative politics more broadly. Intimating that every piece of gun regulation, no matter how trivial, is ultimately connected to a plot to disarm the American population, the slippery slope argument is itself conspiratorial. But, unlike many of the conspiracy theories that circulated in the 1960s and its aftermath, the slippery slope argument rests less on solving a perplexing puzzle of mismatched facts and bizarre circumstances (e.g., who was really behind the assassination of JFK?) and more on asserting a common enemy and their common goal: liberal gun control advocates who wanted to disarm Americans by any means necessary. As political scientists Nancy L. Rosenblum and Russell Muirhead contend in *A Lot of People Are Saying*,[16] the ascendency of Trump to the US presidency arguably mainstreamed a distinctive brand of conspiracist thinking centered on questioning the basic nature of political reality. Legitimated by Trump and amplified within social media echo chambers, by the end of 2020, conspiracist beliefs had become uniquely prevalent on the Right: seven out of ten Republicans believed that a Deep State was at work to undermine Trump, and as many as two-thirds of Republicans believed that Biden fraudulently won the presidency (a claim debunked by the failure of the Trump administration to overturn the election results through the US court system).[17]

Conspiracism reflects the general ethos of anti-elitist sentiment among conservatives, but it also invigorates that sentiment with a sense of control, empowerment, and assuredness. Put differently, conspiracism is as much about locating truth as it is a way for restoring a sense of self-in-control. It allows its adherents to reclaim a sense of truth in a world perceived as intractable (even if this truth about how the world works is paradoxically wrapped up in skepticism). It empowers its adherents by demonstrating their unique access to truth (they are uniquely skeptical and, thus, politically astute). And, it reinforces their political righteousness by doubling down on the nefarious opportunism of their opponents (e.g., "Trump didn't lose the election in 2019, Biden stole it"). It is not incidental that conspiracy thinking emphasizes fringe or far-flung theories, ideas, or assertions; the very fact that these theories appear fringe or far-flung demonstrates the rugged individualism of its adherents as deliberate and dedicated fact-vetters. It also distinguishes them from their political opponents, who are seen as dupes to whatever the elite establishment tells them. Paradoxically, this means that conspiracism is noncommittal: rather than articulating an alternative, adherents can silence or stigmatize those challenging the status quo by simply raising doubts about the intentions and integrity of their opponents. In 2020, this style of political debate helped excuse adherents from taking seriously the critiques forwarded by Black Lives Matter activists—or even explicitly choosing sides for or against white supremacy. In other words, conspiracism can serve not to make meaning per se but rather to circumvent the urgent questions of collective action and of democratic deliberation by providing *through knowledge* the self-reliance that guns provide *through force*.

CHAPTER 2

Conspiracism for the People

The year 2020 introduced a number of new turns-of-phrase: the *quarantini*, the *coronacut, zoombombing, virtual happy hour*, the *COVID 15, coronapocalypse*, the *Before Times, doomscrolling*, and, finally, *COVID deniers*. The latter described those who disregarded public health guidelines, believing the virus to be an overblown hoax or conspiracy and themselves to be inured to it. Flaunting conspiracies around the virus and downplaying public health recommendations, many conservative figureheads led the charge for coronavirus denial. The Republican and former presidential candidate Herman Cain, who refused to wear a mask, attended a large public rally for Trump in Tulsa, Oklahoma, in June 2020,[1] and later tweeted that "PEOPLE ARE FED UP!" about mask policies. Gun rights advocate, musician, and Trump loyalist Ted Nugent called the coronavirus pandemic "scammy" and "not a real pandemic."[2] And former President Trump undermined CDC guidance by promising a magical reprieve from the pandemic: in February, he wagered that it is "going to disappear. One day it's like a miracle—it will disappear."[3]

Many conservative Americans followed suit. Compared to race, geography, gender, and age, political affiliation explained the largest gap in what activities—going to the grocery store, gathering with friends, getting a haircut—people were comfortable undertaking amid the pandemic.[4] As the virus's trajectory unfolded over 2020, Republicans were far less likely to see the pandemic as a major threat to personal health and the health of the US population as compared to Democrats,[5] and Democrats were also far more concerned about contracting and spreading the virus.[6] By mid-2020, the vast majority of Democrats believed that masks should be worn all or most of the time in public (86%) as compared to barely half of Republicans (52%).[7] To wit, some people attended so-called COVID parties hosted by someone who had tested positive for the virus;[8] others simply disregarded public health recommendations. Brian Lee Hitchens, a taxi driver in Florida, and his wife Erin, a pastor, oscillated between believing the virus was an all-out hoax and thinking it real but overblown. They refused to take heed of public health recommendations, like masks and social distancing.[9] Labeling the pandemic a "scamdemic"[10] and frustrated with coronavirus restrictions, Tony Green of Texas[11] decided to hold a family retreat at his lake home. Also from Texas, William Bloom declined to wear a mask; he "didn't believe in it" and "didn't think it would affect me."[12] Herman Cain died of COVID-19 complications,[13] as did Erin Lee Hitchens and William Bloom. Ted Nugent, Donald Trump, and Tony Green all suffered severe ramifications from contracting the virus; Nugent reported that "I thought I was dying,"[14] while Trump and Green each had to be hospitalized. Meanwhile, Green survived, but his family retreat ultimately turned morbid: not only did at least 13 other family members test positive for the virus, but two died.[15]

The conspiracist thinking that made denial of the pandemic sensible, however, was hardly confined to it. Rather, it seemed increasingly visible in all corners of political life throughout 2020, serving as a means to make sense of everything from Black Lives Matter protests to Donald Trump's electoral loss. Some fell so deep into conspiracist thinking that they embraced "big tent conspiracy theories," like QAnon, united by the Deep State conspiracy theory that—in the description in the *New York Times*—"former President Trump is facing down a shadowy cabal of Democratic pedophiles"[16] (a claim that persists despite no evidence). For many onlookers, conservatives were acting out the conspiracist tendencies that historian Richard Hofstadter labeled the "paranoid style" in US conservative politics[17]—a pathological scourge on liberal democracy's promises of popular sovereignty and political equality. Indeed, people like Jake Angeli—the so-called QAnon Shaman who entered the Capitol Building on January 6, 2021, bare-chested and wearing a headdress of fur and horns, and who was later diagnosed with an array of mental health problems[18]—reinforced the stereotype of conspiracy adherents as narcissistic, unhinged, and aberrant.

The Jake Angelis of the Right are evocative archetypes of conspiracism, but they misleadingly suggest that conspiracist thinking is fundamentally fringe to the democratic order of things. Rather, conspiracism—and the populist search for an enemy that it often articulates—has been the bedfellow of American democracy since its inception.[19] As legal scholar Mark Fenster[20] reminds us, conspiracism "is not foreign to democracy" but, like populism, is an "aspect of the 'perpetual contest' of democracy."[21] As anti-democratic as its manifestations might appear, conspiracism is an expression of a wish shaped by the principle of popular sovereignty: to shrink the impassable gap between ruler and ruled by championing the self-rule of the people as the authentic vehicle of equality, freedom, justice—and truth. Put differently, conspiracism can provide the political language for grappling with difficulties inherent in consensus-based, representative politics[22]—in Fenster's words, a "populist theory of power."[23] If populism is a political circuitry by which exclusion, especially racist and nativist exclusion, can become embedded within democratic thought by shrinking the confines of "the people" to exclude the "enemies of the people," then conspiracism provides its motherboard—the set of narratives, rationalities, and sentiments that designate certain people as public enemies and that justify their exclusion from "the people." For this reason, Fenster reminds us, conspiracism is ambivalent: it exposes fundamental, and real, flaws in democratic political order, but it habitually does so through a fundamental misrecognition and simplification of power relations, often exacerbating the moral absolutism and social bigotry that stand to undermine liberal democracy.

Through the looking glass of gun politics, we can engage and better understand contemporary conspiracism from the bottom up—how it becomes appealing to its adherents, how they embrace and express it, and with what consequences for American democracy as an inclusive enterprise. Gun sellers embraced deliberate unawareness as a mark of political perceptiveness; doubled down on their own experiences despite expert knowledge attesting otherwise; and turned to skepticism as a means of avoiding discomforting and discordant political realities. A political language as well as a meaning-making practice, gun sellers' conspiracist thinking prioritized skepticism over consensus, emphasized experience over expertise and, ultimately, elevated conservative ideals—self-reliance, anti-statism, and individualism—as markers of full citizenship. At the same time, conspiracist thinking helped to stifle dissenting voices as well as the elites that appear to validate or vindicate them, including those voices calling for collective responses to social problems (i.e., public health officials) and those voices pressing for racial equality and justice (i.e., Black Lives Matter protesters and activists). Amid the fraught relationship between conspiracism and democracy, conspiracism served as a civic tool that gun sellers used to make sense of, and respond to, unsettled and unsettling political realities.

The Conservative Couriers of Conspiracism

Attempts to understand today's conspiracist thinking often revolve around one key figure: Donald Trump. As political scientist Mark Brewer remarked, "it is hard to imagine a better fit for the populist theme of conspiratorial threat than Donald Trump."[24] Brewer explains: "populism needs an enemy, and in many instances that enemy is engaged in a conspiracy to harm the people, to take from them what is rightfully theirs and destroy their way of life."[25] Under Trumpism, that enemy has often taken the form of racialized minorities (immigrants, people of color) and the elites that are believed to coddle them (liberals, Democrats, progressives). Loud proponent of Birther-ism (the debunked claim that Obama was not born in the United States and thus unqualified to be president), progenitor of "fake news" and "alternative facts" as household terms, and disregarder of inconvenient evidence in arenas from public health to electoral procedure,[26] by 2020 Trump had earned a unique moniker from one of the journalist outlets he most reviled: the New York Times designated him as "Conspiracist in Chief."[27]

Trump is a crucial figurehead in understanding the proliferation of conspiracist thinking on the Right today; however, conspiracism has had much deeper roots in conservative thought. Take the so-called Deep State narrative—the idea that nefarious shadow forces are working to undermine American government from within and must be stopped by a strongman leader like Trump. As media scholars Whitney Phillips and Ryan Milner[28] note, this narrative derives its power from "a centuries-old belief that embedded within every rung of society are demonic elements whose sole, nefarious purpose is to undermine Christianity and, indeed, Western Civilization itself." This worldview— predicated on a stark binary between good and evil that is expressed today in conservative corners through a denouncement of all things liberal—reflected and reinforced the conspiracy thinking that has characterized the contemporary conservative movement since its incarnations in the 1950s. As early as the 1950s, conservative media activists justified the need for alternative channels of political discourse— newspapers, radio shows, publishing houses, and eventually television networks—by decrying the presumed liberal bias they saw in mainstream media and championing a populist stance that elevated the voices of "real Americans."[29] Conservative outlets' blending of "the liberal bias story and the populist story" (as media scholar Reece Peck[30] describes it with respect to Fox News) not only allowed conservative media to adopt an "outsider" status despite its access to economic and political resources;[31] it also allowed space for conspiracist thinking to flourish as an explanation for the ascendancy of liberal policies, politics, and politicians. Purged of liberal bias, this network of conservative media created an insular ecosystem of knowledge that fed off of itself: "existing separately from established media enterprises meant conservatives in media turned to one another to expand audiences, spread publicity, and bolster content . . . to provide evidence for claims, conservatives would cite one another."[32] By the turn of the twenty-first century, these efforts would culminate in Fox News, a "fair and balanced" cable news network that championed conservative ideologies "not by convincing the public that Fox was going to be politically neutral, but rather by hollowing out the very concepts of 'balance' and 'objectivity' themselves"[33] in favor of "truthiness" and "alternative facts" felt to be true, even if they were not, in fact, true at all.[34]

With the help of media activists and politicians, conspiracist thinking became woven into the fabric of conservative politics, coordinating different swaths of conservatives—from evangelical Christians to gun-toting libertarians—into similar styles of political reasoning. But rather than signaling brash anti-intellectualism, conspiracist thinking served as the basis for a "popular intellect" that "embrace[d] lay forms of knowledge such as personal experience in an attempt to perform (and construct) a working class brand of intellectualism," to borrow from communications scholar Reece Peck's study of Fox News punditry.[35] As I would find in my interviews, gun sellers mobilized conspiracist thinking to assert skepticism and even deliberate unknowing as forms of agency and to regard first-hand and second-hand experiences as the best sources of truth—even if, or perhaps especially if, they contested expert truth.

Suspicious Times

The gun sellers I interviewed were largely conservative and often vociferous fans of Trump. However, although they often enthusiastically echoed Trump's talking points, their embrace of conspiracist thinking couldn't be reduced to a simple story of political brain-washing. Rather than a form of "false consciousness" that seeped into the minds of the unwitting or deluded, conspiracist thinking emerged as a *tool*, a folk theory-of-knowledge that allowed conservatives to navigate their political realities, including the insecurities and uncertainties they faced in 2020.

The pandemic had split open a gash of uncertainty at a level that, as gun sellers understood it, was largely unfamiliar to Americans. Aaron, a white and Hispanic gun seller in California, noted, "we think we are isolated and that can never happen here. But realities of the world—and I get it, we've been lulled to complete peace and tranquility, I mean the last major thing like this that happened was 9/11. I mean . . . that was a long time ago." Dave, a white gun seller in Florida, agreed: "nobody's ever experienced going to a store and not being able to get toilet paper, seeing all the meat gone, and so I think there was some fear of civil unrest because they thought people were going to go out and try to steal their toilet paper, or food, or something." In Arizona, Liam, a white gun seller in his thirties, put it in apocalyptic terms, noting that, "You don't know what's next. Is this a pandemic that's going to wipe us out? Is this the apocalypse? A lot of people truly thought this was an apocalypse, and they needed to protect their stuff, you know? 'We have food, we have toilet paper, we have water—but what's going to keep someone with a gun from getting it?'"

The confusion, insecurity, and uncertainty called for answers, but from whom? Rather than turn to political and scientific elites for guidance, gun sellers felt they were responsible for discerning the truth of their political realities. They emphasized the burden of sifting reality from the fake news they saw promulgated by mainstream media. For example, gun sellers often offered that they no longer watch "mainstream"[36] news channels:

> If the media wants to be biased, that's okay for them to be biased. They should at least tell you they are biased. . . . let's take the big one: CNN! How many times have they had a story where it's been proven bogus? (Liam, white, Arizona)

> Quite frankly, I don't even watch the corporate media. I just have no interest in that nonsense and that propaganda. I don't care if you are watching Fox News or CNN, it's all lies. (Carl, white, California)

> I don't watch the alphabet channels, or CNN, but you know, I do catch some news, on talk radio and also on TV with Fox News. (Leonard, white, Florida)

These and other gun sellers emphasized that they resisted believing out of hand the information circulated on social or mainstream media, as well as information disseminated by experts within media, government, or the scientific establishment. In this way, gun sellers distinguished themselves as being deliberately "out of the know,"[37] that is, removed from what they see as the distortions and lies emanating from the mainstream knowledge-producing institutions within American society, such as mainstream media. This, in their view, positioned them as *more* "in the know" than those—particularly liberals, as will be unraveled in the next chapter—who thoughtlessly and sheep-ishly consumed mainstream media outlets.

In contrast to consuming mainstream media, gun sellers tended to value knowledge gathered through their own efforts, searching the Internet for relevant historical anecdotes, policy white papers, and statistics. One gun seller described looking up past CDC reports; another mentioned researching crime rates since the early 1990s; still another discussed extensive learning about gun laws from YouTube and other Internet-based crowdsourcing. Traditionally a term to describe the work of trained scientists, some gun sellers used the word "research"[38] as a commonplace practice that described a deliberate, bottom-up acquisition of knowledge as opposed to the humdrum consumption of information via government dictates and media headlines. While people across the board turn to the Internet to seek out certainty beyond the confounding headlines, this approach to knowledge appears to have a distinctively right-wing flair. As sociologists Ruth Braunstein, Jen Schradie, and Francesca Tripodi[39] show in separate studies of the politics of conservative knowledge-seeking, conservatives approach digital space as a means of consuming and proliferating the "truths" they see as obscured, twisted, or misrepresented by mainstream media by engaging a wide array of sources: blogs, alternative news media, YouTube videos, podcasts, Twitter and Facebook feeds, as well as online platforms aimed at conservatives, like Gab and Rumble.[40] Interestingly, this emphasis on direct access to knowledge resonates not just with a stylized democratic celebration of popular sovereignty but also, as Tripodi suggests, with religious practices among protestants that root one's relationship to truth in individual biblical study.[41] Thus, far from being "'tricked' into supporting Trump" (or other conservative politicians and platforms), Tripodi[42] argues that conservatives draw on this distinctive brand of media literacy—resisting elitist accounts and instead drawing on what they consider to be "primary sources"—to "carefully and meticulously construct . . . a political reality."

Among gun sellers, this "do-it-yourself" orientation toward knowledge appeared to serve as a means of enhancing a sense of control and a feeling of independence from elites. Consider how Liam explained his cool-handed approach to the pandemic: "I'm not a real panicky person, and maybe that's my problem. I don't give a lot of credit to the media. I don't give a lot of credit to what people expect me to think." In bucking people's expectations about what he's "expected to think," this gun seller seized a brand of agency that allowed him to resist the "panic" that he saw in those around him. Refusing to follow the recommendations of mainstream media, science, or government, gun sellers' conspiracist thinking validated alternative sources of knowledge rooted in individual experience and initiative that allowed gun sellers to celebrate the informed individual (as opposed to, say, the field of science) as the ultimate adjudicator on fact versus falsehood.

According to their own accounts, long before 2020, many of the gun sellers I interviewed had approached media elites with consternation and assumed that the information disseminated through these channels would be biased, motivated, or simply not credible. Indeed, this style of apprehension already had been fostered for decades by protracted campaigns among conservative think tanks, politicians, and leaders—using tactics borrowed from corporate entrepreneurs[43]—to question scientific consensus regarding climate change, stem cell research, and gun policy. Meanwhile, conservatives (but not liberals) have exhibited marked declines in confidence in knowledge-producing elites since the 1970s.[44] Further, the news media itself has changed to facilitate anti-elitism in journalism: "the lines between activist and journalist, news and rumor, and new and old media are not only blurred but also made increasingly obsolete,"[45] as Khadijah Costley White, author of *The Branding of Right-wing Activism*, notes.[46] Coming on the heels of Trump's routine degradation of elites, particularly media elites, as treasonous and anti-America,[47] the pandemic was easily poised to validate the apprehension that many gun sellers already brought into 2020. Any uncertainty in news coverage could be read as evidence of elite fear-mongering and disinformation, and indeed, there was plenty of uncertainty: the media scrambled to keep up with, and distill for public consumption, the fragile and ever-changing scientific consensus about the pandemic.

Rather than follow public health guidance developed by scientists and disseminated by mainstream media, then, gun sellers entertained a variety of theories—ones that often transformed the pandemic from an unfortunate happenstance into a nefariously instigated global crisis for the benefits of elites within and outside the United States. Responding to what they saw as exaggeration, misinformation, and even outright fabrication, they forwarded a different social construction of coronavirus, one that recognized the virus not as a global pandemic threatening widespread death but as a fearsome plot hatched by opportunistic politicians. A few gun sellers were partial to a particular explanation. Eli, a white gun seller in his forties in Arizona, explained,

> The hospitals are definitely getting a kick-back from saying that it's coronavirus, and putting them [patients] on intubation rather than saying it's just the flu. So the money aspect is there for them. Do I think it's a pandemic? No. I do not. I think it was made in a lab in China, and they did have Dr. Fauci and former President Obama funding it.

Supplying a motive (profit) and a means (a lab in China that manufactured the virus), this gun seller pulls together a "just so" story of the coronavirus's global entrance featuring a host of allegedly nefarious actors. The story echoes classical conspiracism:[48] it aims to uncover the hidden truth behind the stories that mainstream media tell, oftentimes by appealing to xenophobic or racist characterizations (in this case, situating Obama as a fundamental threat to the United States through his collusion with China). Such characterizations appeared throughout 2020 in some conservatives' insistence on calling the virus the "Kung Flu" or the "Chinese virus," which have helped inflame anti-Asian racism and hate crimes against Asian Americans in the United States from the start of the pandemic.[49]

Eli's story uses conspiracism to tell an ultimately simplistic tale of "good and evil": forces of evil (Obama, China) are engaged in a long-term plot to destroy America in any way they can. Like Eli, most gun sellers saw coronavirus as so much more than a mere pandemic, and they absolutely questioned whether government responses were reasonable versus opportunistic. However, for most gun sellers, their embrace of conspiracism was more fluid, much nimbler, and less committed than Eli's brand of classical conspiracism. In other words, most gun sellers were not die-hard conspiracists in any traditional sense; they did not adhere to a holy grail of truth beyond the pale of elitist lies. Rather, they elevated skepticism as they entertained many possible narratives involving bad actors, especially involving liberals and Democrats, bent on harming the United States. Most gun sellers, in other words, ascribed to what political scientists Nancy L. Rosenblum and Russell Muirhead[50] label the "new conspiracism." Rather than focusing on the answers, they got lost in the questions—satisfied not so much with the special knowledge gained by believing in a conspiracy theory but rather by the special status gained by believing that one is not a dupe to experts and elites.

No Smoking Gun

To most gun sellers, the coronavirus pandemic presented an unnerving blend of fact and fiction, somewhere between hoax and horror. Conspiracism did not provide a smoking gun, or an absolute Truth (with a capital T), as much as it opened the door for gun sellers to draw on familiar narratives (such as political opportunism) and first-hand experiences (specifically with coronavirus) as they embraced skepticism and resisted experts and elites. Gun sellers used conspiracist thinking not as a means of asserting certainty or locating some infallible truth. Rather, they found comfort in the self-assured, and at times self-congratulatory, skepticism that conspiracist thinking entailed.

Consider Greg, a white gun seller from Arizona, who—like Eli— found the timing and origins of the coronavirus pandemic suspicious:

> I guess I am probably one of them that believes that it's too convenient that it came when it did, and whether it was intentional by China or another country that doesn't like us or internally . . . I try not to be a conspiracy theorist, but . . .

Disavowing his own identification as "a conspiracy theorist," Greg skates across multiple possibilities for the coronavirus's "convenient" arrival, ranging from intentional malfeasance by China to internal (that is, US-based) scandal. He's right that he isn't a conspiracy theorist—at least not in the classical sense, as a conspiracy theorist would have settled on a particular conspiracy like Eli did, a concrete kaleidoscope of facts and interpretations that could render the cacophony of 2020 into coherence. Rather, he's an adherent to a nimbler style of conspiracism—an agile skepticism that approached the coronavirus pandemic as a frustrating blend of fact and fiction.

Unlike a stereotypical conspiracy theorist, most gun sellers were apprehensive about dismissing coronavirus as an all-out hoax. Instead, they disclosed earnest ambivalence as they tried to make sense of the virus. Because I wanted to understand the extent to which they accepted the mainstream messaging surrounding coronavirus, I directly asked gun sellers about claims that coronavirus was a hoax. They equivocated. Richard, a white gun seller in California, told me: "I think it's really overblown. Kind of a hoax—but with a little bit of truth to it." Billy, also a white gun seller in California, likewise hedged: "It's not a hoax. I mean, people are ridiculous. Absolutely not a hoax . . . but the news makes it more scary. The 24-hour news cycle that people get sucked into, the constant Facebook, and the Twitter reports . . . it makes everything worse, frankly." Coronavirus may or may not have been an "engineered virus," as Andrew, a biracial gun seller in California, pondered; it may or may not have been released from a "Wuhan lab," as Robert, a white gun seller in Florida, pontificated. Whether coronavirus was a hoax seemed to gun sellers beside the point.

Rather, what rallied the interest (and skepticism) of gun sellers was not so much coronavirus itself but what they saw as the politically opportunistic *use* of the virus by elites in government, in the media, and in science. As Peter from Arizona offered, "I think it's real. I don't think it's a hoax. But I think people are grabbing on to it, using it for something." Political opportunism provided a powerful narrative through which to short-circuit an unnerving lack of knowledge regarding coronavirus and assert skepticism as a politically astute stance. Dave in Florida, for example, worried less about the virus and more about "immunization camps" that he believed could follow: "I think it really is very similar to what the Nazis did to the Jews—they acted, nobody knew what was going on, and they acted like it was all for their good, and they were given these things, we're going to take you to take care of you, here—and nobody knew that they were getting slaughtered."[51] Frank, an Arizona gun seller who described himself as American Indian and white, admitted he was "one of those people that they talk about that's definitely a risk for serious complications and probably death." But, he said that after the initial shock of the pandemic wore off, his view shifted: "you know it's really, really being used as a tool to manipulate the population, and get people more and more open to government controlling the little things in life."

For Frank, Dave, and others, conspiracist thinking helped tame unknown, and fearsome, realities into the terrain of the known. Talk of an "immunization camp" or government control over "the little things in life" fit into a familiar template of conservative thought that has long deemed government tyranny a central threat and liberal propaganda a principal means by which that threat takes shape. Conspiracist thinking, from this perspective, was a check on political opportunism, and in this way, conspiracism resonated with, and complemented, armed individualism (discussed in chapter 1): for gun sellers, both were means of resisting excess government and political tyranny in the form of elitist control.

But gun sellers did not merely regurgitate the well-worn narratives of political opportunism long propagated within conservative circles. Rather, these well-worn narratives became sensible to gun sellers because they resonated far more with their first-hand experiences than the accounts they associated with scientists, politicians, and media elites. Gun sellers relied on personal experience as they fielded knowledge claims—mimicking the style of truth-claims prevalent on conservative news networks like Fox News that emphasize personal experience and family history.[52] Gun sellers who did not contract the virus could point to their imputed immunity as evidence of elitist chicanery; as Richard in California told me, "I've been around thousands and thousands of people, shaking hands, never worn a mask, nothing—and I couldn't be better." Likewise, gun sellers who contracted the virus but survived it became even *more* convinced that the real danger was not the virus itself but the deluge of misinformation and manipulation the virus had unleashed.

For example, Craig, a white gun seller in Michigan, explained that his skepticism grew in part out of his first-hand encounter with coronavirus:

> The virus is real, I'm not going to deny the virus. But I feel like the media hypes it up way more than it is . . . I think it's way overblown. Like looking at numbers, it's highly survivable. Um, so I just

think—it's the media, and the government trying to scare people. And keep them kind of under control. I'm not denying that the virus is real—because I had it. But to be honest with you, I've been sicker in years past with other stuff. Flu, pneumonia, whatever.

Most people who have coronavirus survive it; many who contract it have mild symptoms. Craig's first-hand encounter with the coronavirus reflected a commonplace experience of the virus as well as the broad range of its seriousness and lethality. Rather than recognizing that his experience could have turned out differently, Craig used this first-hand experience to call out media and the government as fear-mongers "trying to scare people." Shoring up a sort of "pull yourself up by your bootstraps" individualism, Craig concluded that if he didn't get that sick himself, there couldn't be that much reason to worry about the virus— other than what the government and media did.

Kenneth, an Arizona gun seller who identified as Cherokee, also contracted the virus, and like Craig, he used his first-hand experiences— and that of his friends—to stake out his own skepticism. As he told me,

My wife had the COVID-19 in early April, and then I got it in late June. I got it in late June . . . So it's a real disease, it's a real thing. The genesis of it is kind of an interesting thing for us. Both of us had symptoms that were very flu-like. I want to say I know 30 people who have had it in southeastern Arizona, and their symptoms [were] very similar to ours, so we're hearing news reports . . . and it doesn't jive with what our experience is. We're not saying it's not real, it's not deadly—it's just that it is different. And so—it makes it hard to understand what's really going on with the coronavirus. And certainly I feel like as a business owner, as an American, that there is some government overreach, and I'm very concerned about the idea that the state of Arizona has a law that suspends the state legislature when there is an emergency like this.

Similar to Craig, Kenneth's personal experiences and the experiences of his friends led him not to jump on board with precautions aimed at quelling the spread of the virus but instead left him concerned about government overreach—"as a businessman, as an American." Without a proverbial "smoking gun"—a clear and present danger that could link coronavirus to death and destruction rather than sickness and survivability—those who had a first-hand brush with the virus found it sensible to downplay its severity.

Gun sellers rejected fake news, questioned the status quo, discerned first-hand and second-hand experiences into truths, and imputed malign motives to elites by wit of their sheer skepticism. Conspiracist thinking—particularly the skepticism it sowed regarding the opportunism of elites—allowed gun sellers to acknowledge the virus as veritable while also doubting its seriousness and even to suggest that the real threat came not from the virus but from the responses to it (i.e., the cliché that "the cure cannot be worse than the disease"). In other words, conspiracist thinking allowed gun sellers to adopt a different social construction of coronavirus than the one they saw in mainstream media: an opportunistic power grab rather than a terrifying pandemic. Accordingly, conspiracist thinking provided gun sellers a way to navigate the dilemma they faced in early 2020: how to respond to a life-threatening pandemic in a way that did not endorse infringements on the individual rights and freedoms they defined as central to that very life that the pandemic purportedly threatened. And in doing so, conspiracist thinking did not just misconstrue *belief* but also fostered *disbelief*: that is, it fused a desire for a particular democratic order—one dogmatically protective of individual liberties—with the dismissal of those who would seem to challenge the righteousness of those desires, such as public health experts and, as we shall see, protesters for racial justice.

The Privilege of Disbelief

As the world was reeling from a once-in-a-century pandemic that destroyed bodies, families, and communities; ravaged careers, businesses, and supply chains; and provided newfound grist for the partisan rancor and political division seething across the globe and especially in the United States, an African American man named George Floyd was brutally strangled to death by a group of police officers in Minneapolis on May 25, 2020. The slow and deliberate murder was caught on tape;[53] its sheer callousness, its utter disregard for any semblance of proportionate force, its lack of appeal to anything resembling a just enforcement of law compelled even those within the police community—often quieted by the so-called Blue Code of Silence[54] that discouraged officers to speak out against fellow police—to condemn the killing as unjustifiable murder. Outside of public law enforcement, the torturous killing of Floyd ignited a summer of outrage. The police brutality of 2020 put a blindingly bright spotlight on the persistence, the prevalence, and the sheer wickedness of anti-Black racism and white supremacy in the United States. Weighing the ramifications of ignoring public health recommendations aimed at preventing the spread of coronavirus with the consequences of ignoring yet another police killing (also a public health crisis), millions gathered, marched, and sometimes rioted for Black Lives Matter; formed and forwarded calls to defund the police, dismantle racism, and remake America; and joined reading groups and discussion circles on white fragility and racial inequality and engaged their friends and families to do the same. Millions of people—including white people in predominantly white areas of the country, in contrast to previous iterations of anti-racist uprisings in the United States[55]—found America's systematic racial inequality to be as unacceptable as it was undeniable.

And yet, many found ways to deny. Trump referred to the push to recognize the racist underpinnings of the United States—past *and* present—as "toxic propaganda" and "a twisted web of lies," wagering that "left-wing mobs have torn down statues of our founders, desecrated our memorials and carried out a campaign of violence and anarchy."[56] Trump's denouncement of Black protest as a left-wing plot to destroy America was far from novel; rather, it recycled the Civil Rights–era belief among many whites that the Civil Rights movement was a communist conspiracy, a belief that "allowed whites to more easily justify their opposition" to efforts at integration.[57] Likewise, Trump denounced the 1619 Project, an initiative spearheaded by the *New York Times Magazine* to recenter slavery and its consequences in American history,[58] and wrote an executive order to ban critical race theory in federally funded programming, which has subsequently spurred a flurry of state-level book bans and other restrictions on free speech.[59]

Following Trump, conservative news media and Republican supporters propagated conspiracist thinking that crowded out recognition
of the systematic injustice that drove the mass protests. Perhaps George
Soros, the billionaire investor and philanthropist, was paying protestors,
covering the costs to have them bused to cities across the United States,
and even supplying them with bricks to destroy police precincts.[60]
Likewise, maybe the viral video of 75-year-old peace activist Martin
Gugino being shoved to the ground by police without provocation was
not an indication of police brutality but rather a clever "false flag" stunt
orchestrated by an ANTIFA provocateur.[61] Perhaps the displays of
anger, frustration, and grief were not the pent-up result of the protracted
injustice built into the US system but rather the connivance of people
set on destroying American society. Maybe George Floyd wasn't even
dead—or maybe he *was* dead, but his death was the result of a scheme
involving counterfeit money and drug trafficking in a local night club
that was so elaborate the FBI was involved.[62] And if that wasn't enough,
the voices of people of color who had concerns about the protests
could be raised up to reinforce the notion that the protests were misguided. For example, recall from chapter 1 how Ben, a white gun seller
in Michigan, referenced minorities he knew who disapproved of the
Black Lives Matter protests to help justify his own misgivings: "From
minorities, and from Black women actually . . . [I hear] that a large
number do not support the Black Lives Matter protests or rioting or
any of that." The style of thinking deployed to make sense of the
pandemic—rampant skepticism, a strident faith in political opportunism, and a reliance on first-hand experience—was reshuffled to discount the voices of those collectively mobilized against racism in
American society.

Though the Black Lives Matter movement included multiple factions, took shape in various manifestations, and intersected with adjacent
mobilizations (such as the Defund the Police movement), gun sellers
treated the Black Lives Matter movement as an umbrella, catch-all term
for the protests, uprisings, and riots that occurred during the summer of
2020. Lacking the first-hand experience that would make racism palpable,
many found the national focus on the Black Lives Matter movement

unsettling and suspect. Several believed that the protests were amplified by virtue of biased mainstream media coverage, as evidenced by a "sudden" lack of coverage of the pandemic. As Arizona's Liam told me,

> I don't want to be that conspiracy theorist guy, but I think a lot of things are dictated by the media. Because now you have these riots going on, and all of a sudden you aren't hearing anything about COVID . . . it all of a sudden seemed like—"well, now we have to force race, racism as an issue. And now we have to spread these riots and panicking."

Brenda, a white gun seller in California, who admits she "never saw this [the simultaneous pandemic closures and civil unrest] coming," likewise told me, "It's odd to me now that we have this new issue [the protests], that corona[virus] has taken such a back seat to society now." Carl, a white gun seller also from California, sarcastically quipped, "the corporate media is telling you that the virus can't infect you if you protest, but it can if you go have lunch . . . somehow the virus skips protests." Meanwhile, Mark, a white Michigan gun seller, believed that the protests revealed liberal hypocrisy by providing an irresistible temptation for opportunistic Democrats to rally constituents. Describing Michigan Governor Whitmer's response to the armed protesters who rallied against the lockdown orders in Spring 2020,[63] months before the Black Lives Matter protests, he recalled,

> She was telling everybody that we were going to have a massive spike in coronavirus cases because of the [lockdown] protest [in Lansing, MI]. Well, now [during the Black Lives Matter protests] she goes over to Detroit area, which is a predominantly blue area and supportive of her in terms of voting, and she marches with them in a protest that is ten to fifteen times larger than the one that was at the [Michigan] capitol grounds. And none of the coronavirus stuff was even mentioned.

The double standard gun sellers like Mark saw in media coverage of protests and political responses provided an opening for gun sellers to raise additional doubts about the protests themselves.

Gun sellers further questioned how the protests took hold across the United States, even within communities not known for protests.

Already predisposed to view collective action with skepticism,[64] gun sellers found the apparent coordination across locales suspect in itself.[65] Consider Phil, a white gun seller in Michigan who saw protests and riots develop across his state. Admitting that "there's a lot, a lot of uncertainty," he paused as he considered "the reasons of [behind] the riots, the violence, and things like that." He struggled to put his thoughts into words: referencing rioting and property destruction in Grand Rapids, he found it unnerving "for riots to sprout across the country, in an almost synchronized manner, and turning to violence." As he opined, "On a Saturday, they burned down eight or ten police cruisers [in Grand Rapids]. You know, that just doesn't happen in the Midwest outside of Detroit and Chicago." The contrast is illuminating: Detroit and Chicago, cities with large African American populations that have served as specters of urban violence, rioting, and uprisings at least as far back as the 1960s, are set apart from Grand Rapids, an idyllic mid-sized city set in rural western Michigan known more for its earnest flash mobs and lip dubs[66] than any political fury. In outlining the uncanny synchronicity of the protests and riots, Phil flirted with conspiracism as he referenced "some kind of underlying dark force":

> There's [pause] clearly a perception that there is some kind of underlying dark force behind them, right?
>
> [You mean behind the riots?]
>
> Behind the riots.
>
> [Do you mean, some kind of organized, there's funding or sort—]
>
> Yes. That's what people feel like.

"Underlying dark force" was an ominous, almost biblical way of characterizing the protests, uprisings, and riots that resonated with a history of characterizing anti-racist activists as enemy-insiders,[67] a history that activated a popular, if unconscious, association of Blackness with evilness.[68] In entertaining the possibility of a conspiracist explanation for the protests and riots, Phil was careful to just lift up the edges on this line of reasoning, both offloading conspiracist thinking onto others ("that's what people feel like") as well as searching for a bit of assurance from me (". . . right?"). Phil is noteworthy *not* because he demonstrates the hardcore leanings of a die-hard conspiracist but rather because he demonstrates the ease with which conspiracist thinking can assist in transforming protests from acts of political voice to stunts orchestrated by an "underlying dark force."

Peter, a white gun seller in Arizona, was also concerned about the synchronicity of the protests; as he sardonically asserted, "I'm not wearing a tinfoil hat right now, but I see our society continuing to devolve and disintegrate as we know it." Noting that "there might be some organization behind it," Phil largely saw within the "protests, marches, riots, whatever— I'll just generally call them mobs" an emergent "mob mentality": "it's like . . . multiple one-celled organisms, or even white blood cells. They just inherently know how they're supposed to do something. And their resilience to changes from the other side and being able to change tactics without any formal communication or organization? It's mind-numbing." This reasoning had the effect of dismissing the protesters as beholden not to a deliberate set of political beliefs but to some "underlying force" that compelled them to act—whether from above or from below.

Zeke, a white gun seller in Florida, likewise believed that the pandemic and the Black Lives Matter protests were at least as much political maneuvers as they were legitimate concerns. Speaking at the end of July, he maintained, "I'm not convinced that the last 60 days or so, or 50 days or so, or whatever it is, is being driven by the virus. I think it's being driven by the political climate." Like Phil and Peter, Zeke focused on a set of circumstances that he thought simply did not add up: "When you've got ANTIFA . . . and then a mayor of a particular city saying— 'well, you know, let's let them go! [decline to prosecute]' And to see the mayor of the city [Washington, DC] painting a billboard on one of the most important streets of our country, painting BLM just to do it." Craig in Michigan took a similar tact, though he more explicitly connected the surge in protests, and mainstream media's coverage of the protests, to a protracted attempt (plot?) to undermine Trump and castigate his supporters. As he reasoned, "And as far as the civil unrest—uh, you know? . . .

I think the media portrayal of all of this [the civil unrest especially amid the 2020 elections] is going [to be] that the Right is racist and bigots and this and that." To illustrate, Craig provided a laundry list of elite attempts that failed to thwart Trump's rise: "I think the media just hates the fact that this guy just came out of nowhere and was able to accomplish stuff . . . the impeachment didn't work, the Russian collusion didn't work, coronavirus didn't work, so they gotta go onto something else." The Black Lives Matter protests, as far as Craig reasoned, were just the latest attempts to undermine Trump's bid to "Make America Great Again," as the populist slogan goes.

The notion that world-historic protests were merely the makings of biased media, the work of an "underlying dark force," or the outcome of nefarious political agendas allowed many gun sellers to discount racial inequality and white supremacy as the political fault lines that 2020's summer of unrest and rebellion asserted them to be.[69] Not only did most gun sellers fail to hear in the Black Lives Matter protests a "call for full and equal inclusion in the social contract rather than for breaking it," as legal scholar Susan Liebell put it;[70] they also used that demand— and the collective form they saw it taking—as reason to be suspicious of their political voices. Conspiracist thinking helped render unfathomable the idea that so many people could come together by their own wits to rally against white supremacy—and, instead, made fathomable the prospect that protesters, rioters, and rebels were dupes of a left-wing plot to undermine the integrity of the United States.

The Truth About Guns

In late August 2020,[71] Kyle Rittenhouse, a white 17-year-old from Illinois, traveled to Wisconsin to attend a Black Lives Matter protest being held in the aftermath of the police shooting of Jacob Blake.[72] Armed with an AR-15, he wasn't there to join the protesters; he was there to support police, who also supported him based on the words of encouragement he received from officers[73] before he killed two protesters later that evening. Soon thereafter, Fox News's Tucker Carlson took up the case in his nightly news segment. Furrowing his brows in his trademark style of forced gravitas, Carlson treated the import of Rittenhouse's lethal actions as both self-evident and inevitable: "How shocked are we that 17-year-olds with rifles decided they had to maintain order when no one else would?"[74] For Carlson, the anti-racist protests were not expressions of political voice but rather were riotous threats to public safety; framed in this way, he asked his viewers, "are we really surprised that looting and arson accelerated to murder?"[75] In posing that rhetorical question, Carlson conveyed what many within conservative circles saw as the obvious import of arming up amid civil unrest: Kyle Rittenhouse, and perhaps any American who turned to guns in search of security, acted on a natural proclivity for self-preservation. The appeal of the gun was deemed straightforwardly undeniable. Rittenhouse was ultimately acquitted in late 2021,[76] and for some on the Right, he was not merely exonerated, but also elevated as "a folk hero": "For millions, he's become a *positive* symbol, a young man of action who stepped up when the police (allegedly) stepped aside."[77]

When it came to Kyle Rittenhouse and other armed white Americans who used their guns in reckless, negligent, or even criminal manners amid the civil unrest of 2020, where was the skeptical stance that many conservatives brought to bear on the coronavirus pandemic, the Black Lives Matter protests, and eventually the results of the 2020 presidential election? Instead of galvanizing skepticism, the iconography of Kyle Rittenhouse as a white teenager standing up to hordes of Black Lives Matter protesters galvanized many conservatives' sympathies through the circuitry of whiteness that, as scholars of race have analyzed, the Rittenhouse case illuminated.[78] And listening to gun sellers, I soon realized that Kyle Rittenhouse couldn't be the enemy within conspiracist thinking because he was, rather, its *avenger*—an exemplar of the heroic individualism that designated some Americans as "good guys with guns" willing to wield violence against those they deemed acute threats (in Rittenhouse's case, Black Lives Matter protesters).

The individualistic ethos of gun culture[79] and the truth-seeking individualism that gun sellers espoused both offered similar benefits: *control over inherently uncontrollable, chaotic, and uncertain contexts.* Consider how these two Arizona interviewees explain the appeal of guns in terms of "control":

> It's a new, different fear that they cannot control, [and gun buyers are] doing whatever they did to gain control. (Peter, white, Arizona)

> I think a lot of people just let that fear of *what if?* seep into their heads . . . People just kind of said, I want to make sure that I'm in control of this. And I think that's what people were doing to—is that they were buying something [a gun] because they wanted to feel like they were in control of something. (Ian, white, Arizona)

For both Peter and Ian, the desire for a gun is a desire for "control"; these interviewees understood gun buyers *not just* as purchasing a firearm *but also* as purchasing the feeling of security that a firearm could bring them. Amid the arresting insecurities—the "new, different fear" and the *"what if?"*—they saw guns as a means of installing control. Recall Robert, the Florida gun seller profiled in the introduction, who explicitly connected the relationship between conspiracist skepticism and gun rights, summing up guns as the "only guarantee":

> I've been using the words "fake news" for a while now, on both sides of the aisle. And I think that has caused the uncertainty, and when you have uncertainty, you have to have a guarantee, and the only guarantee in this country is the right to protect yourself.

Robert links the insecurity of not knowing with a more fundamental insecurity, jumping from "fake news" to "the right to protect yourself" by alluding to a desire for a "guarantee." In doing so, he points to the flexibility of guns as a solution to all kinds of uncertainty, distilling a crisis of knowledge into the issue of self-defense—literally jumping the gun by asserting the firearm as a go-to solution to the uncertainty caused by misinformation and disinformation. In the same way that conspiracist thinking transforms an array of disparate knowledge claims and uncertainties into an insistent skepticism, the gun—or rather, the individual ethos *attached* to the gun—takes disparate kinds of insecurities, fears, and anxieties and melds these to a question of self-defense. For many of the gun sellers I interviewed, conspiracism, like armed individualism, was thus a way of asserting self-reliance, self-governance, and self-determination. In other words, gun sellers "used" conspiracism similarly to the way many gun owners "used" their firearms: both to satisfy a need for security and to affirm a particular set of political values and allegiances.[80] In either instance, conspiracism and armed individualism similarly transform a defensive posture into one of empowerment, control, and even order—whether the empowerment of skepticism or the empowerment of self-defense.

Conspiracism (or gun politics, for that matter) isn't fated to reinforce conservative notions of self-made individualism—after all, there is a great deal of conspiracist thinking on the Left as well as many historical examples of conspiracism that bend the arc of empowerment toward collective, rather than individual, efficacy.[81] But for the gun sellers navigating 2020's multilayered crises, conspiracism asserted an allegiance to a set of beliefs, values, and worldviews that resonated with armed individualism, affirming that conspiracist thinking represents "not merely markers of psychological quirks, alienation, or psychopathology, but rather of shared core associations—similar to issue ownership."[82] Contemporary conspiracism ties into conservative politics because it reinforces an overarching orientation toward knowledge, knowledge-seeking, and knowledge-vetting that aligned with conservative ways of being. Emphasizing their singular authority as knowers, adherents to conspiracism saw themselves as uniquely knowledgeable, particularly skeptical, and doggedly discerning with regard to knowledge claims as they spliced willful not-knowing with proactive self-education. And in doing so, conspiracism provides a subtle, but powerful, defense of armed people like Kyle Rittenhouse, who was understood by many conservatives not as an inexcusable agitator of white supremacy and thus a distressing threat to democratic order (as he was largely understood by liberals and leftists), but rather as a heroic individual valiantly willing to protect "the people" (that is, the "real Americans") from the public enemies that putatively threaten that order.

I Am Not an Expert but I Am a Thinker

Whether evoked in the mainstream media or by conservative gun sellers themselves, the term "conspiracy theorist" has a stigma attached to it: it conveys a certain degree of unhinged-ness, of gullibility, of delusion. No one wants to be labeled a conspiracy theorist. Yet, during 2020 and into 2021, the coronavirus pandemic, the Black Lives Matter uprisings, and democratic instability all provided powerful focal points for conspiracist thinking. A political language as well as a way of knowing, gun sellers' conspiracist thinking prioritized skepticism over consensus, emphasized experience over expertise, and, ultimately, elevated conservative ideals—self-reliance, anti-statism, and individualism—as markers of competent citizenship.

Contemporary conspiracist thinking, as unraveled in this chapter, is well captured by the phrase *"I am not an expert, but I am a thinker,"* as media scholar Reece Peck describes conservative intellectual culture.[83] While conspiracism is a broad-based style of political reasoning that can be found throughout US history (and across the globe, for that matter), at this historical moment, conspiracism in the United States is disproportionately endorsed by conservatives.[84] Perhaps this is because, although conservatives and liberals alike found the vertigo that has characterized 2020 unnerving (albeit for very different reasons), the conservative movement has been more effective in harnessing the populist sentiment that springs from democracy's flailing.[85] This populist sentiment has taken a variety of forms—calls to "Make America Great Again"; flirtations with authoritarianism, nativism, and white supremacy; disdain and distrust toward elites (e.g., "drain the swamp"); and, as this chapter reveals, conspiracist thinking that buttresses conservative values.

Listening closely to how gun sellers *use* conspiracism reveals one means by which knowledge is politicized and political reality is navigated. Conspiracism provides a means of empowerment amid confusion and chaos, a source of solace, satisfaction, and some self-assured smugness. It is a way to shore up individual efficacy despite the dwindling power of the individual to rise to the occasion of public problems in need of a collective solution—such as a pandemic or white supremacy. Conspiracism thus responds to a contradiction fundamental to liberal democratic order—namely, the gap between the sanctity of self-rule and the reality of representative politics, experienced as a mismatch between what people hear from politicians, scientists, and journalists and what they encounter in their everyday lives. Conspiracism provides a means of addressing this mismatch by taking up a scathingly skeptical stance toward elite knowledge claims, dismissing alternative political viewpoints, and reinforcing the preeminence of the individual as a political knower.

But among the conservative gun sellers I interviewed in 2020, conspiracism was a motivated means, reinforcing and justifying an emphasis on individualism as a means of empowerment: the brand of conspiracism documented in this chapter presumes, and reinforces, the non-negotiable authority of the individual and individual beliefs, experiences, and values as a source of political power. Rather than celebrating consensus as a means of decision-making and acknowledging difference as a source of political truth, contemporary conspiracism takes issue with elite knowledge claims by championing the preeminence of individual rights and freedoms—and threatens an illiberal deepening of the democratic cult of the individual refracted through the American politics of race.

Thus, while conspiracism may emerge as a response to built-in tensions of liberal democracy, it also stands to outstrip liberal democracy from within. As we shall see next, conspiracism helps to clarify why, despite the unity and solidarity that 2020's multilayered crises could have elicited among Americans, many instead transformed these crises into a partisan war with their political opponents.

Partisanship

Partisanship describes a sorting of life into opposing camps of believing, of thinking, and of living, and it has increasingly shaped attitudes about a wide variety of issues, including our attitudes about each other—and, ultimately, about ourselves. Political partisanship, as Pew noted in 2019, "continues to be *the* dividing line in the American public's political attitudes, far surpassing differences by age, race and ethnicity, gender, educational attainment, religious affiliation or other factors."[1] By 2019, Democrats (79%, up 18% from early 2016) and Republicans (83%, up 14%) had given each other increasingly "cold" or "very cold" ratings on a feeling thermometer developed by Pew; the majority of Republicans see Democrats as closed-minded, unpatriotic, and immoral, while three-quarters of Democrats see Republicans as particularly closed-minded.[2] Strikingly, 79 percent of Americans believe we have little trust in one another.[3]

Consider partisanship in the context of the coronavirus pandemic. Setting itself apart globally as a viral hotspot, the United States has also distinguished itself as the most divided country among advanced economies[4] with regard to public opinion about its government's response to coronavirus. Republicans' (but not Democrats') concerns about getting coronavirus, having to be hospitalized, or spreading coronavirus to others[5] dropped dramatically over the course of 2020. These differences in concern translated into everyday behavior,[6] with Republicans much more at ease in attending crowded parties, indoor sporting events, eating at a restaurant, or spending time with friends and family inside their homes.

Or consider the politics of racial justice and the Black Lives Matter protests that pressed those politics in the summer of 2020. In one 2017 poll, Democrats and Republicans differed by a striking 45 points on whether "the country needs to continue making changes to give blacks equal rights with whites," while a full 50-point gap separated Democrats from Republicans on whether "racial discrimination is the main reason why many black people can't get ahead these days."[7] In the midst of the Black Lives Matter protests in June 2020, a full 82 percent of Republicans thought "some people taking advantage of the situation to engage in criminal behavior" had contributed a "great deal" to the protests (only 39% of Democrats thought so),[8] and Republicans in the majority viewed the protests as "largely" violent (Democrats viewed them as "mostly" peaceful).[9] By September 2020,[10] only 19 percent of Republicans surveyed that month expressed at least some support for the Black Lives Matter movement, as compared to 88 percent of Democrats. As the 2020 presidential election neared, the all-too-immediate politics of public health and race animated the extreme partisanship that unfolded with the election. Just a month before the election, roughly 90 percent of voters believed that "a victory by the other candidate would lead to *lasting harm* to the nation"; roughly four-fifths of both Trump *and* Biden supporters thought that priorities and "core American values" divided them.[11] These data suggest a profound shift. Political opponents were not simply political rivals in the equal playing field of democratic contest; they bordered on un-American, perhaps unfit to play the game of democracy at all. In other words, partisanship represented not just the stakes that divided up political community from within; it also represented the boundaries of political community from without.

Perhaps, then, it should come as no surprise that gun ownership has become one of the most striking axes along which profound partisanship gets expressed.[12] Among a panoply of issues, no political topic is more divided by partisanship.[13] Maybe that is because, in an inescapably partisan world, the gun doubles not just as a means of protecting oneself existentially but also as the means of protecting oneself from the threat posed by the political opposition.

CHAPTER 3

America Unmasked

In March 2020, *The Truth About Guns* ran a story headlined: "Ammopocalypse now! And Other COVID19-induced Hysteria."[1] Despite the boon for gun sales that the pandemic inaugurated, the story drew a line between "firearms enthusiasts" and everyone else eager to buy guns amid the sudden advent of the pandemic: "While many firearms enthusiasts have maintained their preparedness for these scenarios, most people haven't thought that far ahead."[2] Neither panicked nor paranoid, gun enthusiasts understood themselves as *prepared*—unlike the new gun buyers of 2020. As a matter of personal responsibility, they had embraced the gun as an instrument of everyday security; they weren't so naïve as to need a pandemic to illuminate the necessity of a gun, even if they admitted that they hadn't quite envisioned the apocalypse to take the shape it did in 2020. And given their strident skepticism toward political, media, and scientific elites, they hadn't fallen into the trap of believing the government (or anyone else) would be there to save them. Prepared and proactive, reasonable and resolute: these are the qualities that—at least in the view of those who embraced gun rights—uniquely distinguished the American gun owner.

This political identity—the gun owner—is crucial for understanding how gun politics has become an expression of partisanship. As sociologist David Yamane[3] has noted, owning a gun does not in itself make one a "gun owner"—a lesson that gun sellers themselves both learned and taught as they navigated the surging gun purchases of 2020. Nevertheless, political scientist Matthew Lacombe reminds us that gun attitudes and gun ownership have been increasingly linked to conservative beliefs and Republican Party identification since the 1970s.[4] While liberals certainly own guns,[5] the political identity of the gun owner as conservative represents a decades-long outcome of the National Rifle Association's maneuvers—alongside the contemporary conservative movement more generally—to weld the platform of gun rights to the broader agenda of the Republican Party.

Gun sellers sold guns, but they also marketed a particular political orientation to guns—one that considered guns as objects of cool preparedness, self-reliance, and individualism in the face of danger, uncertainty, and chaos. In contrast to the long-time gun owners who surged into their stores in reasonable (as gun sellers saw it) anticipation of gun regulations and bans amid election-year uncertainties, the new gun owners who flooded their stores during the long 2020 were often seen as hysterical, naïve, ignorant, and even hypocritical—or, to use the shorthand of gun sellers, as *liberals* ill-equipped to exercise the right to keep and bear arms. In other words, gun sellers enlisted partisanship as a way to parse out who could claim the identity of gun owner and all that it implied politically, socially, even morally.

As I listened to how gun sellers understood themselves amid the chaos of 2020 and how they used this understanding to define themselves against those they saw as panicked and gullible, I realized that the rampant partisanship that had long shaped gun rights politics[6] was taking a distinct form in 2020. Partisanship is an expression of political difference—a necessary element of liberal democracies. After all, to function as a deliberate space that captures popular will (even if imperfectly), liberal democracy requires *both* a tolerance for conflict, disagreement, and impasse *as well as* an embrace of universal commonalities that link up citizens into a polity. Extreme partisanship, however, reneges on both of these requirements by transforming political difference into a Rorschach test for deciding who is a political friend and who is a political enemy (with little room for anything in between). Not simply a disagreement in opinion, a difference in party allegiance, or even a divergence in lifestyle, contemporary American partisanship has saturated people's political lives, shaping how they find and hold onto a sense of security, how they know what they know, and how they relate to the different people with whom they share society, whether or not they agree.

This chapter starts by examining how gun sellers themselves understood growing partisanship in the United States—a problem that, like most of us, they could see but could hardly solve. It then traces how partisanship intersects with armed individualism and then with conspiracism. It follows gun sellers back into the gun store, exploring how partisanship provided a tool for gun sellers to police the boundaries of gun culture as conservative terrain, even—or especially—as they encountered a surge in liberals wanting to purchase guns for the first time. Then, the chapter unpacks how gun sellers propped up the mask as a partisan device that symbolized—in their view—a sheep-like, rule-following liberal mindset that contrasted with the freethinking conservatism represented by the guns they sold. Often branding political opponents as incompetent and ill-equipped rights-bearers, the partisanship of 2020 as expressed by gun sellers edged away from democratic ideals that deemed every citizen an inherently equal bearer of rights— and remade rights, not as the founding rewards of democratic citizenship, but as the unequal earnings of political loyalty to conservative ideals.

The Partisanization of Everyday Life

Though partisan rancor seems endemic to the American polity, it wasn't always this way. If people in the United States today could time-travel to the 1950s, they would encounter lethargic, disinterested Americans who, in the words of the sociologist C. Wright Mills, "pay no attention to politics of any kind. They are not radical, not liberal, not conservative, not reactionary. They are inactionary. They are out of it."[7] The inactionary ethos of American politics would not last for long. Conservatives would soon reject this lethargy—what they characterized as the liberal establishment—and take on bipartisanship as one of its pernicious manifestations.[8] As historian Nicole Hemmer,[9] author of *Messengers of the Right*, notes of conservative politicians in the 1960s, "they saw bipartisanship as one of the fundamental flaws in post-war politics, particularly because it had congealed around nonconservative policies." During the next several decades, this rejection of bipartisanship would swell into one of the defining attributes of the Republican Party, guiding conservative politicians to reject liberal ideology while they debated social issues like abortion, gay rights, and guns; deliberated on public spending from welfare to the arts; and transformed once-banal procedures, such as confirmation hearings, into forums for political theater. Whites, particularly white men, have increasingly identified as Republican over the years, although whites and men *across parties* seem particularly willing to embrace partisan rancor,[10] as men are more likely to not just disagree with but also dehumanize their political opponents,[11] and whites' emotional investment in politics is more likely to center around anger.[12]

The conservative rejection of bipartisanship would not be confined to politics "proper" but would also take shape as a partisanization of everyday life. Illustrating the penetration of politics into "nonpolitical" life, a 2019 Pew Research poll found that 61 percent of Republicans and 54 percent of Democrats said members of the opposing party "probably don't share many of their other values and goals" beyond politics proper.[13] As sociologists Daniel DellaPosta, Yongren Shi, and Michael Macy show, partisanship captures a lifestyle-based divide that expands beyond the typical boundaries of politics into markets and culture.[14] This expansion is obvious to anyone who has trekked into a gun store—pro-NRA signage, conservative slogans, and even Trump paraphernalia reveal the politicization of the business of selling firearms to gun enthusiasts. Even previously apolitical markets and spaces have now been saturated with political signaling. For those conservatives unnerved by the association of high-end coffee with liberalism, they can now comfortably shop at outlets like Black Rifle Coffee (the "Starbucks of the Right," ventured the *New York Times*[15]), Covfefe Coffee and Gifts in Maine,[16] and Conservative Grounds in Florida.[17] (Liberals, for their part, can shop at outfits like Starbucks, which markets coffee by appealing to diversity and inclusion, green capitalism, and community uplift.[18]) As Conservative Grounds co-owner Cliff Gephart noted to the *Washington Post*, "it's a place for conservatives to feel welcome . . . it's about a conservative lifestyle."[19] Politics has swelled beyond a set of beliefs to shape lifestyles—hence the grain-of-truth stereotypes of the "bird hunting conservative" and the "latte liberal."[20]

This partisanization of everyday life both reflects and is reinforced by geographical sorting that has increasingly isolated Americans ideologically, a process that began in the 1970s according to journalist Bill Bishop, author of *The Big Sort*.[21] Since then, communities within the United States have only become more politically homogeneous as people have increasingly "voted with their feet" by seeking out places that "feel" comfortable. For liberals, this has often meant highly educated, more anonymous, and more racially diverse urban places; for conservatives, this has often meant less populated, less educated, whiter communities in suburban and rural areas with high levels of volunteerism. Conservatives did more of the moving, but the result has been the same for both sides: people are more likely than any time in American history to live in communities with politically, socially, and culturally like-minded people.[22] As Bishop summarizes, "the way Americans sorted themselves created a new kind of cultural separation. People living in different cities literally had different ways of relating to family, to government, to strangers, and to religion."[23]

The sorting of Americans into communities, markets, and media spheres has made partisanship even more entrenched than it may have otherwise been.[24] Social psychologists have long anticipated just why. Experiments have shown that like-minded groups don't moderate themselves; instead, they cohere around ideas and opinions *more* extreme than any individual started with.[25] Add to that plummeting levels of trust in institutions—political and otherwise—since the 1960s,[26] an erosion of local, broad-based civic organizations, and the expansion of social media as key platforms for political engagement,[27] and you have a stage set for "wild" polarization, especially with the likes of a political fire-starter like Donald Trump. By 2020, Bishop's 2009 words rang startlingly truer than perhaps when they were first penned: "Americans segregate themselves into their own political worlds, blocking out discordant voices and surrounding themselves with reassuring news and companions."[28]

Less Than Human

Negatively polarized—"we hate the other team more than we love our own," as conservative commentator David French lamented in *Divided We Fall*[29]—Americans have entered territory that social psychologists have longed warned us about. In 2016, roughly 45 percent of Republicans and 41 percent of Democrats said the opposing party's policies "are so misguided that they threaten the nation's well-being";[30] by 2019, 64 percent of Republicans and 75 percent of Democrats said members of the opposing party were "closed-minded."[31] As French describes, "a person can have a high degree of character, kindness, and personal integrity, but if they hold to ideas at odds with the opposition, they'll be demonized and vilified as morally defective—often with more vitriol than if their failings were 'merely' personal."[32] As French's commentary illustrates, we are deeply worried about our partisan divides—even as many of us participate in perpetuating them: by the end of 2020, roughly 80 percent of people—regardless of party affiliation, and thus surely including many of those who would attest to the closed-mindedness of their political opponents—said they were concerned about partisanship.[33]

Jake, a white gun seller from Florida, illustrated this balancing act between partisan indignation and indignation over partisanship that many of us are caught between. Throughout our conversation, he recognized flaws on both sides of the political spectrum, but revealing his own political bent, he considered liberals, democrats, and leftists as distinctly intolerant. For example, he splits his family between "die-hard liberals" (the only kind of liberal Jake mentions in this context) and "conservatives":

Unfortunately, the die-hard liberals will not communicate with the conservatives—even though we don't ever talk politics! Nobody in my family talks politics at [family] events, nobody cares! Their opinions are up to them, we still love them for it—but they don't feel the same way. And I feel that that's indicative of how the country is today. You've got people that just don't care [about you] if your opinion is not the same as theirs: *you are less than human.*

Here, Jake summarizes not just what partisanship *is* but also how it *feels*—the sting of feeling "less than human" by virtue of one's political standing. Jake views his family's political dynamics as mimicking American political rancor in miniature: the "die-hard liberals" refuse to engage with their conservative counterparts and assume, mistakenly, that conservatives can't help but bring politics into family events. Bemoaning the political partisanship of his liberal family members, Jake advances a key distinction between conservatives and liberals: while conservatives can practice some degree of compartmentalization with regard to their political beliefs, liberals lack this skill of self-control and self-awareness. Conservatives are capable of "loving" their family members regardless of their opinions, but liberals don't seem to be able to do the same. Instead, Jake bewails, "you've got people that just don't care [about you] if your opinion is not the same as theirs—*you are less than human.*" In Jake's view, the problem with partisanship came down to a problem with liberals—specifically, liberals who unfairly judge, wrongly dismiss, and ultimately debase their conservative counterparts.

Other gun sellers had similar quips about rising partisanship, usually condemning the judgments of Democrats, liberals, and leftists toward Republicans, conservatives, and right-wingers.[34] For example, Craig, a white gun seller from Michigan, complained about the ease with which media labels "the Right" as "racist" (as discussed in chapter 2). Arizona gun sellers Frank, who described himself as American Indian and white, and Peter, who identified as white, both used the phrase "Orange Man Bad" to caricature liberal resistance to Donald Trump's Republican rise; the term captured how—as they believed—liberals had unfairly written off Donald Trump and his supporters. Meanwhile, Ron, a white Arizona gun seller who described himself as "relat[ing] more to the Republican side," lamented: "it's just getting more polarizing. And so with the election coming up, you either love Donald Trump or you hate him. You know? There doesn't seem to be really any in between." Gun news outlets likewise reiterated this partisan rancor and blamed Democrats for its propagation; proclaiming that Democrat politicians want "penance" from gun owners, *Ammoland* asserted: "One thing that Second Amendment supporters need to understand: Anti-Second Amendment extremists hate you."[35]

All of these bombastic comments have the ring of cliché, but anyone who has paid attention to American politics over the last decade can recognize that Jake's sense of being dismissed as "less than human" taps into a palpable and pervasive political emotion in the United States—and this is a feeling that liberals share about their conservative counterparts, too. Dehumanization has occupied an increasingly central role in American politics. Overtly racist tropes that denigrated the Obamas—the first African American first family—as unfit for office routinely depicted them as subhuman or ape-like, including a West Virginia official who called Michelle Obama an "ape in heels" in 2016 and other racist "jokes."[36] Dehumanization, as the egregiously racist treatment of the Obamas intimates, has long been employed to malign and justify mistreatment of people who are already marginalized along the lines of race, gender, nationality, and sexuality. As exhibited in debates on crime, immigration, terrorism, transgender rights, and other issues,[37] dehumanization still shapes the overall tone of American politics. But if racist, sexist, homophobic, and transphobic discourses have been increasingly (if in fits and starts) recognized and denounced as hate speech, political identity remains one of the few acceptable targets of sheer intolerance. This helps explain why, as political scientists Alan Abramowitz and Jennifer McCoy show,[38] partisanship reflects and reinforces racial resentment. The point here isn't to equate partisan rancor with hate speech associated with racism, sexism, homophobia, and transphobia as much as recognize that partisanship provides an acceptable outlet for forms of anger and aggression that may be otherwise stigmatized.

During the 2016 election cycle, to take one example, dehumanizing rhetoric was replete across the political spectrum as Donald Trump and Hillary Clinton campaigned for the US presidency: political scientists

James L. Martherus, Andres G. Martinez, Paul K. Piff, and Alexander Theodoridis found dehumanizing phrases—"treasonous rats" and "Frankenstein monster" (liberal leaders denouncing conservatives); "the ultimately cowardly sacks of garbage" and "not even people" (conservative leaders denouncing liberals)—taken up by conservatives and liberals alike.[39] This politics of dehumanization represents, as Martherus and his co-authors[40] note, "a new form of partisan polarization." As they write, "partisans are willing to explicitly state that members of the opposing party are like animals, that they lack essential human traits, and that they are less evolved than members of their own party."[41]

Jake is right to name dehumanization as a pervasive and perverse element of contemporary American politics, but his focus on liberals as its main drivers reveals something about how partisanship animates conservative politics. The appeal of slogans like "Make America Great Again" draw their power, in part, from the view that the "real America" has been left behind as liberal cities thrive and minorities—gender, sexual, racial, ethnic, and religious—have gained expanded (if precarious) political rights and economic standing. In her study of Scott Walker's rise in Wisconsin, political scientist Katherine Cramer argues that economic, cultural, and political displacement (whether real *or* perceived) has invigorated resentment against so-called liberal elites.[42] Read against this backdrop, Jake's insistence that liberals view conservatives as "less than human" has echoes of resentment rooted in a fear of being left out or left behind politically, culturally, and economically. Partisanship provides a language for articulating political insecurities amid the loss of traditional sources of power. This helps explain why Jake plays into partisan divides even as he tries to reject them: the presumption that liberals, leftists, and Democrats are closed-minded elitists not only legitimates antipathy toward them but also voices the underlying political, cultural, and economic anxieties that fester below the surface of contemporary American politics.

Instead of addressing these political, cultural, and economic insecurities explicitly, however, partisanship often does little more than point the finger at one's political opponents. Partisanship represents release without resolution. Rather than inviting productive spaces for political debate and deliberation (as political difference can and should do), today's partisanship has instead incited arenas like right-wing blogs, conservative talk radio or, for that matter, gun stores, transforming them into what Sarah Sobieraj, Jeffrey Berry, and Amy Connors call "safe political spaces" for conservatives. These "safe political spaces" take the libertarian mantra of "don't ever tell me what to do"[43] to the limits of tolerance by providing a forum for forms of expression (including but not exclusively toxic, bigoted, or hateful speech) that many conservatives see as unduly curtailed by liberal culture. Unlike the liberal "safe spaces" that provide a forum for expressing vulnerability without fear of further marginalization, these conservative "safe spaces" protect against a different kind of fear, the fear that one might be labeled as "racist," "sexist," "homophobic," "transphobic," or—as Jake would understand it—"less than human" for one's political beliefs.

Polarizing Guns

Like almost every gun seller I interviewed, Andrew, a biracial gun seller from California, was puzzled by the new wave of gun buyers that rushed into his store in 2020. He could understand these new buyers insofar as they were motivated by an ordinary yearning for security, a sense—as Andrew paraphrased—that "I have to buy these [guns] because tomorrow my door might get kicked down by someone who is motivated by lockdowns and shortages of supply to feed their family or get what's mine, kill me to take my supplies. Kill me for my food." At the same time, they differed markedly from the gun buyers who comprised previous surges. As Andrew told me, "I've been through gun sale surges before. The presumptive Hillary election was a huge gun surge. And then before that, Obama. . . . those were mostly gun owners or at least gun enthusiasts saying, 'I better buy these . . . guns before they outlaw them.'" To purchase a gun in the context of an upcoming election or even in the aftermath of an active shooting,[44] as Andrew saw it, was not an impulsive reaction to collective panic but rather a reasonable, calculated, and even rational expression of one's commitment to being prepared.

In line with what gender scholars Cynthia Belmont and Angela Stroud have described as "apocalyptic masculinity,"[45] Andrew and other gun sellers repeatedly associated their "usual" clientele—and themselves—with preparedness, praising them because they were "already prepared" (AZ), "prepared for *anything*" (FL), or "prefer[ed] to be prepared" (CA). Jake, the Florida gun seller, justified his own stockpiling habits by appealing to his fatherly obligations: "I'm just a normal dad trying to raise my kid in a country that's safer for what I've done. And so yeah, I have my own couple thousand rounds of ammunition, . . . you know, 223, 556, 9 mm." Neither a hysterical panic-buyer nor a paranoid doomsday prepper,[46] Jake presents himself as a responsible dad who has made a calm, cool, and collected decision to hold onto guns and "thousands of rounds of ammunition" as a means of keeping himself, his family, and even the country safer.

Gun sellers saw themselves in terms of cool-headedness—a characteristic they decidedly did *not* see in many of the new gun buyers of 2020. Instead, they often perceived these new gun buyers as panicked, naïve, hysterical—frantic and fearful, in contrast to the stoic attitudes of their "typical" gun clientele.[47] Consider how these gun sellers in California, Florida, and Michigan convey the desperation of these new gun buyers:

> Many of our anti-gun would-be customers were upset [about having to undergo a waiting period and thus delay taking possession of their guns] to the point of getting red in the face and shaking. (Andrew, biracial, California)

> People were reacting with a sense of urgency, you know, and then . . . product was drying up and that was driving people to make sure that "they better get while they could" type of thing. (Paul, white, Michigan)

> I could tell [that someone was a first-time gun buyer] by the way they look at [the gun]—there's kind of this deer in the headlight on them, you know? (Rodrigo, white Hispanic, Florida)

Each of these excerpts reveals how gun sellers saw in first-time gun owners an excessive emotionality and troubling ill-preparedness: afraid, bewildered, desperate, even visibly angry, on the one hand, and ignorant and naïve, on the other hand. Foolhardy and also a bit hypocritical (at least, as gun sellers saw it), rookie gun owners were desperate to acquire a firearm that they had naïvely deemed unnecessary prior to 2020.

While gun sellers saw panic buying in anticipation of the election of a Democrat as reflecting calm, cool, and calculated foresight given the possibility of impending gun control,[48] gun sellers saw the gun buyers of 2020 as irrational, impressionable and, often, dependent on the initiative of others. Gun sellers described the gun sale surge during the coronavirus pandemic as panic buying and even a "knee jerk reaction" (MI), and they saw new gun buyers acting out of desperation and irrationality, not unlike the panic purchasing taking place with other consumer goods. Janet, a white Arizona gun seller, compared the urge to buy a gun to the panic over toilet paper: "it's the same reason people went out to buy 50 things of toilet paper. They didn't need it to wipe their ass, they wanted to have it in the closet." Or, as Michigan gun seller Josh, a white immigrant, reasoned, "there was really not an underlying reason to buy anything, except people watching too much TV and looking at dystopian future movies and things like that." Lacking their own sense of self-direction, new gun buyers followed the lead of others who were buying guns, swayed by the crowd or taken in by the media's portrayal of impending crisis. Nathan, a white gun seller from Arizona, remarked that he saw "a herd mentality," while Carl, from California, described it as a "'do as you're told' mentality."

As I listened to gun sellers, I realized that partisanship was shaping how gun sellers experienced the 2020 surge in gun purchasing—albeit in a much different way than in other surges. While excessive emotionality and panicked hysteria are stereotypically associated with women and marginalized men in society at large, for gun sellers, such behaviors were explicitly captured by the ultimate partisan insult: "liberal." Though they were enthusiastic about new gun owners, gun sellers bemoaned the liberal and left-leaning clientele who came along with the gun purchasing surge. One California gun seller characterized the new purchasers as "flat out anti-gun people, Bernie Sanders supporters, people who six months ago wouldn't be a mile near a gun." Some gun sellers reasoned that while the liberal first-time gun owner might be buying a gun, what they were really doing was blindly following their friends or their political leaders in a moment of panic. One Arizona gun seller joked that the reason liberal gun buyers were buying out the 12-gauge shotguns was "because that's what Joe Biden told them to get."[49] Another California gun seller quipped at just how out of touch the new liberal gun buyers were by labeling them liberals even among other liberals: "We saw people . . . leaning toward a liberal, more anti-gun kind of stance. Even their liberal friends [were] like, *what do you mean you aren't prepared?*" Meanwhile, Kenneth, a Cherokee gun seller in Arizona, acknowledged at least one liberal gun buyer who broke from this herd mentality—only to reinforce it further. Suggesting that liberals were sheep-ishly unwilling to stand up for their political beliefs in the face of friends who might disagree, Kenneth referenced a friend who was "a little bit more on the liberal side" who bought a gun *on the condition that Kenneth not disclose the purchase to the buyer's other liberal friends.*

Sometimes, these put-downs explicitly emasculated new gun buyers by pegging their very decision to buy a gun not on their own inner resolve but on a woman's initiative.[50] As Dave, a white Florida gun seller, noted, "a lot of them really came out and said, 'I don't like guns, I never wanted to have a gun, but somebody—my parents, my wife—somebody said I need to get a gun. And so I need a gun.'" Some gun sellers took this sentiment a step further, deriding new gun buyers whom they saw as dependent on their wives' permission to purchase a firearm. As Andrew in California explained, "The wife allowing it in the home was a huge driver . . . Mama says you can now. . . . it is kind of a joke within the retail gun industry about what 'mama' wants." For Andrew (and a few other gun sellers who also explicitly made this point), the act of buying a gun for the first time represents *not* an embrace of the ethics of self-reliance and independence celebrated within pro-gun circles; rather, it represents an emasculating need for permission—a woman's permission.

Gun sellers prized the newfound *demographic* diversity of gun buyers, as already explored in chapter 1, but seeing many of these new gun owners as excessively emotional, often ignorant, and even hypocritical, they hardly celebrated these new gun owners' *political* diversity.[51] This is a subtle distinction, as the surge in political and demographic diversity among gun buyers came hand in hand: the gun buyers of 2020 were almost certainly less likely to be white men and more likely to be first-time gun buyers[52] who themselves are more likely to be liberal than existing gun owners.[53] (And it's worth remembering that while a startling one-in-five to one-in-two gun purchases in that year have been estimated to be from first-time buyers,[54] probably at least half of the people coming in to purchase guns and ammunition were still long-time buyers.) It wasn't that gun sellers necessarily doubted new gun buyers' immediate reasons for buying a gun; after all, anxieties surrounding social disorder (often rooted in racial politics of the War on Crime) as well as political uncertainty (especially surrounding upcoming elections) have motivated Americans to turn to guns for decades. It was not the *why* but the *how* that seemed to provoke gun sellers. As gun sellers drew stark contrasts around these new gun buyers, they were spryly abridging a more complex scene—of new and long-time gun owners, of white gun owners and gun owners of color, of men, women, and sexual minorities—into a story of partisanship. Partisanship, in turn, allowed them to assert their *own* guns as rational responses to chaos and disorder while *simultaneously* deriding the desperation and panic of the new liberal gun buyers they found coming into their stores.

But in treating the "liberal mindset" (as one gun seller described it) as antithetical to gun ownership, gun sellers did not just complain about their new liberal customers; viewing them as both a political and a safety liability, gun sellers proactively tried to convert new gun buyers into the kinds of responsible gun owners that not only embraced guns but also ascribed to conservative values.

The Gatekeepers of Guns

As the 2020 surge unfolded, gun rights organizations, firearms training outfits, and Second Amendment news outlets recognized the need for educating first-time gun buyers in firearms safety—a task made all the more difficult by virtue of the lockdowns that kept people away from firearms classes and shooting ranges. The National Shooting Sports Foundation "urge[d] gun owners to keep firearm safety a top priority" and made "safety resources widely available as gun and ammunition sales increase, especially among first-time firearm purchasers,"[55] stating that "guns are flying off the shelves these days, but at the same time the most important commodity in the firearms marketplace is free and invaluable: That's responsible and safe firearm ownership."[56] Likewise, Tim Schmidt of the United States Concealed Carry Association (USCCA) told Fox News, "with that right comes a tremendous responsibility, and that responsibility is to be trained. [. . .] If you're watching this and you just bought a gun for self-defense, get training."[57] Representatives of the gun industry like the NSSF, leaders in firearms training like Tim Schmidt, and most of the gun sellers I interviewed converged on a clear concern: that the new gun owners of 2020 must be educated in the basics of firearms safety. But as I was to learn, this concern was about responsible firearms safety, but it was also about much more. By emphasizing "responsible firearms ownership," gun sellers also opened the door for partisanship to shape how they engaged the new gun buyers in their stores.

Gun sellers told me that they proactively vetted gun purchasers as they grew more and more concerned about firearms training amid the surge in new gun buyers. Describing the mentality of an irresponsible gun owner, Brandon, a white gun seller in Florida, admitted that he turned people down who came to his store looking for a gun:

> I cannot tell you how many people I have turned down for buying a gun because they straight up told me, "I'm never going to look at this thing again. I'm not getting training. Just show me how to work this thing in that shit-hits-the-fan kind of situation so I can kill someone if I have to." And I say, I'm sorry I cannot sell you a gun! I have a conscience, and I can't do it!

This seller's words reveal the crucial role that gun sellers play as gatekeepers of guns, gun rights, and gun safety. Panic buyers may be suddenly interested in purchasing guns, Brandon acknowledged, but without the resolve to train to become a responsible gun user, they are a threat to themselves, to others, and even—as some gun sellers noted—to the future of gun rights.

While at least one gun seller I interviewed quipped that "I'll sell a gun to anyone," most were much more circumspect about ensuring gun buyers understood what they were getting themselves into—and refused to sell if not. Janet, a white gun store owner in Arizona, refused sales to buyers she saw as unprepared for firearm ownership, even as—she told me—her local gun community shamed her for her cautious approach. Detailing one incident, she recalled,

> I don't care if you go to my class, or [another class], but you need to come back and demonstrate that you can hold a gun, and then I'll revisit it. One woman said, "well how am I supposed to protect my family?" I said, "You are a little late to the party—you should have thought of that before."

Meanwhile, Rebecca, a white gun seller in Michigan who identified as a Democrat (one of only a few interviewees who did so), explained, "we are very hesitant selling to brand new shooters that have zero experience. Without any prior training. . . . I don't think that people understand the power that's behind that—that as soon as you pull that trigger, it could change your life forever." Echoing these gun sellers, one writer for *The Truth About Guns* noted, "Personally, I wouldn't loan a non-gun owner anything . . . because I'd be worried that someone in that family would accidentally hurt themselves or another family member with it. And guess where they would then point their finger afterward if that happened."[58]

This emphasis on responsibility—from Janet's refusal to sell a gun to untrained buyers who lived with children to Brandon's rebuff of customers who had little interest in maintaining safe firearms habits—should be commended, as gun sellers are uniquely positioned within the American terrain of gun rights to promote safe storage practices, gun training, and basic proficiency in the safe handling of firearms. Of course, gun sellers have a built-in professional motivation to embrace safety, training, and responsibility—their continued livelihoods, after all, depend on it. Either way, there's no reason to doubt the sincerity of this commitment—not least because it was in their market and moral interests.

But this commitment did double duty. In addition to representing an earnest embrace, gun sellers' emphasis on safety, responsibility, and training often served simultaneously as a partisan put-down that designated liberals as unfit for Second Amendment rights. After all, within pro-gun circles, the language of "responsibility" often appears alongside independence and self-reliance—as code for a conservative ethic that celebrates self-determination and eschews dependency. Though they celebrated the demographic diversity of the gun buyers of 2020 (see chapter 1) and, with that, the democratization of gun rights they saw unfolding in their stores, gun sellers nevertheless policed the limits of that newfound diversity through an emphasis on "responsibility." As Nathan of Arizona told me, "responsible gun owners make responsible citizens." Irresponsible people, as Alex of Florida digressed, "have no business buying guns!" When I asked him to clarify, he zeroed in on their sheep-like incompetence: "There are a lot of people who are buying guns, who are influenced by media, television, TV shows, uh, the Internet. And they shouldn't be owning firearms." Josh in Michigan relished his ability to deny a sale based on his evaluation of a would-be buyer's fitness. Explicitly connecting his political conservatism to his business ethics, he noted,

> I'm a staunch conservative, there's no question about that—I never made a secret of that to anybody. Now, I tell you there are certain people that come to my store that will never walk out with a gun. They shouldn't have a gun. And the beautiful thing is that—nothing in the federal statutes says that I'm forced to transfer a gun to anybody . . . Yes, I believe that the Bill of Rights is as close to absolute as there is, okay? But I also think that citizens in general need to be responsible to preserve their rights. And if it's a person where I believe it would be harmful for them to have it, it's not here that they are going to buy it.

Josh's words show how—legally, politically, even morally—gun sellers are positioned not just as sellers of guns but brokers of gun rights,[59] who at turns help or hinder the process of exercising Second Amendment rights for the people who come to their stores looking for a firearm. Rather than a free-for-all with respect to gun rights, gun sellers articulated parameters on who and how gun rights can be exercised. The commitment to responsible gun ownership thus opened up space for gun sellers to navigate the dilemma raised by 2020's surge of new gun buyers, who were decidedly more liberal and less likely to be white men than existing gun owners: embrace them (and whatever transformations they might bring to US gun culture) or reject them (and protect US gun culture as conservative terrain). Appealing to "responsibility" as a code word for partisanship,[60] they could draw lines around who should not be trusted to safely handle a gun that putatively eschewed demographic bigotry (such as racism) while upholding political bias (in the form of partisanship).

Though not everyone explicitly connected the kind of "responsibility" needed to own a gun to political attitudes, it was hard not to see a peculiar brand of partisanship at work—one that divided not just agendas and ideas but also people themselves along party lines. Several gun sellers validated this hunch. Frank, who sold guns in Arizona, connected a person's politics with their ignorance about guns: "I would have to say a lot of people that I would call 'liberals' and 'Democrat'-type people know nothing about guns, but they want a gun." Rodrigo, a white Hispanic gun seller in Florida, also explicitly connected people's political stances to their fitness as gun owners:

> They are the people—all the people that [people] say shouldn't have guns, they are the ones coming in to buy guns! Everybody else already had their gun, I hate to say it so plainly like that, but I had a kid walk into my store with a Bernie Sanders shirt on. I got a Trump 2020 poster here, I got all kinds of shit here! This kid says, "Oh I need a gun! I want to use the gun show loophole!" I had to stop him—he left out of here almost crying. I am very confident that I converted him to grow up in the little time I had him, and he actually left here thanking me for Trump [laughs].

Rodrigo's point that "everybody else already had their guns" stakes out a line between the "real" gun owners who already had firearms and those who were now desperate to acquire a gun. To make the point, he presents a vivid caricature of a liberal looking to buy a gun: a "kid" wearing a "Bernie Sanders shirt" who ends up "almost crying" when confronted with his own political shortcomings. It's a powerful image that combines political immaturity and excessive emotionality. For his part, Rodrigo puts himself in the role of political evangelizer: he helps the "kid" "grow up a little" by "converting" him to Trumpism.

Rodrigo wasn't unique; gun sellers frequently made partisan jabs against the liberal gun owner. Alluding to panic as a by-product of a "more liberal way of thinking," Liam, a white Arizona gun seller, told me that "There are a lot of people that are more liberal in their way of thinking . . . [I'm] coming across people that have never thought they'd need it, they are all of a sudden panicking that they don't have one." Ian, a white gun seller who also lived in Arizona and often sold to people who had migrated to the state from California, told me, "In California and some of these other super-liberal states . . . the people have always kind of depended on the government for protection, and then once they realize that they couldn't do that, suddenly it became—I better get a gun, and I better get one quick!" In linking liberal attitudes with a panicked lack of preparedness, Liam and Ian draw on, and deepen, partisanship as a mark not simply of one's beliefs but also of one's fitness in the quest for acquiring a gun: after all, the responsible gun owners had already prepared with their own stash of guns and ammunition.

Being fit to own a gun, as many gun sellers suggested, reflected both *technical* ability (i.e., to safely use a gun) as well as *political* proficiency (i.e., to embrace the conservative politics of which gun rights are a part)—a sentiment that also appeared in gun rights news outlets. One *The Truth About Guns* article wagered, "We need to welcome these new gun owners and those who now want to be to the side of those of us who keep and bear arms . . . But we must also teach them this: With these rights come responsibility." The piece went on to stimulate a number of disclaimers that went "a step further" than understanding "gun safety, safe handling and the nuances of gun laws in his or her state":

Never again should you vote for an anti-rights politician.

Never again should you support a candidate who says "I support the Second Amendment but . . .".

Never again should you support the banning of commonly used tools like modern sporting rifles and standard capacity magazines.

You must only support candidates who stand firmly for the Second Amendment on principle. There is no room for equivocation.

Remember, welcome the newbies. This is our chance to show them how they've been led astray.[61]

Throughout 2020, gun news outlets ran celebratory headlines (e.g., "Second Amendment Supporters Welcome the 2020 Class of New Gun Owners!"[62]) that exuded more than a hint of *schadenfreude* at the "gun-grabbers' nightmare" represented by the surge in new gun buyers (e.g., "Nothing Makes Gun Grabbers Angrier Than Hundreds of Thousands of New American Gun Owners"[63]). Yet this excerpt takes a more ambivalent tone, instead explicating clear expectations for these new gun owners: with "no room for equivocation," new gun owners should be ready to step in line to "only support candidates who stand firmly for the Second Amendment." Given the alignment between the mainstream gun lobby and the Republican Party, this is a conspicuously concealed cry for partisanship—one that gives new gun owners a loaded choice between taking "responsibility . . . a step further" or continuing to be "led astray" by anti-gun politicians.

Reflecting the sheer power of partisanship to reframe armed individualism from the inside out, much of the gun community throughout 2020 celebrated the power of guns to equalize across nearly all identity categories—race, gender, sexuality—except one: partisanship. Even though they could have simply embraced liberal gun owners as a boon to the overall cause of gun rights (and gun sales as well), gun sellers instead often approached new gun buyers with some partisan apprehension. As gatekeepers of guns and all they represented, gun sellers used partisanship to draw boundaries in their gun stores that transcended mere disagreements in political values. Making sense of these first-time gun buyers who knew little about guns, who perhaps never deeply considered armed self-defense, and who were comprised—as Gabe, a white gun seller in Michigan, told me—of "a lot of left-wing people," gun sellers did not just recognize political differences in who was buying guns during the 2020 surge versus their "typical" clients. Rather, they deployed partisanship to draw boundaries between responsible and ir-responsible gun owners—and thus reinforced the linkages between gun rights and conservative ideology.

But gun sellers saw liberals, leftists, and democrats not only as incompetent rights-bearers; they also saw them as incompetent *knowers*.

When Knowledge Becomes Partisanship

Listening to gun sellers, I learned that partisanship went far deeper than I had realized before 2020. Of course, I knew that partisanship could deeply divide people in terms of *what* they believe. I hadn't totally grasped, however, how deeply partisanship could divide people in terms of *how* they come to believe what they believe. This transformation in the politics of truth was already well under way in the 1990s, when conservative media fostered "an environment where 'facts' were losing their truth power as they were increasingly judged not by their internal merits and methodological soundness but rather by the partisan affiliation (perceived or actual) of the institution producing them," according to scholar of conservative media Reece Peck.[64] "Truthiness," by the early 2000s, became shorthand (at least, among liberals) for a dominant communication style among conservatives that prioritized "emotion over information," as historian Nicole Hemmer[65] put it—even as it was exactly this emphasis on "emotion" that, as I found in my interviews, conservatives reviled among liberals. By the time I interviewed gun sellers in 2020, I found a new iteration of this politics of truth: a brand of conspiracist thinking (as discussed in chapter 2) that prioritized skepticism, celebrated first-hand experience, and affirmed an anti-elitist approach to knowledge. But conspiracist thinking didn't just reflect and reinforce a commitment to armed individualism; it also opened the door for knowledge to transform into partisanship.

Knowledge—what people know, and how they come to know it—had become a vehicle for asserting partisan divides. For gun sellers, it allowed them to scorn liberal counterparts as uninformed, unreasonable, and emotional—in short, as politically gullible and dangerously naïve subjects rather than the freethinking citizens that gun sellers understood themselves to be. To illustrate, take Ron in Arizona, who acknowledged that politics are inherently "skewed": "liberal or conservative, Democrat, right wing, left wing, whatever you want to call this stuff, it is skewed both ways. It's not just one." But with a laugh, he pulls back on this professed even-handedness: "I certainly think that the liberals are crazy, but that's my opinion [laughs]! If I have to generalize, I just don't see a lot of rationality in terms of what is being said . . . they thrive on feeling and emotion. So, if they feel it, it must be real."[66] According to him, this emotive impressionability—the "selective" recognition of facts[67]—is a key source of liberal opportunism:

> I feel that the Left, or the liberals, are more selective on what's gonna immediately benefit them. And it's been shown! And that's where I believe that this is only for their own personal benefit, their agenda, or their views, or their political stances—they are ultimately not going to change.

In a similar fashion, Steve, a white gun seller in Florida, bemoaned liberals' inability to face the facts:

> For some reason, they don't look at real science. Now, they'll scream all day long "Believe scientists!" But when you point out some piece of science to them, they run and hide their head in the sand.

Both Ron and Steve appeal to the empiricism of research and science [68] (i.e., "it's been shown!"; "real science"), but they do so not just to assert a stance on a particular policy issue, such as gun rights. Rather, their goal is to associate liberals with a way of knowing that they see as neglectful of facts, excessively emotional, and ultimately opportunistic.

This partisan divide over facts—including beliefs about how people come to value facts—had been widening before the pandemic, but the pandemic would ultimately reveal the divide for what it was: an unyielding chasm. Indeed, not only did the pandemic not bring Americans together as many had initially hoped, but it also provided them with a new symbol for partisan division. For those on the Right, the rejection of this symbol communicated a skepticism toward knowledge claims that conveyed their antipathy vis-à-vis liberal, media, and scientific elites alongside their conservative political allegiances. This symbol was, of course, the mask.

It is difficult to recall just how little political meaning anti-viral face masks held before the pandemic, even among conservatives. In early 2020, the mask was merely one item in a list of "coronavirus defense supplies," as an *Ammoland*[69] story described it in the first days of March; some defense manufacturers, like Versacarry, switched their production to focus on "face masks and face shields," a move that earned even-handed reporting from *The Truth About Guns* in early April.[70] But the mask soon fell under the grip of partisanship. Rather than an undertaking of community care, the vast majority of gun sellers saw masks as indicative of their wearers' naïveté and their inability to think for themselves (a tidy reversal of the kind of independence and self-reliance that the gun is understood by gun rights advocates to communicate about its bearer).[71] Rodrigo and Dave, both in Florida, did not just ridicule the pronouncements surrounding masks, but also took them as yet another illustration of "people's" gullibility:

> People are just dumb. They believe everything, and manipulating the people—our biggest threat right now is the media and its ease and power to manipulate huge amounts of masses of people. People are manipulated into all kinds of stuff. Look the other day—the United States Air Force, the Air Force, came out and said aliens are real! And nobody batted an eye—nobody cared! *Aliens are real,* and nobody said anything! Wash your hands, wear a mask—and aliens are flying around and nobody cares? So I've lost all hope. (Rodrigo, Florida)

> "Don't wear masks. Don't wear masks, they aren't going to help." "Now, everybody wear a mask. You gotta wear a mask!" You know? Which is it? Masks don't work, or they do work? And it changes all the time. It's just like—one year they'll tell you not [to] eat something, the next year it is good to eat. They don't know, they just make crap up, and people buy it until they come out and say something else. (Dave, Florida)

Both Rodrigo and Dave communicate a cynical state of the world, predicated not just on rampant misinformation but also on the credulity of people to "buy it until they come out and say something else." Mask-wearers were dumb, credulous, even paranoid—as Paul remarked in June 2020 when he told me that women seemed disproportionately likely to wear them: "some of these ladies with these masks—there's people who are really paranoid still."

Other gun sellers used politically charged language that described mask-wearers as rule-followers of the worst kind—comparing wearing a mask to "getting on the train" to a Nazi concentration camp, as Arizona gun seller Nathan[72] did,[73] or calling mask-wearers "sheep," a widespread partisan insult among conservatives to label Democrats, liberals, and leftists as followers rather than freethinkers. As Leonard dismissed his political opponents on the Left, "they've been fed a bunch of malarkey by their so-called handlers, who are the liberal news media and the Nancy Pelosi's of the world and the Adam Schiff's of the world, so they don't really know what's true." Likewise, Bryan, a white gun seller in Arizona, referenced a YouTube video called "It's just a mask!,"[74] posted by a user whose tagline read "The truth is what you should be looking for people. Don't just accept that something is true." As Bryan explains, "[The video] is talking about the rights that are being taken away. 'It's just a mask! Don't be a jerk! It's just a mask!' [in a sarcastic tone.] But we've accepted it like sheep! [laughs], you know?" Bryan found the video's political satire useful for explaining how people allow their rights to be "taken away": even though the real threat to liberty, in Bryan's estimation, is the pressure to mask up, it's the anti-maskers who are scolded and shamed as petty "jerks," making it all too easy for people to "accept" rights infringements "like sheep." The mask—and the willingness of the gullible to wear it—provided Rodrigo, Dave, Bryan, and other gun sellers with a concrete means of drawing a line between themselves and the "dumb" people (Rodrigo's words) who are "following orders, even if they defy logic . . . [and] living in fear" (as *Ammoland* surmised of the "Mask Brigade"[75]). As political scientist Francesca Tripodi[76] summarizes, resistance to public health measures signaled a "call to freedom," while "compliance" indicated "a form of (forced) submission."

Not surprisingly, gun sellers bristled at the notion of requiring their customers to be masked; as Nathan in Arizona illustrated by exposing what he saw as faulty science behind masking, "I wasn't going to tell someone, 'You can't come in without a mask.' Because wearing a mask just keeps my spit in my mouth. It really doesn't do anything about keeping someone else from getting sick." Just a handful of gun sellers required their employees, let alone customers, to be masked. And while no gun seller I interviewed banned masked customers from entering,[77] some did convey—to me and, as they intimated, to their customers— that whether to mask or not was not simply a personal choice but also a loaded question. As Liam in Arizona illustrated, "if you want to wear a mask, wear a mask, if you don't want to wear a mask, don't wear a mask. You know what I mean? It should be left to the citizens. But at the same time, I know a lot of people depend on the government for answers." Anyone could choose to wear a mask, Liam seemed to say, but in making that choice, they also communicated the kind of person they were—the kind that who "depend[ed] on the government for answers." Other gun sellers, like Brad in Arizona, communicated the same sentiment to his customers by example: "I always tell them, if you feel like you should wear a mask, wear a mask. And I tell them I'm not going to be in a mask, but you are more than welcome to wear one." The politics of masks exposed a fine line that gun sellers walked as they asserted themselves at once as *defenders* of personal choice but also *rejecters* of choices that communicated gullibility, sheep-ishness, and, ultimately, epistemological unfitness for the kinds of rights and freedoms that gun sellers saw themselves as embracing through their celebration of guns *and* their repudiation of masks.

In 2020, not wearing a mask imparted the same message as holstering a gun:[78] for conservatives, both were signals of one's capacity for cool-headed self-reliance and independence that conveniently and visibly differentiated them from the ignorance, hysteria, and naïveté they saw in the Democrats, liberals, and leftists who embraced masks, as they often understood it, as an attempt at "virtue-signaling."[79] Thus, the gun and the mask revealed two sides of the same partisan coin—each conveyed an unmistakable verdict about their bearers' political merit as a competent, rights-bearing, and knowledgeable citizen. As an *Ammoland* story mocked-then-condemned the putative mask-wearer and the politicians they followed: "Your rights end where my feelings begin, and I'm afraid of a virus, afraid of guns, and afraid of freedom. That is why you have to do what I tell you to do. Or not . . . This so-called 'epidemic' is a wakeup call. . . . I will not be a politician's slave, even if the politician is wearing a white lab coat and a surgeon's mask."[80] Knowledge is not just power—it is also partisanship.

The New Partisanship

A few years ago, two political scientists named Nathan Kalmoe and Lilliana Mason decided to ask survey-takers to respond to a series of statements about their partisan opponents: whether they were "downright evil"; whether they should be "treated like animals"; whether they "deserve any mistreatment they get"; and more.[81] They wanted to show that partisanship had morphed into something distinctive—not merely dislike for one's political opponents, they wagered that partisanship had begun to justify a perverse pleasure in the misfortune of one's political opponents and even an embrace of harms against them. Their study showed that Democrats *and* Republicans expressed shocking indifference to the well-being of their political opponents, with 20 percent of surveyed Democrats and 15 percent of surveyed Republicans agreeing that the country would be better off if large numbers of the partisan opposition "just died."[82] The questions, let alone the findings, should be striking. And yet, the study reinforces what scholars have increasingly found across a wide variety of contexts and methodological approaches: partisanship has come to represent a new kind of division, one predicated less on differences in political beliefs and more on degrees of political exclusion. We are so far from the notion that we can "agree to disagree" that we can barely stand to be in the same room to have the disagreement in the first place.

Prior to 2020, the gun store was certainly one of those proverbial "rooms"—a highly politicized market that people flocked to or, depending on their political persuasion, vehemently avoided. The multilayered crises of the long 2020, however, brought a markedly different kind of gun buyer into the room—people who were less likely to be white, less likely to be men, more likely to be first-time gun buyers,[83] and who, in turn, were more likely to be liberal than long-standing gun owners.[84] Gun sellers on the front lines of the 2020 surge thus faced a dilemma: embrace these liberal gun owners as part of a new, perhaps post-partisan, chapter in American gun politics, or double down on gun politics as conservative terrain. Many gun sellers chose the latter, turning to partisanship to make sense of these new gun owners. Unlike my conversations with gun carriers in 2010 for my book *Citizen-Protectors*, which rarely included the kind of partisan rancor that was commonplace in 2020, partisanship saturated my conversations with gun sellers. While the gun carriers I met in 2010 at times expressed excitement at the prospect of converting a "Berkeley liberal" (as they assumed of me, given that I was pursuing my PhD in sociology at UC Berkeley at the time) to the side of gun rights, the gun sellers I encountered in 2020 couldn't help but convey a deep aversion to their presumed political opponents— including me, based on the (at times, quite amusing) insolent declines I received in response to some of my requests for interviews. Further, with gun sellers, I almost never started the conversation about partisanship; I didn't have to. They dependably brought up the gulf of character that they saw dividing them from Democrats, liberals, and leftists. Partisanship served as the modus operandi by which they made sense of their political boundaries—forging the line between "us" and "them" through the only form of bigotry that can be openly flaunted throughout American politics today: that based on political identity.

Partisanship serves as a civic tool to draw boundaries about political rights and levy limitations around political inclusion. Accordingly, this chapter unmasks partisanship not simply as a set of beliefs, but as an everyday practice that guided how gun sellers parsed out worthy and unworthy gun-bearers-cum-rights-bearers. Mobilizing partisanship as a practical guide for assessing their fellow citizens, gun sellers exposed the contemporary imbalance between two at-odds requirements for liberal democracy: an embrace of the inherent political equality—and political value—of one's fellow citizens, on the one hand, and a celebration of difference, on the other hand. Rather than hold this tension in productive place as a way of generating political consensus (e.g., finding commonality amid the proverbial resolve to "agree to disagree"), gun sellers often reinforced the impasse that extreme partisanship has become. No doubt, they bemoaned the closed-mindedness of contemporary political discourse (as many of us do), but they often did so by chastising their political opposition (again, like many of us), entrenching partisanship in the very act of condemning it.

In this regard, gun sellers were not so different from other Americans—on the Left *or* the Right. Gun sellers provide a window into contemporary conservatism, but the appeal of partisanship as a way of organizing our political lives is, ironically, surprisingly non-partisan. The purpose in focusing on gun sellers, then, is not to suggest that partisanship flourishes only on the Right or to merely document *that* partisanship divides Americans politically (a well-established finding). Rather, focusing on gun sellers helps illuminate *how* this divide is distinctively enlivened on the Right in intersection with armed individualism and conspiracism. And, as we will see next, while partisanship may blanket the political spectrum, partisanship on the Right intersects with armed individualism and conspiracism to distinctively shape how gun sellers imagine and engage liberal democracy and the promise of political pluralism upon which it depends.

Democracy

As a political system that promises equity, freedom, and justice through popular sovereignty, democracy is often treated as a uniquely Western export. However, democracy has never been confined to the West—nor has its meaning been straightforward or uncontested. Democracies of one form or another existed in China, in the Middle East, in the Indian Subcontinent, and across Africa before taking shape in Athens to spark the centuries-long political movement in democratic thought and practice in the West.[1] Once it arrived in the West, Aristotle and Plato feared democracy could lead to mob rule.[2] Always the strategist, Machiavelli saw it as a powerful vector of state legitimacy. Alexis de Tocqueville distilled it into a noble embrace of political equality. John Stuart Mill saw democracy as a system of political representation best suited for the pursuit of liberty. John Locke and Jean-Jacques Rousseau found it to be the political form of an innate yearning for liberty and rights—a natural capacity for freedom distorted only by society's chains. Thomas Jefferson's thinking on the subject theoretically celebrated the pursuit of social and economic equity, the sanctity of self-rule, and the value of political resistance central to democratic order, but he betrayed each of these values in practice as he politically justified indigenous genocide, personally owned and raped enslaved peoples, and espoused a variety of racist views.[3] He was not an aberration: the social contract that provides the foundation for liberal democracy in the West relies upon, as Charles Mills[4] would argue, an implicit racial contract that excludes people of color from full civic membership. W. E. B. Du Bois[5] recognized that democracy's promise could only be fulfilled by universalizing the franchise to women and African Americans and by expanding the principles of democratic decision-making to industry. And, rethinking democracy from the perspective of non-violence and anti-colonial resistance, Mahatma Gandhi rejected the focus on individual rights altogether and instead emphasized the self-sufficient and self-reliant community as the bedrock of democratic governance.[6] But for all the nuances, ambiguities, and reinventions throughout the long history of the idea and its practice, democracy's contemporary meaning in the United States seems to have amply shrunk: a 2021 *New York Times* crossword reduced democracy to one simple act—the vote.[7]

Writing on the practical utility of democracy's conceptual vastness, political theorist Bernard Crick noted, "It is easier to say when a government or any other form of authority is acting undemocratically than to say when it is acting truly democratically."[8] Illustrating that insight, Harvard legal scholar Michael Klarman identified a list of indicators for democracy's decline in the United States under its 45th president, Donald Trump: attacks on free speech, undermining credibility of press, direct threats to reporters, attacks on the judiciary, politicization of law enforcement, overt use of government for private gain, overt racism, the endorsement of violence, the erosion of transparency, open admiration of Vladimir Putin and other autocrats, and explicit efforts at delegitimizing elections through words and deeds.[9] Recognizing that "today's autocrats are not your grandparents' autocrats,"[10] Klarman acknowledges that the line between democratic leaders and autocrats-in-the-making is blurry. As Klarman notes, "Because no single measure appears outrageous, citizens may not recognize the danger to democracy—the proverbial frog failing to notice it is slowly being boiled alive."[11]

But in fact, many Americans did recognize a danger to democracy—just not the danger outlined by Klarman and other defenders of liberal democracy. One poll conducted in mid-2021 found that more than three-quarters of Republicans, and even more so for Trump voters, saw "democracy under threat"—a figure that far outpaced Democrats and Biden voters.[12] The conservative consternation about democracy's decline has largely centered around a fixation with electoral integrity, reducing the messy and multifaceted potential of democratic governance into a one-dimensional act of voting fit for a crossword puzzle. Today, the vast majority of Democrats and Democrat-leaners see voting as "a fundamental right that should not be restricted in any way" (78%)[13] and feel that "everything should be done to make voting easy" (85%),[14] according to Pew surveys taken in the months following the January 6th insurrection. But the same surveys revealed that two-thirds of Republicans and Republican-leaners said that voting is a "privilege"[15] and 71 percent believed that "citizens should have to prove they really want to vote by registering ahead of time."[16]

This sentiment isn't new. Though the right to vote was conspicuously absent as a right of citizenship in the original formulation of the US Constitution, the Fifteenth Amendment was ratified in 1870 to bar voting discrimination based on race in the aftermath of the formal abolition of slavery. But enfranchisement was resisted by states across the country, especially in the South. Draconian tests to ascertain voter fitness, austere administrative hurdles to determine voter eligibility, and brazen voter intimidation became preferred machinery of white supremacy, whitewashing the entrenchment of white political power into a mere defense of democratic institutions.[17] Despite the 1965 Voting Rights Act, many Republican leaders have carried on this legacy by casting wide access to voting as a threat to democracy and elections themselves as the weakest links in the precarious chain that connects the will of the people to their governing institutions. They have pushed for legislation that would make the act of voting more difficult for the most disenfranchised groups in American society, decried legitimate election results as fraudulent, and initiated lengthy resource-intensive audits of elections that rarely overturn electoral results.

The headlines today regularly warn that democracy is under siege; they say that now is "A Make-or-Break Moment for Our Democracy" (*Washington Post*);[18] that "Elections Officials Fear for the Future of American Elections" (CNN);[19] and even that "The Rest of the World Is Worried About America" (*New York Times*).[20] But whose democracy is it, anyway?

CHAPTER 4

At the Edge of Democracy

For Americans who thought the central mandate of the Centers for Disease Control (CDC) was to safeguard the public health of the country, the conservative outcry against the agency from March 2020 onward may have seemed sudden and unsettling. Charging the CDC with a variety of grave wrongdoings, some conservatives decried the CDC for incompetence, while others saw more sinister machinations. Some of these claims have been baseless (e.g., the CDC's inflating death counts[1]); others amplified CDC actions and statements as evidence of deliberate misconduct, such as the CDC's off-the-cuff consideration of federal vaccine mandates,[2] their discrediting of unproven treatments such as Ivermectin as an alternative to vaccines and masks,[3] and their reach into arenas[4] that seemingly exceeded the CDC's public health mandate. While the CDC was hampered from the inside out by the political meddling of the Trump administration and the reticence among CDC bureaucrats that it inevitably produced,[5] conservative leaders in politics and the media largely magnified the CDC's fumbles. Tucker Carlson of Fox News ridiculed the CDC's inconsistent messaging around masking, saying, "[The CDC is] protecting us from this pandemic? ... They don't even know what their own director is saying."[6] Another Fox News pundit, Laura Ingraham, blasted the CDC's mask guidance: "this mask thing has been a charade from almost day one ... No one believes [the CDC]. When people say, 'the CDC says,' it's not exactly considered the good housekeeping seal of approval anymore."[7] For many conservatives, it all added up to a clear conclusion: the CDC couldn't be trusted. Indeed, from April to September 2020, trust in the CDC among Republicans dropped dramatically, from 90 percent to 60 percent.[8] By the middle of 2021, only 27 percent of Republicans said they "greatly trust" the CDC in contrast to 76 percent of Democrats.[9] While the *Washington Post* succinctly stated that "2020 has been a disaster for the CDC,"[10] this disaster was largely driven by conservative incredulity.

Gun politics provides crucial clues for understanding the roots of conservative outrage against the CDC—a linkage explicitly drawn by a May 2020 *Ammoland* quip that "lies about hydroxychloroquine [a discredited coronavirus treatment . . . are] just like lies about guns."[11] The groundwork for the conservative rejection of the CDC in 2020, in some ways, had already been laid by the National Rifle Association and the broader gun rights community. From the late 1980s into the 1990s, the CDC became a reviled target for gun rights advocates, as the NRA's *American Rifleman* began encouraging its readers to oppose the CDC's use of funding to research gun deaths. In democracy's tug-of-war between public good and individual liberty, the CDC became a battleground for asserting the non-negotiable preeminence of gun rights. Motivated gun rights proponents of the 1980s and 1990s found themselves combing through peer-reviewed studies and painstakingly tearing apart research methods, but as they did, they found the basic tenets of the public health approach advocated by the CDC to be fundamentally at odds with their own embrace of gun rights as a cherished symbol of autonomy and self-preservation. Gun rights advocates were riled by the CDC's emphasis on minimizing population-level risks associated with the prevalence of firearms—an emphasis that, as gun rights advocates saw it, reduced guns to harmful pathogens rather than crucial means of protection. As the NRA described it, the CDC's aim was to "conduct anti-gun pseudo-scientific studies disguised as research."[12]

In 1996, when the US Congress passed the Dickey Amendment to forbid the CDC from conducting research that would "advocate or promote gun control,"[13] it looked like the NRA had won a critical battle against the CDC. And by 2020, it seemed that conservatives were waging all-out war. But this war against the CDC was really a war against the state itself—seen in turns as incompetent, overreaching, and indulging the fears and insecurities of an unfree people. From this vantage point, to oppose the CDC was to defend the heart of American democracy and the individual rights and freedoms it was supposed to espouse. In democracy's unsteady balance between public good and private right, the former would thus take a backseat to the latter: according to this conservative take, any "public good" achieved through the sacrifice of personal freedom wasn't a public good, but rather personal freedom's perversion.[14] The CDC was just the latest crucible.

If gun politics helps us unearth the roots of 2020's outrage against the CDC, gun sellers might help us grapple with the political imaginations that animate conservatives today, imaginations that have led them to oppose mask mandates, vaccine endorsements, and other public health precautions while at the same time deeming democracy under grave threat. To do so, this chapter starts by examining the state as conjured by gun sellers, revealing a broad consensus that, to reference the well-known Ronald Reagan quote, "Government is not the solution to our problem, government is the problem."[15] Every one of the gun sellers I interviewed—even the handful of gun sellers who identified as liberal, left-leaning or Democrat—universally expressed anti-statist sensibilities that undergirded their embrace of armed individualism. Gun sellers differed, however, in how they transformed these anti-statist sensibilities into markedly different understandings of politics. Rather than a unitary imagination, I found three distinctive political imaginations that informed gun sellers: a libertarian imagination (which centers on a celebration of individual rights as the preferred remedy to social ills), an illiberal imagination (which rallies around an exclusionary vision of "the people" to resuscitate a bygone era of American democracy), and an eclectic imagination (which brings together elements of conservative and liberal politics by emphasizing individual rights alongside collective responsibility). These imaginations all contained some degree of democratic allegiance to popular sovereignty as an inherent political value—we could, if we stretched the definition of "democracy," call each a democratic imagination. Yet, these different imaginations compelled starkly different understandings of political belonging and civic engagement. As it turns out, democratic sensibilities—an allegiance to popular sovereignty, for example—can buttress inclusionary and justice-oriented sensibilities as well as exclusionary and bigoted credos. By exploring the plurality of political imaginations within a conservative arena, this chapter shows that the United States faces not simply a breakdown in liberal democracy's appeal but competing visions of democracy that stand to fundamentally redraft the parameters of citizenship and civic engagement.

The State of American Democracy

Throughout 2020, conservatives' vocal cries against the efforts of Democrats to address the coronavirus pandemic could be heard at all levels—from Trump's tweets that Michigan, Minnesota, and Virginia should be "liberated" from the stay-at-home orders[16] issued by their Democrat governors to the perspectives of conservatives like Bryan, a white gun seller in a small town in rural Arizona. I interviewed Bryan in July, well enough into 2020 to appreciate the full ramifications of the pandemic. When I asked him to sum up the pandemic as he understood it, he was quick at the draw: "it's the government seeing how far they can push the people . . . Never before in history have people been quarantined for being well." He chastised people—liberals—for sheep-ishly following guidance on wearing masks. He referenced Tucson's reputation as a liberal stronghold in a largely conservative state to explain his relief that he didn't live under a "city government like Tucson" that mandated masks: "luckily our city council says . . . we're not going to play those games." Yet, he bemoaned the faith that so many had still placed in the CDC, going "off topic"—as he admitted—to quip about the public health institute:

> That's what I feel that so many people are doing [accepting CDC guidance "like sheep"; see chapter 3]—the CDC, I know [this topic] isn't on guns, but the CDC has said that wearing a mask *may slow down the coronavirus*. Now there's two optimal words there: "may" and "slow down."

Bryan focused on those words—"may" and "slow down"—to suggest that the CDC has finessed the scientific knowledge on coronavirus to justify an infringement on people's rights—symbolized by the mask. Bryan's concerns about the CDC may not seem directly related to guns, but for many within the gun rights community, these concerns about CDC mask mandates evoked the same issues about rights and regulation as guns do. Ben, a white Michigan gun seller, drew a direct line between mandatory masks and gun bans:

> Does social distancing and masking matter? Sure, it could. But I don't think it needs to be mandatory. People say that this is about saving lives . . . It's like with guns—let's ban guns. Well, I know history and I know the nefarious intent, but a lot of people don't.

Distinguishing himself from those who don't know "history" or "the nefarious intent," Ben put masking and gun bans in the same category of troubling government action.

Though their focus was the CDC and public health mandates, Ben and Bryan both voiced a broader skepticism surrounding the state that has gone hand-in-hand with pro–Second Amendment sentiment at least since the 1960s.[17] Gun rights advocates have long justified their defense of the Second Amendment in a basic calculation of risk amid a resource-strapped state: captured in mantras like "I don't dial 911!" and "When seconds matter, the police are only minutes away," they acknowledged that the government, no matter how well-intentioned, likely will not be there to get Americans out of trouble should it find them.[18] Gun sellers across the board likewise recognized that the state often failed to protect Americans, who could not rely on state safeguards or provisions in their time of greatest need. Even the handful of liberal gun store owners I interviewed—like Rebecca, a white gun seller in Michigan, and Kyle, a white gun seller in California—thought that many Americans, especially Democrats, suffer from a misplaced faith in state efficacy: "I do feel like we are all spoon-fed that 'you're fine, you are going to be taken care of'" (Rebecca); and "most people in that environment [city-dwellers who consider themselves Democrats] kind of train themselves to think—'there's a lot of people here, there's a lot of cops, there's a lot of firefighters, there's a lot of emergency response, I shouldn't have to worry about things if things went bad'" (Kyle).

Meanwhile, Sam, a white Hispanic gun seller in Michigan and also a liberal, worried about state overreach: "I do agree that people have a fundamental right to defend themselves . . . and ultimately . . . it's not really up to the government to tell people, in most cases, what they can't, should, and shouldn't own." For gun sellers, including these left-of-center gun sellers, guns serve as the stopgap between impending danger and personal vulnerability amid the presumption of a feckless state at risk of overstepping its boundaries.

The appeal of guns, then, was inextricable from an apprehension surrounding the state. But to Bryan and Ben, the state was not merely threatening in its absenteeism. It also threatened with its uninvited appearance in realms, such as public health, that threatened to curtail freedom and control lives. This resonates with broad sentiments among gun rights advocates; sociologists Angela Stroud[19] and Jonathan Metzl[20] both found in their respective studies that conservative supporters of the Second Amendment oppose gun control as a "fundamental threat to liberty," part of a broader opposition to "governmental control" that often doubled as a defense of the prerogatives of white men.

For the gun sellers I interviewed in 2020, government responses to the pandemic were understood through an overarching trepidation regarding government control. As Frank, an Arizona gun seller who described himself as American Indian and white, said of the pandemic, "it's really, really being used as a tool to manipulate the population and get people more and more open to government controlling the little things in life." Some gun sellers were particularly vocal about the erosion of economic freedom via lockdown orders, arguing that the state actively incentivized government dependency while purportedly criminalizing independence. As Steve, a white gun seller in Florida, explained with exasperation, "these people want to work! They're [the government] putting people in jail for wanting to work while they're telling people, 'sit at home and let the government take care of you.' Which is 100% totalitarian, tyranny, dictatorship, communism, socialism—every bad thing you can think of." And rallying partisanship, conservative gun sellers equated the stripping of individual rights with liberal, progressive, or Democrat-run jurisdictions. Referring to Democrat-dominated states, Liam, a white gun seller in Arizona, quipped, "[those states] are more for, 'let's take those rights from people.'" Steve euphemistically described "maybe even a large" group of power-hungry Democrats as "some real evil people . . . trying to seize power": "[they] think that's a good thing [that they are in power because] . . . all of the rest of us are rubes and need to be controlled, and they're the ones to control it."

In the view of these gun sellers, government control did not just *leave* people defenseless; it proactively *created* defenselessness. Riled by requests to wear masks, by lockdown orders, and by the state agencies— the CDC as well as state and local governments—that justified their recommendations and mandates as good for public health and in the interest of the public good, gun sellers lamented that the state did not just endanger bodies but also souls: the state clipped freedom *and* the capacity for freedom, leaving a polity—recall what Frank said "more and more open to government controlling the little things in life." Where some saw merely the headaches of liberal democracy—namely, the inconvenience of having to adjust one's behaviors for the sake of the greater good—many gun sellers often saw the menaces of tyranny.[21]

Gun sellers converged on a deeply held suspicion of the state. And yet, their understanding of the state as at once overbearing and underwhelming did not exhaust their political imaginations. Indeed, despite their agreement that "Government is not the solution to our problem, government is the problem" (to quote Reagan again), they varied meaningfully in terms of how they understood and engaged the ideals associated with liberal democracy (such as equality, justice, and liberty), how they balanced collective efficacy against private initiative, how they drew boundaries around civic inclusion and belongingness, and, ultimately, how they articulated "the people" as a justification for who gets to participate in politics and how. Their political imaginations— described here as libertarian, illiberal, and eclectic—indicate different orientations to politics even among conservatives, reminding us[22] that conservative thought is comprised of diverse political sensibilities rather than a dogmatically monolithic ideology.[23] Each of these political imaginations is "democratic" in the (admittedly limited) sense that each relies on some rendering of "the people" to legitimate a wide variety of political actions, beliefs, and principles, including those—such as exclusionary voting regimes—that are incompatible with *liberal* democracy. This requires that we suspend our disbelief regarding the meaning of "real" democracy to understand how democracy operates at the micro level, not as a principled political system but as a messy ideological framework. The purpose here isn't to adjudicate on what "really" constitutes democracy, nor is it to hash out battle lines between pro-democracy liberals and anti-democracy conservatives—or vice versa, depending on your political slant. Rather, my objective is to explore the edge of democracy—and how, by blending armed individualism, conspiracism, and partisanship, gun sellers parlayed the well-worn principles of democracy along that edge. Accordingly, I profile a handful of gun sellers whose political stances particularly epitomized each imagination. But remember, these imaginations crisscross conservative gun rights discourse (particularly the illiberal and libertarian imaginations)—and should be understood as distinctive, but not mutually exclusive, ways of understanding politics, rather than ideological straightjackets. Gun sellers—like everyone else navigating democracy—can hold multiple, even contradictory ideologies, as they make sense of the political world around them.

The Libertarian Imagination

Peter saw himself as a maverick. A white gun seller in Arizona, he boasted that he was a member of the Liberal Gun Club; he said he refused to "choose a team" when it came to political divisions, telling me, "I easily walk down both of those paths." A political optimist, Peter identified an opportunity for unity in the mess of 2020: "this is that unifying moment where we all kind of need to be in this together and set aside whatever your bias is." For Peter, unity was found not in our collective circumstances but in our shared individual rights. Describing his conversations with people on the Left and the Right,[24] he made this political connection: "if you want to truly protect your rights, then you got to realize they are for everybody. They are for everybody."

A maverick indeed, he saw the establishment Left *and* Right as equally at fault for putting other people's rights on the chopping block in the hopes that theirs will be protected—and used his unique position as a purveyor of gun rights to remind people across the aisle of this political truth.[25] Peter was well aware that his gun store and training outfit doubled as a political forum to engage people during the high-stakes crises of 2020—a twenty-first-century manifestation of the eighteenth-century salons that birthed civic society. Embracing the opportunity, he was almost evangelical in his earnest hopefulness that he could awaken people politically. And for Peter, guns were at the center of this political work: they constituted the medium through which he could engage his fellow citizens; they represented the ultimate right among rights (e.g., "if you keep doing this [infringing on other rights], you are not even going to be able to have the ability to protect yourself"); and they served as a potent instrument of personal transformation and liberation.

As he told me, "I'm in the business of selling guns and training, and you'd think I'd want people to be scared out of their fucking minds all the time! And that's not my job. My job is to empower people." Whether providing gun training to people who have experienced violent crime first-hand or shaking people out of their propensity to see themselves as "perpetual victims," he saw guns, and the individual empowerment they entailed, as a means of awakening. Speaking of those who "put themselves into the victim role quite easily," he bemoaned that "they've never had the experience to learn that they have that capability to do . . . to do really cool things. And to be brave." Catching himself—"not that carrying a gun is brave by any means, I'm not saying that"—he nevertheless places guns, and the politics of rights they imply, as key vehicles on the road to personal empowerment.

Peter relied on individual rights as a means of transformation, liberation, even enlightenment. His politics left little space for a productive or positive government role. Admitting that "I see our society continuing to devolve and disintegrate as we know it . . . a perfect storm," he sprinkled conspiracist reasoning throughout our interview—joking, at one point, that "I'm not wearing a tinfoil hat. *But.*" He was bemused over the odd "coincidence" of a virus coming from China given "the things that they have to control their people"; he paused over what he described as the "pervasive disinformation campaigns to elicit a certain response . . . like Portland and Seattle [two sites of anti-police protests]." In his view, the multilayered crises of 2020 could serve as an awakening—not simply to the inefficacy of the state but also to its very illegitimacy. At one point happily wagering that the coronavirus pandemic had "delegitimized our government . . . both sides, in different ways, have delegitimized it in their heads," he saw in 2020 an invitation to return to the roots of American politics: "That's our genesis . . . to not trust the government. Our country was born from that." His words echoed a story in *The Truth About Guns* that ran with the headline, "Why Americans Love Liberty More than Safety":[26] "The American character does not like authority. A nation born in rebellion, a country founded by exiles and a people possessed with a pioneer spirit do not respond well to dictates on their movements. It goes against everything that's American."

Peter illuminated the hopes and aspirations of the libertarian imagination—an imagination that relished the potential of 2020's crises for redrafting people's relationships with their government and deepening their commitment to individual rights as vehicles of transformation and liberation. Though Peter have been a member of the "Liberal Gun Club," his membership indicated not so much an openness to liberal thinking (the substance of his politics suggested anything *but* that) but rather an earnest attempt to spread the gospel of individual rights through gun rights. This earnestness was echoed in a story in *The Truth About Guns* asking gun owners to "Be Goodwill Ambassadors to your Neighbors, Community": "By showing our neighbors that gun owners aren't a bunch of hermits with racist, sexist, xenophobic tendencies that some in society try to label us, we all win. Be nice to all your neighbors, even the less polite and welcoming ones."[27] Peter—and Andrew and Carl, described below—blended an appreciation for guns as a vehicle of self-reliance, a penchant for anti-elitist skepticism, and an optimistic style of partisanship that engaged political opponents in the hopes of converting them.

Peter was far from the only one who articulated this libertarian imagination—although perhaps he did so most memorably. As in my interview with Peter, empowerment in the face of incompetent and even nefarious government forces animated my conversation with Andrew, a biracial gun seller in California. At the heart of his embrace of gun rights was his refusal to turn away from the anguish of others. He acknowledged the anguish and distress of people in disasters like Hurricane Katrina and was outraged by those who were "disdainfully dismissive" of other people's "suffering." He lamented the hate crimes that surged throughout California against Asian Americans, driving people into his store to buy guns. He worried about how climate change would make survival in "an arid environment" like California wretched in the aftermath of the "Big One" (the earthquake that scientists have long predicted). Emphasizing personal responsibility and self-reliance, Andrew responded to each of these hardships with an explicitly individualistic appeal to empowerment. Recall Andrew's words from chapter 1: "I tell you I delight when I put a gun in the hands of any marginalized or discriminated minority group. I believe that is *exactly* what the gun is for. So that they can defend themselves and stand as an *individual* even against oppression." In the face of government incompetence and nefariousness, individuals—empowered through their exercise of rights— could stand up. As he summarized, "I don't own guns, I don't train with guns, I don't sell guns because I hate people—it's quite the opposite. I love people. I cherish life."

What Andrew didn't love, however, was the nefarious actors who had created chaos with the pandemic. In a conspiracist take on the coronavirus pandemic, Andrew blamed the coronavirus on "botched lab controls" that China "covered up" with the help of its "puppet organizations, including the World Health Organization . . . which made the spread and exposure worse," and he bemoaned political "opportunism" of "social progressives and governmental progressives . . . some of them, without even understanding the ends of their own, the endgame of their own agenda," in addressing the pandemic. He admitted at one point: "I'm sorry to sound like a tinfoil hat-wearer." Yet, sensing that the pandemic had broken the myth—as he saw it—that government action can replace personal responsibility, Andrew was hopeful that 2020 had "shifted" people: "it will have a lasting impact, that's what I think. And what I hope for, what I am praying for, is that this has fundamentally shifted gun politics for a generation." While he emphasized guns and gun rights, he also saw a broader moment of awakening into personal responsibility and self-reliance: "My hope is that on a societal level we have shifted somewhat." As he explained, "I hope that enough people—even if they didn't go buy a gun, and that's the key! Even if they didn't go buy a gun!—they made some other kind of preparation, [and] the notion of providing for their own personal safety and security has been personalized for them."

Ben, a white gun seller in Michigan, likewise saw 2020 as a moment for political transformation regarding people's relationship with their government and their rights. Though he explicitly rejected that the coronavirus was released as part of a "conspiracy . . . to wreak havoc," he saw the government's response to the pandemic, particularly the executive orders from Michigan Governor Gretchen Whitmer, as "a political thing from the start," as described in chapter 1: "it was just 'snap your fingers!' And BOOM! Your rights are gone." Positioning himself beyond rigid partisanship even as he fixated on the "liberal mindset" as a particular scourge on American politics, he recognized that "people who are very hard left or very hard right—there's no nuanced views, there's no argument, it's just that's what they are, that's what they think." They might not see the pandemic as the wake-up call that it is, but Ben told me that he has "seen a different change" in the "people who are more nuanced, who have a mixture of ideas, and [who] can look at both sides of the coin." When I asked him to describe the shift that he witnessed, he responded by emphasizing an expansion of personal responsibility: "I think a lot of people rise up to that level of responsibility. So I think when people get a gun, it changes something—about how they view the world. Short term, I don't know—but in the long term, I think so . . . I think guns are really a steppingstone out of the liberal mindset."

As became clear during our interview, Ben's concern with the "liberal mindset" revolved around rejecting what he saw as a slovenly dependence on government, rather than a dogmatic embrace of Republicans over Democrats. As he said, "it's not just a Republican–Democrat or left–right thing." To illustrate, he pointed to Reagan's support of gun control to dispel the narrative that "Republicans like to tell themselves—[that] they are the pro-gun party." He recognized that "there's people that will gladly call the cops on their neighbors because people have more than six people at their house. That's not something that is one party or the other. There are people who favor statism on both sides."[28] Ben's words indicate a skeptical stance toward public law enforcement and strong-arm state action—a libertarian take, as we shall see below, that contrasts starkly with the endorsement of state violence within the illiberal imagination.[29] Rather, rejecting what he called "that whole 'I want it done but do it for me' attitude," he saw private initiative and personal empowerment as adequate for addressing the structural impasses exposed in American society over the course of 2020. Accordingly, he saw the Black Lives Matter protests and the Defund the Police movement as yet further examples of government dependency, rather than a demand for collective transformation: "they want to make a difference but they want someone else to do it—like vote someone in to fix the problem, or call the police, or have the government fix the problem without doing something themselves." He offered an alternative to the demands of Black Lives Matter protesters rooted in personal responsibility and private initiative: "You are protesting the government to do something for you, but you could do a neighborhood clean-up or neighborhood watch." As mentioned in chapter 1, Ben appreciated the surging numbers of African Americans in his store buying guns as a means of self-protection—and an embrace of individual over collective solutions. From his perspective, guns were a race-neutral implement that mobilized individual rights as the solution to racial injustice, including police violence—even as cases like the murders of Ahmaud Arbery or Philando Castile reveal guns as lethal instruments that achieve the very opposite end.[30]

Together, Ben, Andrew, and Peter illustrate a libertarian imagination: seeing government as an apparatus of control rather than the guarantor of freedom, they were faithful to the promise of individual rights, personal responsibility, and private initiative as a means of empowerment, often drawing on conspiracist thinking to reinforce their apprehension of collective initiative. Framing the state (and the politicians and bureaucrats who worked within it) as nefarious, opportunistic, or manipulative, Ben, Andrew, and Peter each defined civic engagement fundamentally around the transformative potential of individual rights—rights that stood not just as a *means* of popular sovereignty but an *enactment* of popular sovereignty in themselves. As they saw it, individual rights and the empowerment they entailed were available for anyone who had the political courage to embrace them—even if many people, especially liberals, declined to rise to the level of personal responsibility necessary to take them up. Thus, though they clearly disdained the "liberal mindset" (in Ben's words) and leaned right as they extolled the transformative power of individual rights, they maintained a vision of the people that included those liberals who had "awakened," and they often took pains to criticize "both sides" of the political spectrum.[31] Declining to take up partisanship in its most rigid, exclusionary, and rancorous form helped maintain the hope that 2020 could serve as a wake-up call for people—wherever they might be on the political spectrum—to celebrate the individual as the quintessence of popular sovereignty and eschew collective action as a thinly veiled mechanism of tyranny and control. These gun sellers certainly didn't embrace liberal thinking—they were plenty partisan—but in adopting a more open-minded partisanship, they didn't fundamentally write off liberals as beyond political salvation, either.[32]

But not all gun sellers took up partisanship with this grain of optimism. In contrast to this libertarian imagination, the gun sellers who expressed an illiberal imagination blended armed individualism, conspiracism, and partisanship in their most dogmatic and rigid forms, asserting not tentative hope but rather deepened pessimism surrounding American politics and American democracy.

The Illiberal Imagination

Nearly every answer that Eli, a white gun seller in Arizona, gave to my questions exuded a profound pessimism about American life—and the threat that Democrats posed to it. Did he consider coronavirus a pandemic? "No. I do not." Then where did the virus come from? "I think it was made in a lab in China. They did have Dr. Fauci and former President Obama funding it." But for what end? "I think it is a political ploy. The economy was doing great, and come time for the end of the election [cycle], *they [the Democrat establishment] can't have that.* That would make our current commander-in-chief [then-President Trump] look good. And possibly get re-elected." What was the ultimate goal of this ploy, then? The "ploy," as he saw it, would start with Biden's apparent nomination, but "come time for elections, he's going to fall ill and won't be able to run." We were talking in the summer of 2020, months before the November electoral defeat of Trump by Biden. Sarcastically admitting that he had a "funny feeling" someone else would step in, he wagered that Michelle Obama would run: "then she will appoint Barack under her." The hidden agenda of 2020, as Eli saw it, was to effectively reinstall Obama as president-cum-tyrant—a feat that would contradict constitutional term limits and spite the ethos of electoral democracy. Two election cycles after Obama vacated the office of the US presidency, this fear continues to reverberate: in anticipation of the 2020 election, an *Ammoland* article subtly evoked recent elections past by noting, "it appears now we're at another election battle for the soul of our country."[33] Obama represented an existential threat for conservatives like Eli—a stance that sociologists Adia Harvey Wingfield and Joe Feagin[34] have attributed to a "hard racial framing" rooted in fears and anxieties about the waning power of whites in America. But in Eli's mind, his fears were fundamentally about the erosion of democracy, which justified, from his perspective, his fixation on the Obamas and liberals more generally.

From the presidential power grabs he believed were unfolding before his very eyes to the lockdown orders he observed across the country,

Eli was indignant about the loss of freedoms, of rights, and ultimately, of America itself: "last I knew, this was still America. We had all the freedoms that the Constitution and the Bill of Rights have given us. And they're just being squashed." Eli saw the chaos of 2020 as just the latest in a long line of machinations among power-hungry Democrats, and he felt that "it shouldn't take much more for the general public to wake up and see it." But unlike Peter, Andrew, and Ben, he wasn't so hopeful about people waking up. As he saw it, "They've always—most of them have depended on the government. And they're all for the bigger government." Exuding cynicism about his fellow citizens, he bemoaned, "we are slipping closer and closer into socialism. And the next step is going to be communism." Similar to his take on Obama's conspiratorial takeover of American government, he had worked out an account of just how easily those "next steps" could be taken based on the apparent "need" for a vaccine:

> "We need a vaccine." Now, "we need to have our eyes retina-ed and scanned." And, if we don't have a vaccine, we can't go to the store. "We need the vaccine!" Hitler used that same tactic during his reign and got everyone onto the trains! And took them straight to the gas chamber!

Here, Eli deploys the terror of the Nazi regime as a moral ultimatum to oppose liberals and liberal ideology. The references to Hitler might seem overblown, but they are not unusual within conservative politics; for decades, gun rights advocates have routinely referenced Hitler's efforts to confiscate firearms as an argument against gun control and gun regulation.[35] Rather than a mere denunciation of genocide and genocidal regimes, Wingfield and Feagin[36] argue that this uptake of Nazi iconography—comparing Obama to Hitler or vaccine mandates to death camps—signals an illiberal turn in conservative politics. It downplays the scope and scale of Hitler's genocidal terror and also helps justify exactly what Nazis stood for: a flat-out opposition to the pluralistic politics, including multiracial democracy. Decrying what liberals *have* done, these references to Nazis, fascism, and Hitler also shape conspiracist thinking about what liberals *could* do, animating Eli's apocalyptic view of American society as teetering on the edge of collapse.[37] Blaming leftists and anti-racist activists, he saw little hope for peace heading into the US presidential election: "the Black Lives Matter movement is still going to be running rampant. ANTIFA is going to be running rampant . . . It's just gonna get worse. Even with Trump [in office]." He saw civil war on the horizon "if Trump wins."[38] And if he loses? "It's just gonna be worse. Downright turning into communism." Like his references to Hitler, Eli didn't use communism to refer to the threat of an outside force, like the USSR under the Cold War; instead, for Eli, communism served as shorthand for enemies that threaten the United States from *within*.[39]

As I listened to Eli, I realized that despite some similarities with libertarian-minded gun sellers like Ben, Andrew, and Peter, Eli's understanding of American democracy—and the stakes of the current political moment—were fundamentally at odds with theirs. Eli's sensibilities illustrated a very different political imagination—an *illiberal* imagination. The illiberal imagination conjured up "the people" in narrow and divided terms—between those who believe in and will defend a nostalgic vision of America (i.e., "Make America Great Again") versus the progressives, Democrats, and leftists who are vulnerable to liberal lies and who feed off government dependency.[40] Deeply pessimistic, the illiberal imagination motions toward a bygone era of American democracy, replete with freedoms and rights. But, unlike adherents to the libertarian imagination, the path toward defending that version of America laid not in the rights and freedoms that make up democracy, but rather in strong-armed tactics and a strongman leader[41] like Donald Trump necessary to protect "the people" at the heart of democracy. If violence was inevitable—whether the violence of civil war or the violence of tyranny—as Eli believed it was, then Trump was more than just another presidential candidate in yet another election cycle in the centuries-long progression of American democracy. Rather, Trump was the only bulwark standing between democracy and tyranny, between rights and dependency—indeed, between Eli's America and Hitler's Germany. If the Democrats insisted on playing dirty (as Eli was convinced they did), then democracy could only be defended by the likes of someone like

Trump. This stance opened the door for what legal scholar Michael Dorf calls "insider violence," a term he uses to describe political violence threatened, supported, and/or perpetrated not by agitators outside of government but rather by those aligned with an "insider" faction of government, such as the Republican Party, in order to "intimidate one faction of the government [or, one side of the political divide] on behalf of another."[42] At democracy's apparent endgame, the ends justified the means.

As another interlocutor for the illiberal imagination, consider Alex, a white gun seller in Florida. He also looked to Trump as a strongman leader[43] to reinstall the conditions of order he saw as necessary for American democracy, even if securing those conditions of order came through anti-democratic means. As he saw it, "We don't like social unrest in the United States! We the people—the people who vote, the people who actually go and vote and pay taxes, we like order!" Instead, he saw disorder all around him. Though he declined to accept anarchy as inevitable (e.g., "Are we on the fall of the United States—falling into some anarchy? No. No."), he foresaw the "collapse" of the economy and worried about rampant lawlessness: "this COVID thing, because it is so politicized, has made everybody think that it's legitimate to break the law. *Including* Black Lives Matter." Rather than a protest movement, Alex saw something sinister and conspiratorial in the Black Lives Matter movement. Alex viewed the movement as something uncanny and unnerving, despite his self-professed lack of knowledge about it. Noting that "I don't like civil unrest," he admitted: "I don't know a lot about Black Lives Matter. In other words, I actually don't watch much news or anything. But I smell it—how's that? Does that work for you? I smell what it is." When I pressed him further, he adopted a conspiracist stance by connecting Black Lives Matter to the "propaganda" that he witnessed "all of a sudden" and for the "first time" in the United States under the Obama administration: "There's misinformation. There's slanted news. And there's propaganda. And for the first time, I was hearing propaganda. And it's like, *this is interesting, this is propaganda in America!*" Like Eli, Alex likened Obama to an un-American tyrant.

Though less explicit than Eli in tying up the threads of civil unrest and social disorder into an account of power-hungry Democrats, Alex was much more explicit than Eli about the role of violence as a means for restoring order.[44] Defining the "duty of government in America" around the obligation "to serve the common defense. To serve and protect. Protect the people," he asserted a violent ethos at the heart of democracy's existence: "*a show of force works. . . .* If you convince your opponent that you mean business, and that you will not tolerate a certain kind of misbehavior, they'll find other avenues—which hopefully are better—to make their case." With his conclusion that "a show of force works," Alex's take on the Black Lives Matter movement echoes how, across American history, individuals and organizations representing the interests of white Americans have historically framed Black uprising, rebellion, and protest as an existential threat and justified violent repression accordingly.[45] For his part, Alex largely wondered why Trump "took so long" to intervene in what he saw as "seditious" Black Lives Matter protests erupting across the country, particularly in Seattle:[46] "The minute you have people deciding that . . . we're going to have a police-free zone [Trump should have intervened] . . . The social unrest, which has gotten out of control, I'm surprised that Trump didn't intervene ahead of time."

Returning to the mantra he repeated throughout our interview— "We like order!"—Alex did assert an important disclaimer on the rule of law: "I believe in order. But for everyone. Including those in power. And the rule of law. And if you break the law, then you better have a really good reason. And the only reason is for life." Here, Alex illuminates that democracy, as a political system accountable to the people "who vote and pay taxes" and who "like order," depends upon a willingness to enact violence—albeit as a last resort—when societal conditions demand it. In doing so, Alex acknowledged the possibility of, even the *need* for, a shift from civility to violence—a viewpoint echoed in a *The Truth About Guns* article that laid out one path ahead for Americans who had "grow[n] impatient with heavy-handed authoritarianism": "First, the uprising will take place with angry phone calls, letters and public condemnation. Eventually, if and when the soapbox uprising fails, a cartridge box uprising could be next. And nobody wants to see that happen."[47] As another *The Truth About Guns* headline by the same writer put it, "If police won't stop the violence and looting, America's gun owners will."[48]

Like Alex and Eli, Joe, a white gun seller in Florida, also found political decline seemingly everywhere he looked. Seeing rights infringed upon and eroded all around him, he believed the American people were changing from the inside out: "we're going in that direction with the people who see their rights being taken away and their ability to protect themselves being taken away, and being okay with . . . all the socialist ideas becoming more and more a part of our lives. And it's just . . ." He paused with exasperation. His political pessimism contrasted sharply with the political hope exuded by the libertarian imagination; instead, he viewed many Americans as "lost causes" (so to speak). An *Ammoland* article echoed Joe's stance by comparing current threats to "fundamental rights and liberties" to Americans with an insidious virus:

> There is another virus in our midst that is more horrific . . . Many Americans have a natural immunity to it. Most, unfortunately, do not. It is endemic to our Nation but rarely mentioned. There is no known cure for those who contract the disease. And, for those who succumb to it, the virus turns a person into a numb, unthinking automaton, an obedient drone.[49]

With no cure and widespread susceptibility, the plague of tyranny infected "most" Americans and made them unfit for American politics: "numb, unthinking . . . an obedient drone." Perhaps that helps explain why, instead of placing his hopes in the transformative embrace of individual rights (as under the libertarian imagination), Joe placed his bets not on "the people" who were "okay with . . . all the socialist ideas" but on Trump. While Joe liked Trump's platform,[50] he told me that Trump's appeal transcended any one of his particular political stances. Rather, Joe appreciated *how* Trump approached politics. To illustrate, Joe told me the reason he named his hound dog after Trump: "I named [my hound dog] Trump, and it's based on the revelation that the hound dog is howling *all the time*. You hear him howling, and you get tired of hearing him howling because he's just making a lot of noise. [But for the hound dog, that noise] is a challenge. It's always a challenge to the people that are there: this is my territory, and I'm going to protect it. And I think that's what Trump is—he's a hound dog. He'll do what he can to protect his people." Acknowledging that Trump "says a lot of things that he could probably say in a better way," he sees that as a small price to pay for a leader willing to stand up when most Americans have lost their grit. Casting Trump as a strident defender of the people, Joe told me, "I believe that he is pro-American; I don't think he's anti-anybody."

Eli, Alex, and Joe each deployed a language of democracy in their own way, but listening closely to their political sensibilities reveals illiberalism conveyed through democratic principles—a wolf in sheep's clothing, if you will. After all, they raised the specter of "the people," and the protection of their rights and freedoms, but at the same time, they narrowed the scope of civic inclusion, justified strategies and tactics anathema to liberal democracy, and ultimately forged an alternative, illiberal vision of democracy that would become increasingly appealing to right-leaning Americans in general and to Trump's supporters in particular by the end of 2020. Blending armed individualism, conspiracism, and rigid partisanship, they conjured an illiberal embrace of "the people"—one that excluded Obama, the Black Lives Matter movement, liberals, members of the Democratic Party, and others who "were okay with all the socialist ideas." In doing so, they remind us that democracy is only as inclusive, just, and free as the people on whose behalf it is rallied.

The Eclectic Imagination

When I asked Sam, a white Hispanic gun seller in Michigan, to identify himself politically at the end of the interview, I was already prepared for an uncommon moniker, and he did not disappoint: "Gun-loving hippie." It reflected the eclectic nature of his politics I had already heard throughout the interview: though he easily rejected the "ideals of the conservative platform," as he put it, he was libertarian in some regards, "traditionally" liberal in others, and progressive in many others. He considered himself a "big proponent of environmental change and environmental policy," even joking that "if I could have another job, it would be like either a rock star or an eco-terrorist—and then I could combine my love of firearms with the environment [laughs]!" In August 2020, months before a vaccine would roll out, he had already predicted that the American rejection of coronavirus vaccinations would look a lot like the rejection of climate change: yet another example of "government propaganda, [a] government hoax," as he anticipated the opposition, rather than an earnest attempt to address a collective problem that was bigger than any one individual American.

Unlike his conservative gun-selling counterparts across Arizona, Michigan, California, and Florida, who largely saw mask mandates as an opportunity to resist government tyranny and assert the rights of individuals, Sam saw a yawning tear in the collective fabric of American society: "that there's been even so much as a debate over just something as simple as wearing a cloth mask when you go out . . . really speaks to . . . how Americans view ourselves, and how we view each other." Recognizing that "the attitudes of the current administration" led by Trump are "fueling" the debate over masks, Sam laments that "the fact that we are even having an argument about it seems kind of silly." To Sam, the question of whether to wear a mask comes down to a "simple" civic arithmetic based on a prioritization of collective responsibility over individual prerogatives: "even if something as simple as wearing a mask only proves to be 20% effective, and it's not really that huge of a benefit, [but] the cost to me is very minimal. At worst I suffer, or whoever is wearing a mask suffers, a mild inconvenience. It's a net gain." Even though Sam was a strident defender of gun rights, Sam's reasoning would be repellent to most of the conservative gun sellers I interviewed, who would likely decry it as a dangerous slide down the slippery slope of tyranny disguised as mere inconvenience. But it wasn't that Sam didn't understand the threat that government could pose to rights, or that he thought his gun rights were forever secured by the Second Amendment. Rather, his views on guns simply hadn't colonized his political views more broadly: he refused to treat every issue as a possible path to government tyranny.

Only three gun sellers I interviewed identified as left-of-center or—in Sam's words—a "gun-loving hippie." But each of these three differed markedly from other gun sellers. Each tended to have a bricolage of

politics that placed greater emphasis on consensus, collective responsibility, and civic community as they mixed and matched conservative
stances (particularly their pro-gun attitudes) and liberal attitudes. Their
eclectic political imaginations blended anti-statist sensibilities with a
commitment to collective responsibility, a belief in collective efficacy, and
a willingness to take the demands of other citizens as politically legitimate,
and worthy of redress, even if those demands admittedly emanated from
experiences that they could not relate to first-hand. They embraced an
inclusive view of "the people" and resisted attempts at narrowing the
scope of civic engagement, and entertained the possibility that collective responsibility was a worthy political disposition in the service of
the public good, rather than simply a ruse of tyranny. Though they
touted gun rights, their embrace of armed individualism existed alongside, rather than at odds with, an embrace of collective efforts at addressing public health concerns and even, in Sam's case, environmental
justice.

Consider Rebecca, a white gun seller in Michigan who laughed as she
identified as Democrat and opted to call her store "politically neutral":
"we're definitely much more politically neutral than I would say 99% of
the other stores." I could sense that Rebecca was different from the other
gun sellers I interviewed as soon as the subject turned to former President
Obama. Admitting that her family was "very supportive" of Obama, she
suddenly held back for a moment, wanting reassurance that her identity would not be disclosed: "I don't want to be identified— [we] do not
fit in the standard right-wing, pro-gun, 'everyone should be able to have
access to a gun, no background checks.' We don't agree with any of that
kind of stuff." After explaining the anonymizing process (and that she
wouldn't be geographically identified beyond her home state of Michigan), she went on to describe the kind of political environment—a "bla-
tantly racist," "us versus them" environment—that she encountered as
a Democrat working in the highly politicized, conservative space of
gun sales:

> There's just a mentality that we've seen that's been brewing over the
> years . . . I can tell that the tensions are constantly increasing on a

daily basis . . . Everybody's tone and demeanor—it definitely has
gotten angry. We definitely come in contact with some very strange
characters running that business, and I do feel like that's the state
where the world's in right now. Us versus them. Blatant racism.

Unlike the gun sellers who emphasized their opposition to the lockdown orders and promised they'd never close their shop despite executive orders to do so, Rebecca found that the ambivalence of Michigan's
lockdown order had a "silver lining" (her words) in that it allowed her
and her family to shut down their retail storefront, putting some distance between herself and the broader gun culture that had become
increasingly unbearable for her.

No doubt, Rebecca embraced armed individualism; she empathized
with the growing distrust of government and thought owning a gun was
a reasonable safeguard amid police response times that took "minutes
when seconds counted" (to paraphrase the popular pro-gun slogan).
However, she resisted conspiracism and partisanship during our interview,
instead prioritizing collective responsibility and political empathy. Rather
than lend credence to a "slippery slope" of government tyranny, she
explicitly rejected the notion that "the government is out to get us" in
the face of state action that would enhance firearms safety (e.g., background checks): "I would say honestly, like, safety is always our number
one priority . . . when it comes to politicking or people always think[ing]
that the government is out to get us and that kind of stuff, we just don't
really play into that." Likewise, rather than dismissing protesters as left-
wing thugs or dupes of a liberal cabal, she recognized protesters as fellow citizens with the same basic urge for freedom as herself. Regarding
civil unrest, she conveyed neither surprise nor alarm, but rather empathy: "I feel like when, you know, you have a specific minority that's been
oppressed for 400 years, what else are they supposed to do except fight
back when no one is listening to them?"[51]

Similarly, Kyle, a white gun seller and self-described "progressive"
from California, placed public health safety and social justice alongside
his embrace of guns. Rather than consider coronavirus an overblown
hoax or "plandemic" or question public health guidance, Kyle gladly

revealed that he was one of the first gun stores in his area to implement social distancing. He likewise resisted the common conspiracist assumption among conservative gun sellers that the police murder of George Floyd was being exploited for gains by unsavory actors on the American Left. Recognizing that the "civil unrest has been mostly, mostly peaceful protests, and has only been directed towards government officials and police," he described Floyd's murder not as a reason to further embrace conspiracism but rather as a "wake-up" call:

> Granted, that's not new—racial injustice and that sort of thing, that is a very old story. [But] a lot of people are seeing it for the first time, and they are going—wow, this is really a problem. And it's like, "wake up, and thank you." I'm not surprised at all.

As Kyle saw it, the protests following Floyd's murder were the obvious outgrowth of a deeply broken, and deeply divided, society. And rather than seeing civil unrest and coronavirus as blemishes on the otherwise triumphant story of Trump's America (as many conservatives did), Kyle noted, "people were struggling before this, right? It wasn't like everything was peaches and roses for everybody out there." Likening the particular economic difficulties facing "a lot of people living in inner cities" to "gasoline," he describes the film of the police murder of George Floyd as "the spark . . . you basically had gasoline all over it, [and] that spark lit it." He reasoned, "Police keep agitating, and various people are going to get angry, and they are going to basically say—why am I playing by the game if everyone else is cheating?" Kyle saw police violence as the "spark" that pushed people past their point of patience. After all, why wait for the wheels of justice to turn when it's clear that the entire game is rigged and that the cheaters—"police [who] keep agitating"—don't have to play?

Like Rebecca, Kyle rejected partisanship and conspiracism: instead of dismissing those fellow citizens whose actions he couldn't comprehend from his own first-hand experience as thugs or dupes, he recognized in the protests, the riots, and the unrest a commonplace response to intolerable hardship. And in doing so, he saw their acts of protest as sincere political expression—and also acknowledged the political (and socioeconomic) conditions that made that expression urgent. Rather than an instance of partisanship or an opportunity for conspiracist hand-wringing, both Rebecca and Kyle took the civil unrest of 2020 at face value as an expression of political voice[52] and the protesters as fellow citizens.

Rebecca, Kyle, and Sam each, in their own way, pulled together a range of political attitudes that rendered what we might call an "eclectic imagination." Though they were all left-leaning, their political imaginations were informed not just by their left and center-left politics but also by the fact that they straddled political worlds. They cobbled together a cacophony of politics that set them apart from their conservative counterparts in the gun industry but also from their non-gun-selling counterparts in the sphere of liberal politics. They embraced armed individualism and approached guns as a sensible option to address state shortcomings (much like their conservative counterparts), but they also resisted using conspiracism and partisanship as tools for making sense of government action, on the one hand, and understanding their fellow citizens, on the other hand. This separated them from their conservative counterparts who, instead, largely embraced libertarian and illiberal democratic imaginations. This eclectic imagination provides insight into how left-leaning gun sellers inhabited the conservative landscape of American gun culture, and it suggests the kind of political imagination that the first-time gun buyers of 2020—themselves disproportionately liberal as compared to existing gun owners—may develop as they enter that space, too.

Imagining "All the People"

About a year after I finished talking to gun sellers, pollsters in 2021 asked Americans a range of questions regarding US democracy—and uncovered stark misgivings among conservatives.[53] The quintessential instrument of transferring popular sovereignty onto government—the election as democratic norm and practice—was broadly seen as inadequate and even illegitimate. A striking 54 percent of conservative-identified respondents said they were "not at all confident" "that elections today reflect the will of the people" as compared to only 18 percent of self-identified liberals, and that figure surged to 73 percent when combined with those conservatives who expressed "just a little confidence" (again, liberals clock in at just over a third—38%). A full 70 percent of conservatives thought that "Biden did not legitimately win enough votes to win the presidency" (a view shared by only 8% of liberals), and 49 percent of conservatives thought there was "solid" evidence to attest to that belief. Roughly half of people surveyed—51 percent—believed that it was "very likely" or "somewhat likely" that election results could be overturned by election officials because "their party did not win." And on this point, there was some convergence between liberals and conservatives, as the majority of both believed (52% and 57%, respectively) that elections could become largely unfree and unfair—and, instead, mere devices of the ruling party—in the years to come.

My conversations with gun sellers during 2020 reveal how this profound lack of confidence in democratic institutions and practices— from misgivings about electoral outcomes to the increasing view of voting rights as "privileges"—can take shape in the political imaginations of everyday Americans. Among the gun sellers I interviewed, Eli, Alex, and Joe served as interlocutors of an illiberal imagination, illuminating *how* they managed to reject key elements of liberal democracy while maintaining a vision of themselves as defenders of American political values and principles. They cast their political opponents as existential threats to the United States; they dismissed fellow citizens who participated in social movements such as Black Lives Matter as accomplices to tyranny rather than advocates for a more inclusive democratic order; and they justified illiberal means to save America from the pluralistic democracy it has been struggling to become.

But the illiberal imagination was not the only political imagination— even among conservatives. Revealing the variety in political thought even within the Right, gun sellers Peter, Ben, and Andrew provided a window into the libertarian imagination. This imagination replaced the political pessimism of the illiberal imagination with political hope: hope that the displays of government underreach *and* government overreach over the course of 2020 would awaken people—even liberals—to their capacity as rights-bearing individuals. Under the libertarian imagination, guns thus served as a means of maintaining order (an overlap with the illiberal imagination), but guns promised much more to their bearers: for those "honest citizens" (as *Ammoland*[54] put it) who take up the call, gun rights serve as a means of personal transformation and empowerment, a first step in a political awakening that reminded people of their own capacity for self-governance and revealed to them government as a largely unnecessary apparatus of control. Rather than championing the strong-armed statism endorsed by their illiberal counterparts, gun sellers with a libertarian imagination blended armed individualism, conspiracism, and a more forgiving brand of partisanship. The result was a stance stoutly conservative in its embrace of individual initiative (such as gun rights) and its apprehension for collective action (such as government-led change). But despite this partisan disdain, these gun sellers saw their vision as an inclusive one—open to anyone, on whichever side of the political spectrum, who was willing to let go of the "liberal mindset" in defense of individual rights and freedoms.

For their part, the handful of gun sellers who *did* profess to having a "liberal mindset" illuminated a distinctive imagination from their conservative counterparts, one that cobbled together an eclectic stance on politics and a wide-ranging collection of ideas about the relationship between the people and the state. These gun sellers recognized that the state often failed to live up to its promises (like their conservative counterparts), especially with respect to ensuring the safety of everyday people, even as they also recognized collective action orchestrated by the state—public health measures, for example—as legitimate and beneficial to society. Giving little airtime to either conspiracism or partisanship, they saw the value in both private initiative and collective action; they acknowledged that people might understand politics differently depending on where they stand; and as such, they seemed more willing to understand people different from them as fellow citizens with a genuine message that deserved to be heard on its own terms. In other words, they saw difference, including racial difference, as core to democratic politics rather than a threat to democratic order. Rather than simply a reflection of their left-leaning politics, this imagination seemed to reflect these gun sellers' position as political outsiders within a deeply conservative space—a position that compelled them to think eclectically and dispense with dogmatism.

Across my interviews, gun sellers declared a profound skepticism regarding the state—and, if the 2020 surge in gun-buying is any indication, such skepticism was rampant among Americans at large. But even as they started with similar suspicions surrounding the state, gun sellers developed distinctive imaginations, particularly in relation to liberal democracy, as they mobilized the civic tools of armed individualism, conspiracism, and partisanship in different ways. Their imaginations showed, as political sociologist Ruth Braunstein[55] notes in her comparison of liberal and conservative Americans, not just how they "develop[ed] different styles of active citizenship but also view[ed] alternative choices as inappropriate, undemocratic, and even un-American." In illuminating how they used this civic toolkit to navigate the edges of democracy and build conservative culture from the ground up, gun sellers have provided insight into the fault lines of American democracy as an everyday politics. They have also provided a starting point for forging new tools for reimagining, repairing, and restoring a free, equitable, and just political terrain in the United States.

Conclusion: The Democracy We Deserve

There's a specter haunting American democracy—the specter of the gun owner. Policy outcomes, election results, even the very terms of political debate have all been, at some point in the recent past, attributed to the uncanny power of the gun owner to harness American democracy for the expansion of gun rights. In an era in which—as political scientist Jan-Werner Müller[1] notes—American voters have abandoned electoral participation in droves, gun owners stand out for their high levels of civic engagement. Compared to non-gun owners, they are more likely to vote and, when they do, vote Republican; what political scientist Mark Joslyn describes as a partisan "gun gap" has widened threefold since the 1970s.[2] The more guns a person owned in 2016, the more likely they were to vote for the Republican ticket.[3]

The gun owner, then, appears not as foe to democracy but rather its felicitous student. Much more likely to be politically engaged than their gun control–favoring counterparts (not to mention the general American population), gun owners are endlessly reminded by the National Rifle Association and other gun rights groups of their power and prerogative as citizens to shape the democratic process. They are told they must not just vote but be informed voters (hence, the NRA's politician grades); they are informed that politics doesn't only happen on an election cycle, and thus they must be ready at a moment's notice to contact politicians about impending legislation (hence, the NRA's legislative alerts); they are instructed that not just elected politicians but also appointed officials—like judges—are crucial to the political process, and thus elections are as much about fighting a protracted culture war as they are about putting a specific term-limited leader in office (hence, the NRA's increasingly pro–Republican Party messaging). The "engagement gap" between gun owners and non-gun owners, as political scientist Matthew Lacombe[4] argues, is as much a reflection of differences in political commitment as it is a consequence of the NRA's power to construct the gun owner as a political identity.

To be a gun owner, on the NRA's terms, then, is not simply to own and carry a gun but also to be civically engaged in American democracy in a way that prioritizes expanded gun rights (and also increasingly entails other conservative platforms). Despite democratically perverse outcomes (such as the blockage of universal background check legislation in US Congress despite the vast majority of Americans favoring it), the NRA and the legions of politically engaged gun owners it has helped to forge perhaps haven't perverted American democracy as much as diverted it to the cause of gun rights, using the very civic practices—such as voting—that lie at the core of how Americans broadly define democracy. If anyone wishes to bemoan the impact of the NRA—and late-twentieth-century conservative gun rights politics—on democratic culture in the United States, they must start by considering that the NRA didn't break American democracy as much as reveal its breaking points.

But in another sense, the NRA very much *did* change the rules of democracy insofar as it helped to transform the basic parameters of political culture that keep American democracy humming. The NRA celebrated *armed individualism* as it promoted gun carry laws not just as an expression of gun rights but as a response to state inefficacy; it has popularized and normalized *conspiracism*, starting with the spread of "slippery slope" logic that identified the inevitability of gun confiscation in any piece of gun regulation, no matter how seemingly harmless; and it has been a bulwark of *partisanship* as it has increasingly portrayed Democrats to be the party of gun confiscators by virtue of their embrace of further gun regulations or their opposition to expanded further deregulation. Each of these civic tools has helped to galvanize gun owners into a formidable political force that, by the twenty-first century, had convinced many Americans, across the gun debate, that the NRA was nearly unstoppable.

But by the time Trump supporters gathered in Washington, DC, on January 6, 2021, to storm the Capitol Building in a pitiful attempt to

assert the then-president as the victor of the 2020 US presidential elections, the NRA was hardly the powerhouse it once was. Embroiled in
financial scandal and facing outcry from within (among defecting members) and without (from the Attorney General of New York State, where
the organization is chartered), the NRA boasted its strategic decision to
declare bankruptcy and avoid the brunt of its misdeeds—only for a court
to throw out the bankruptcy.[5] Apparently, the US political system—or at
least, a part of it—was fed up with the NRA. And, suggesting the organization's demoted presence in the minds of gun rights advocates, the
gun sellers I interviewed for this book who mentioned the NRA largely
did so in passing, while those who offered more substantive comments
were apt to express their dissatisfaction about the organization's direction. As Ben, a white gun seller in Michigan, exclaimed, "I think they are
the worst gun rights group ever, especially now how poorly they are managed!" If the NRA's political power and popular clout had slipped from
the organization, though, that didn't necessarily signal waning influence.
After all, the NRA certainly didn't claim any connection to the January 6
riots (no major national or federal pro-gun organization did),[6] and the
violence of January 6th largely took place *without* guns (though some protesters had illegally brought guns and bombs with them to Washington,
DC[7]). Nevertheless, the connection between January 6th and conservative gun culture did not run through the gun as a concrete object as
much as a symbol of a broader political project. The display of armed
individualism, conspiracism, and partisanship in evidence on January 6th was undeniably resonant with the brand of gun-centric politics
the NRA pioneered and promulgated since the 1970s—and much like the
NRA's own approach, it was couched in a dramatized devotion to the
primary symbol of American democracy that has served the NRA so well:
the vote.

The Trials of January 6th

The insurrection at the US Capitol Building on January 6th has largely
been seen as a message about American democracy: about its fragility,
precarity, and even illegitimacy in the minds of many Americans (even
as the insurrection, and all other attempts at unearthing widespread

voter fraud related to the 2020 elections, failed to prevent Joe Biden from assuming office as the 46th president that he legitimately won). Rioters assaulted police officers, one of whom was killed;[8] they destroyed property; they traumatized staff, first responders, and elected officials. All told, the riot may cost as much as $30 million—an irony given that excess government spending was one of the charging points of the rioters.[9] But it also brought an incalculable political cost to the American public that will be difficult to repair: violence is now on the table of possible responses to electoral defeat.

Of course, for some Americans, that option was always there—if tucked away as a last resort. The gun sellers I interviewed during 2020 knew as much, as did the gun rights news headlines leading up to the 2020 election that asked, "Want to see what real civil unrest looks like? Try confiscating Americans' guns."[10] By July 2022, nearly 900 people[11] had been arrested for their involvement in the January 6th insurrection on charges including conspiracy, civil disorder, assaulting officers with dangerous weapons, and a litany of others. Many have viewed the government's responses, including the speedy impeachment of Trump a second time for inciting the riot and the hundreds of arrests of participants as well as the ongoing investigation by a special "Jan. 6 Committee" appointed by the US House of Representatives, as a trial of American democracy against antidemocratic forces that have been bred and bolstered within it.

The insurrectionists themselves would likely agree—as would many of the gun sellers I interviewed for this book. Swaddled in silos—of information, of political beliefs, of cultural sensibilities—that made it less and less likely they could imagine half the country voting for Joe Biden, millions of conservatives now believe the election was illegitimate, fraudulent, even stolen. Democracy is a political apparatus that is supposed to require that losers accept their loss, lest they sacrifice their loyalty to democracy on the altar of loyalty to a particular political party or politician.[12] What the losers of the 2020 presidential election managed to do, however, was split the difference: their stated commitment to democracy became the very means by which democratic outcomes could be rejected. Armed individualism, conspiracism, and partisanship facilitated this illiberal mobilization of democracy by legitimating violence as an act of individual empowerment against collective encroachment, recasting the opposition's political expression—whether in the form of protest or policy—as a nefarious power grab, and asserting that one's political foes were not just opponents in the game of democracy but undeserving of participating in that game at all.

Thus, when gun rights advocates tell us in the aftermath of the January 6th insurrection that "the Democrats turned our sense of fair play & morality into weakness and beat us into the ground with our own decency"[13] (from an *Ammoland* story), we *should* hear the echoes of the bombastic political rantings made mainstream by Trump and Trump's Republican Party. But we should *also* hear more than that. Entitled to a bygone America seen as threatened by the Democratic Party and its agenda of multiracial democracy, the insurrectionists and their sympathizers were not just motivated to "Make America Great Again" in some general sense but specifically in a political sense. Multiracial democracy posed the existential threat of disenfranchisement and disempowerment for those invested in the maintenance of racial and gender hierarchies that have historically put white men at the top of the American social order. Themselves disproportionately white conservative men, the insurrectionists wanted the democracy that they thought they had grown up with, and one that they had taken for granted, back: that brand of American democracy that exalted rights, freedom, and justice as universal goods *in principle* but protected those goods *in practice* only when they served their interests, their values, and their priorities. This illiberal entitlement was captured in one yell heard among insurrectionists as they blasted through windows, beat police officers, and intimidated the frontline workers of American democracy: "This is our house!"[14]

As legal scholar Aziz Huq surmised, "The hard instruction of the January 6 insurrection (one of many) is that our constitutional tradition can well supply the inspiration for insurrectionary violence against a fair and legitimate election result at the behest of a manifestly illiberal demagogue with a demonstrated penchant for mistruths."[15] To say that the insurrectionists were anti-democratic, then, wasn't entirely wrong, but it would be giving American democracy a bit too much credit. Most certainly, the insurrectionists revealed just how easily the edges of American democracy can defray into righteous violence. But they also revealed something else: the pliability of democracy as a discourse and an imagination. The January 6th insurrection put American democracy on trial, indeed, however, the lead prosecutor wasn't anti-democracy but rather illiberal democracy. The insurrectionists and their sympathizers, at the core, exposed that mere fealty to "democratic" procedural norms will not resuscitate American democracy in the twentieth century, nor will appeals to procedural norms prepare American democracy for the challenges it will face as US society becomes both more diverse and more unequal. Despite their violent acts and their bombastic rhetoric, the insurrectionists beckon us to consider that it's not a bang that will kill democracy—or at least, the kind of democracy worth saving. What will kill American democracy is the widespread adoption of a whimpering, hollowed out, and loosely democratic imagination motivated by political exclusion, fueled by illiberal tactics, and stoked by strongman leaders. After all, the insurrectionists failed in their attempt to disrupt the certification process on January 6th, but six months later, nearly half of Republican-identified voters believed they were right to try—a "legitimate protest"[16] against a US presidential election that conservatives have continued to view as fraudulent as 2021 marched on.[17]

It's too simple to say that conservatives left democracy—and too naïve to say that democracy left them. Rather, this book shows that while American democracy was threatened from above, political imaginations were reconstructed from below as people mobilized armed individualism, conspiracism, and partisanship. The gun sellers I met during 2020—a year of seemingly "unprecedented" chaos and uncertainty—provided a window into how this unfolded.

The Guns of Democracy

This book draws on conversations with 50 gun sellers across Arizona, California, Michigan, and Florida during the multilayered crises of 2020—crises that instigated a dramatic uptick in gun sales across the country. Ammunition shelves were cleared. The logistical chains that delivered guns from their manufacturers to the holsters of their owners were stymied. Gun sellers found themselves fielding millions of buyers, many of whom had never purchased—or even thought to purchase—a gun in their lives. This great gun purchasing surge has been taken as an adjudication on the well-worn American gun debate: proponents of gun rights have celebrated the surge as an indication of the Second Amendment's continued appeal and relevance (even as they worried about the fitness of the new gun buyers joining American gun culture), while proponents of gun restrictions have braced themselves for the violent fallout of so many more guns in circulation. Though a variety of factors shape gun violence, the surge in purchasing coincides with rates of gun violence unseen in decades, including the single highest increase in the raw number of homicides since the FBI began keeping records in 1960.[18]

Unfolding in American schools, homes, or on the streets, gun violence assumes markedly different shapes and represents markedly different kinds of threats to Americans situated differently along the lines of race, gender, and class. Boys and men of color, particularly African Americans, in socioeconomically marginalized communities, bear its inordinate brunt—a fact often elided in public outcry surrounding mass shootings. Yet, gun violence has a generalized impact insofar as the threat of gun violence weaves fear into the basic fabric of American life—and for that reason, gun violence is not simply a public health issue or a criminological problem but also a political one. As Firmin DeBrabander notes in *Do Guns Make Us Free?*,[19] Americans' high tolerance for the problem of gun violence and the widespread acceptance of more guns as an individualistic solution for that problem generalizes fear of one another as a defining mark of the American polity. With guns increasingly entering the public sphere not just as practical objects of safety and security but also as political symbols of protest, guns have become wrapped up in "Americans' equal freedoms to speak, assemble, worship, and vote without fear," with "citizens (and sometimes politicians) deploy[ing] guns in ways that change how stakeholders and lawmakers engage with each other in politics," as legal scholars Joseph Blocher and Reva Siegal observe.[20] They argue that the result is a tapered and tampered democracy—"one in which armed citizens, who are overwhelmingly white and male, exclude others from full participation in democratic life."[21] The impact of conservative gun culture on American democracy thus runs deep—shaping the heart of our basic political capacities. As Joan Burbick[22] concludes *Gun Show Nation*,

> How much easier it is to believe in the politics of the gun, and to fight for our right to be armed, than to step in front of the gun and build social and civil institutions that sustain our society and promote economic and political justice. The gun is ultimately a shortcut, a strategy to sidestep consent. Our will to engage in democracy is what is at stake. The question remains: Can we put aside the lethal politics of the gun and take up again the challenge of democracy?

Those who embraced guns and gun rights in 2020, however, understood firearms less as a threat to democracy and more as a tool—perhaps the only available tool—for navigating what they experienced as its profound shortcomings. While commentators have often signaled contemporary gun politics as a broad threat to American democracy, my conversations with gun sellers reveal a more fine-grained, and ultimately more complex, relationship between the politics of guns and the politics of democracy. Specifically, these conversations helped reveal just how the gun—specifically, the gun forged as a key object of the conservative agenda since the 1970s—intersects with democratic sensibilities as Americans navigated a bewildering intersection of insecurities, uncertainties, and chaos over the course of 2020. The coronavirus pandemic, the crisis of police violence, and the instability of American politics (and the ways that institutions and individuals responded to each of these) converged into a democratic crucible—an acute moment that exposed the core tensions within the democratic project as they took shape in the specific American context. As scholars of democracy show, the tensions that erupted—between government underreach and government overreach, between the ideal of popular sovereignty and the reality of representation (and the expertise that representation necessarily entails), between the tolerance for conflict and the embrace of universal commonalities among citizens—are inherent, unavoidable, and incontrovertible to the project of democracy. But, as American historians of race and democracy relentlessly remind us,[23] these tensions have taken specific shape in the concrete realities of American structures of racial inequality, exclusion, and injustice.

While political leaders—from Barack Obama to Donald Trump—provide starkly different alternatives for responding to those tensions from the top down, everyday people are tasked with navigating them from the ground up. Rather than automatons obeying the latest dictate of the NRA or Trump, gun sellers provided a window into how conservatives navigate the political impasses they experience. Their gun stores functioned as quasi-political forums to engage, expand, and export a repertoire of civic engagement. They promoted armed individualism as they celebrated the centrality of guns in everyday life as "great equalizers" of safety and security. They adopted conspiracism as they made sense of expert claims—and decided whose knowledge, perspectives, and experiences counted. And, they rallied around partisanship not just as a means of defining their opinions against the views of others but also as a way of defining themselves against the people they deemed outside of "the people" on whose behalf American democracy exists. Far from monolithic, gun sellers' political imaginations at turns celebrated individual rights as the epitome of empowerment, dismissed the voices of their partisan opponents and at times even justified their political exclusion, stigmatized collective action and responsibility, and entertained strongman government and political violence as, perversely, democracy's last hope.[24] Democracy became contested, contrived, and even convoluted, especially as some gun sellers redefined political engagement in such exclusionary terms that it became incompatible with norms of inclusion typically associated with the term "democracy"—a finding that echoes recent studies of conservative Americans, including Ruth Braunstein's *Prophets and Patriots*,[25] Arlie Hochschild's *Strangers in Their Own Land*,[26] and Theda Skocpol's and Vanessa Williamson's *The Tea Party and the Remaking of Republican Conservatism*.[27] Like the conservatives profiled in those studies, gun sellers used the political culture at their disposal to navigate the dilemmas of 2020 as they saw them—and in doing so, they redrafted the substance of democracy itself in illiberal, libertarian, and even (for the handful of left-leaning gun sellers) eclectic terms.

Retooling Democracy

Most scholars taking on the contemporary crisis of American democracy have centered on two kinds of interventions: a fortification of political procedures and institutions and a recommitment to political civility.[28] With regard to political procedures and institutions, there are many forms that these interventions could take: the repeal of the 2010 US Supreme Court's *Citizens United* case alongside campaign finance reform;[29] federal protection of voter rights amid the de facto dismantling of the 1965 Voting Rights Act;[30] the end to the filibuster;[31] the expansion of the US Supreme Court;[32] and more. Underlying these interventions is a hope that fortifying democratic procedures and institutions can take the edge off of American politics and avert a fatal blow to American democracy as it stands.

The call for political civility, however, reflects that protecting democratic procedures and institutions from the top down, however crucial, cannot alone transform the underlying political culture that feeds democracy's decline from the bottom up. As Robert Bellah and his colleagues[33] concluded nearly four decades earlier in their meditation on American civic culture *Habits of the Heart*, "it is evident that a thin political consensus, limited largely to procedural matters, cannot support a coherent and effective political system . . . the only way to find out [whether we can excavate deeper political consensus] is to raise the level of public political discourse so that the fundamental problems are addressed rather than obscured." Unfortunately, an emphasis on civility—as political sociologist Andrew Perrin[34] reminds us—may make politics *feel* better but will not address the tensions that have taken explosive form during 2020 and onward. Conflict, after all, is core to democracy and something we must learn to embrace rather than eschew; norms of civility that frustrate the open expression of conflict may, in fact, backfire into rage—or worse. Further, there is good reason to be angry about US democracy; for centuries, it has functioned as a system that has supported the interests of the powerful (white, landowning men) while facilitating wild injustices against immigrants, women, Black people, indigenous people, people of color, and sexual minorities. Conflict is not the root of the problem; the problem is that the United States still—after more than two centuries—lacks a generative and just means of recognizing and redressing political conflict and transforming it into political consensus.

For what it's worth, this book does not serve as a basis for reimagining democratic procedures or institutions—gun sellers, or any political niche of the American polity, would provide a poor basis for that venture if the goal is to maximize space for deliberative disagreement. But gun sellers *do* help us imagine how to rehabilitate democratic culture beyond flat calls for "civility." Understanding *just how* armed individualism, conspiracism, and partisanship shape political imagination, particularly among conservatives, raises the possibility of forging a different civic toolkit—one equipped to take up the invitation of US democracy to make good on the long-deferred promises of equality, justice, and freedom as the United States becomes a more diverse yet more unequal society. Consider three possibilities for this alternative toolkit: political equanimity, civic grace, and social vulnerability. In the development of these civic tools, I am indebted not just to the scholars cited below, especially Black feminist scholars, but also to those who have fused a commitment to social justice with Buddhist practice, particularly the thinking of Thich Nhat Hanh.[35]

Political Equanimity

Uncertainty, especially in the midst of 2020, became a bad word, associated with fear, threat, and chaos. Something to be avoided or extinguished, uncertainty galvanizes armed individualism, which dangles an elusive sense of control through the specter of the gun. As Robert, the Florida gun seller who opened this book, asserted: "when you have uncertainty, you have to have a guarantee, and the only guarantee in this country is the right to protect yourself." The gun not only promises to restore a sense of control, serving as "a guarantee" to its owner; the gun—or rather, contemporary gun politics—also recasts the effort to extinguish uncertainty as not a thankless endeavor but a worthy and worthwhile pursuit.

But that's a fallow and one-sided understanding of uncertainty. From a different perspective, uncertainty might elicit not fear but political equanimity—a measured tolerance for uncertainty rather than an eager attempt at controlling it. If armed individualism centers the gun as the primary means of quelling uncertainty, political equanimity aims to de-center the gun in order to consider why uncertainty must charge the steep price it does in fear and intimidation. Political equanimity would replace the need for "a guarantee" with acknowledgment of uncertainty as a valuable resource for political creativity and civic engagement. Democracy—an inclusive, multiracial democracy—cannot function without some degree of uncertainty.[36] Rather than "merely a set of abstract principles enshrined in law," as political sociologist Ruth Braunstein[37] notes, American democracy is a "living tradition . . . it is hundreds of millions of citizens trying (and often failing) to put these principles into practice. It is improvisational; it is messy." This messiness isn't an existential threat; it's what helps maintain the integrity of democracy in the first place. Political equanimity can help reframe the seemingly high-stakes tension between government underreach and government over-reach by recognizing that democracy is a process—one that is never settled but, rather, requires creative, collaborative, and constant engagement alongside whatever individual actions we may undertake (such as purchasing a gun) to ramp up our personal sense of safety and security. Political equanimity provides the temperament to weather the vicissitudes of democracy as a necessarily tentative, and always-evolving, political project. It also provides the foundation necessary to breach boundaries and bridge chasms within the polity—that is, to cultivate civic grace.

Civic Grace

Democratic uncertainty cuts deeper than whether we can be assured that our preferred policies and politicians will win at the polling booths: it extends upward, to the machinations of government, but also outward to our fellow citizens as well as inward to ourselves. We can't be certain of the intentions behind the pronouncements of experts; we can't be sure of the inspirations for the actions and attitudes of our fellow citizens.

We can't even be assured that, with more experience, expertise, and time, our own political views won't change dramatically over our lives. And yet, the democratic tension between the ideal of popular sovereignty and the reality of representations means that politics must be a shared good—not simply in the sense that we hold it in common with others (i.e., a "shared politics") but also in the sense that we are willing to let others have a piece of it too (i.e., their "share" of politics) in return for recognition of our own slice.

Conspiracism is one response to this conundrum: it declines the invitation of shared politics by attempting to monopolize political reality and shrink the sphere of who gets to participate in defining it. And in doing so, it stands to erode our capacity for compromise—as it threatens to frame those with whom we might compromise as power-hungry experts or knowledge-deficient dupes instead of our political equals.

Rather than conspiracism, though, we might approach these tensions from the perspective of civic grace. Civic grace speaks to a particular kind of political compassion toward one's fellow citizens. It takes as an act of faith another's sincerity of political expression and legitimacy of political standing. As a temper to conspiracism, civic grace centers on the acknowledgment that we can never walk in another's footsteps; we simply cannot fully grasp—whether from an experiential or expert perspective—just how they've weathered the life that's worn them to the point of their current politics. Civic grace thus means recognizing that while we may disagree vehemently with one another's political viewpoints, we can still approach the paths—experiential, epistemological—that brought people to those viewpoints with the dignity of recognition. This dignity of recognition rests *not* in exonerating or excusing people for a particular political stance they hold but rather acknowledging that each of us is more complicated than what we appear; that our lives are animated by contingencies that have produced not just who we are but also who we might become; that none of us can be written off; and that, therefore, we might all benefit from extending civic grace widely.

Civic grace is one way to make good on historian of African American and American religion Anthea Butler's call to those who are invested in the project of American democracy: "you must join with people you don't agree with in order to make a more perfect union."[38] It resonates with what Bellah and colleagues[39] call "generosity of spirit": "the ability to acknowledge an interconnectedness—one's 'debts to society'—that binds one to others whether one wants to accept it or not [and] the ability to engage in the caring that nurtures that interconnectedness." And as the work of decolonial thinker Frantz Fanon suggests, civic grace is also a radical act of anti-racism: it compels us to recognize in one another not the finitude of stereotypes and preconceptions but rather the profound, and profoundly liberating, resplendence of possibility—the "open dimension"—posed by another human being who is mutually acknowledged as such.[40] Civic grace resists the "living death" wrought by white supremacy, as described by Buddhist practitioner and scholar of trauma, race, and grief Breeshia Wade when she writes that "white supremacy attempts to pervert Black life into a living death through the destruction of possibility, where individual flaws that would naturally be a fleeting moment, a failing, become failure—an all-encompassing state of being."[41] Civic grace disrupts fixity and finality, replacing it with the recognition that not only has the story not ended . . . but that perhaps the story doesn't have an ending at all.

Extending civic grace to others *and* ourselves means acknowledging that we, too, can't be sure of the multitudes we contain or where our politics might lead—freeing ourselves *both* to embrace the principles we hold dear *while also* recognizing that we might be wrong and that, if we are, we too are free to change. Civic grace asserts recognition and appreciation of fallibility as a political value, one needed to sustain our capacity to share our politics with those with whom we may share little else. And as such, civic grace also provides a deeper capacity to recognize with empathy, and redress with intrepidity, how American politics has failed its most vulnerable constituents.

Social Vulnerability

Americans generally do not appreciate vulnerability as a fact of human life. They tend to prefer talking about (and devaluing) weakness, dependency, precarity, and inadequacy—attributes that can be easily chalked up to moral failing, poor choices, or sheer lack of merit. But that doesn't comport with the nature of the human condition. By virtue of being human, we all experience a basic frailty that can't be avoided: the suffering of loss and the experience of pain. Whether it's our material subsistence, our physical being, or our interpersonal relationships, we will all experience—in one form or another—the profundity and finality of loss.[42] "Grief is knowing," as Breeshia Wade reminds us, "that we, too, will die."[43] However we try to deny it or talk our way out of it, we are fundamentally vulnerable.

Despite its inescapable presence, Americans as a whole have an impoverished culture when it comes to acknowledging and addressing our vulnerability to suffering. We embrace chemical addictions that take the edge off of pain even as they isolate us. We turn to consumption as a means of softening the sting of loss—or, in the case of anti-aging products, convincing ourselves that we can avoid it. Many of us consent to social arrangements that ensure that certain people—in American society, disproportionately, Black women—not only are inordinately burdened with their own grief but also are tasked with managing the grief of privileged others.[44] Some of us even turn to religions that help justify a "harsh, uncaring posture toward suffering and disaster"[45] as cruel expressions of God's will, blaming victims rather than extending them our unconditional support. And many become attracted to those ideologies that provide an intoxicating and self-assured illusion of power and control by celebrating a disdain for social connection (redrafted as weakness) and collective care (redrafted as dependency).

Like most dimensions of American social life, the ability to ignore or even accept the suffering of others is compounded by the politics of race. The "racial empathy gap" describes a troubling predisposition for people to discount the suffering of people of color,[46] one explanation for why people of color, and African Americans in particular, are sentenced to more onerous punishment, expected to work through their discomfort or injury, celebrated for mustering "grit" and "resilience" in the face of hardship that would garner sympathy and support in others, and ignored when they scream "I can't breathe" upon suffocation by public law enforcement. The assertion that "Black Lives Matter" is one direct retort to this phenomenon—an assertion that the ruin of Black life represents an immeasurable loss worthy of individual *and* collective grief.[47]

Conspiracism and partisanship, however, serve to short-circuit the grievances, losses, traumas, and suffering of fellow citizens; after all, if you believe that your fellow citizens are epistemologically or ideologically unfit to make the claims they are making, there's no reason to look too closely at their suffering. In extreme cases, conspiracism and partisanship might even struggle to erase that suffering altogether. Conspiracist claims that coronavirus deaths are wildly inflated or that mass shooting victims are crisis actors[48] take the universal pain surrounding the loss of human life and erase it through partisanship and conspiracism; perhaps it is easier to believe political opponents would engage in elaborate and convoluted plots to expand power and control rather than to accept that sometimes, terrible and inexcusable tragedies happen. Such claims are a gravely insulting affront to the real and devastating loss of life, and for those willing to embrace them, they express a denial—a twisted, disturbed denial—that such loss is not just possible but profoundly part of life, especially in the contemporary United States. Meanwhile, armed individualism is often quite explicitly built around avoiding the trauma of gun violence—not just in the sense that guns are embraced by their owners as protectors against the trauma of gun violence *but also* in the sense that the promotion of gun rights, to the extent that it is formulated as a political and social panacea to gun violence (i.e., the "more guns, less crime" mantra), takes its advocates off the hook of having to look closely at the suffering of those, disproportionately people of color, who experience gun violence.

Armed individualism, conspiracism, and partisanship are not *merely* means to avoid coming face to face with the fact of our own suffering and the suffering of others, but that avoidance is most certainly in that political mix. An alternative to this impulse would be to recognize, rather than run away from, suffering as an inherent human experience that shapes and is shaped by our relationships with ourselves and one another and that compels us to recognize our interconnectedness.[49] As bell hooks observed, "true resistance begins with people confronting pain, whether its theirs or someone else's, and wanting to do something to change it."[50] Rather than degrade suffering into—at best—a personal grievance undeserving of collective redress, social vulnerability asserts a fact of universality that transcends our political differences: the fact of our inherent, even if also singular, capacity to experience loss, pain, and suffering. Social vulnerability invites us to remember that this inherency is social in two senses: first, in the sense that it is intimately linked with our need for human connection, and second, in the sense that how we experience this inherency is fundamentally shaped by our social position and the social institutions that structure that position.

I am, of course, not the first to entertain vulnerability, empathy, and love as tools of civic connection that we would be better off embracing. From bell hooks[51] to Brené Brown,[52] visionary thought leaders have called emphatically for our collective need to embrace vulnerability in our work lives, our personal lives, and our political lives. As hooks calls us to embrace love as a political value and practice of freedom, "The moment we choose to love we begin to move against domination, against oppression. The moment we choose to love we begin to move towards freedom, to act in ways that liberate ourselves and others. That action is the testimony of love as the practice of freedom."[53] Centering our shared and singular experiences of vulnerability in our political lives would make good on the promise of love as a political ethic. Doing so would counteract the tendency to discount the pain of others and to avoid the inevitability of our own pain, and it would also provide a basis for imagining a democratic polity—"the people"—founded not on rights and responsibilities, or on privileges and propensities, but rather on our mutual capacity for, and thus shared obligation to attend to, suffering as a defining human experience.

———

The solutions that are offered for the contemporary dilemmas faced by American democracy are often technocratic in nature. They tweak a particular institutional arrangement; they innovate a procedural approach; they remind us of the power of meso-level organizations—such as parties and the media—in safeguarding democracy. These are all useful interventions that can help stack the odds in favor of a fair, just, and equal political system. But by tracing the many lives of democracy in the political imaginations of largely conservative gun sellers, this book has emphasized the importance of everyday political cultures, alongside institutions, in sustaining American democracy. We can rig the dice, but ultimately our democracy rests on the people calling the shots—that is, ourselves.

The historical record shows that our institutions have not kept us from the worst of American democracy. From the beginning, the United States has rested on "a deeply anti-republican embrace of inequality that throughout American history has served to trigger and inflame racial divisions and animosity," as legal scholar Bertrall Ross[54] puts it. Writing in the aftermath of World War I—a war that some Americans believed would make the world "safe for democracy"—W. E. B. Du Bois[55] remarked that:

> It is curious to see America, the United States, looking on herself, first, as a sort of natural peacemaker, then as a moral protagonist in this terrible time. No nation is less fitted for this role . . . instead of standing as a great example of the success of democracy and the possibility of human brotherhood America has taken her place as an awful example of its pitfalls and failures, so far as black and brown and yellow peoples are concerned.

And as we stretch farther back into American history, the lie of the World's Greatest Democracy comes into focus: the United States is a country that was founded through genocidal violence, enslavement, and the disenfranchisement of the majority. What we have inherited is not simply a nation antithetical to the democratic myths it repeats to itself but also a centuries-old culture of denial built up around those democratic myths. Many of the calls to "save democracy" turn on a nostalgia for a democratic Golden Age that, for too many Americans, is not worth returning to. Meanwhile, those of us around today may not have started the fire, but many of us continue to feed it by commission and by omission. We can't exit this predicament simply by pointing our fingers at our political opponents. Across the political spectrum, Americans too often fail to treat the baring of our anti-democratic souls as anything but unfortunate aberration. Over the course of the twentieth century and into the twenty-first, conservatives and liberals have both—albeit in very different ways—used the language of equality, freedom, and justice to obfuscate their abrogation.[56] Far too often, and often regardless of their political allegiances, Americans who would prefer not to reckon with the past simply claim innocence when confronted with resolute evidence of what this country is and what it has been.[57]

Amid American society's penchants for heavy-handed nostalgia for a rosy past or outsized faith in the power of institutions, at some point we—especially white Americans who have benefitted most from the social, political, and economic arrangements of inequalities in the United States—must confront not just the politics outside of us but also the politics within us. Though this book has focused on conservative thinking, many of the core themes examined here extend across the Left and the Right: across the political spectrum, Americans have an aversion to uncertainty, an out-of-place faith in procedure (whether as an ideal or a means of manipulation), and a dwindling desire to do the hard civic work of engaging those who disagree with them in ways that affirm, rather than undermine, the humanity of their opponents.

Merely telling people to give up the guns that can't shoot a virus, to stop believing in their theories, or to forgo the false consciousness of their partisan identities is unlikely a fruitful course of action. That is because attempts to simply stamp out or eradicate the civic tools outlined in this book are unlikely to change people's understandings of the social, political, and economic forces swirling around them, but such attempts are very likely to reinforce the very dynamics that encouraged them in the first place. A better approach would be to put *more* tools in the civic toolkit that can roll back the appropriation of democratic sentiment without replacing one set of illiberal missives with another.

What I suggest here—political equanimity, civic grace, and social vulnerability—would not just help "address" the tensions within democracy but encourage us to *learn to live with* them and even *sustain* them so that they can become the productive, rather than destructive, fuel for the kind of political freedom that thrives *within*, rather than *despite*, difference. After all, democracy is a road to freedom, but it is not free itself.[58] It exacts a risky speculation not just in terms of our electoral processes but also on behalf of our political sensibilities—indeed, a free, inclusive, and equitable democracy can't exist as such *without* that risky speculation. Without political equanimity, civic grace, and social vulnerability, democracy does not necessarily disappear—but it does become more susceptible to converting into a force for unfreedom, exclusion, and inequality.

But who will be willing to take up these tools? Gun sellers—Jake, Rebecca, Andrew, and Peter especially come to mind—lamented, in their own ways, the shallow callousness of contemporary political engagement in the United States that has eroded our relationships with ourselves and with one another. They were far from unaware of the mutual problems we face as a society, but they typically defined these problems in their own terms and from their political vantage points. For that reason, change will likely not come from most of the gun sellers I interviewed—or any group of Americans embedded in one side or the other of our political divisions. While this book has focused on these gun sellers to understand where we *are*, it is the new gun *buyers* of 2020 and beyond—the women, the people of color, and the liberals who all broke the stereotype of the "typical" gun owner in the United States—who are in a position to take up the project of breaking down the political barriers that divide Americans and improvising new ways of engaging in politics and engaging with one another.[59] To the extent that they neither give up on politics nor give in to the pressure to choose political sides, those Americans who straddle political worlds may be the best, and last, hope for reinvigorating democratic culture in the United States and for forging the democracy we deserve. After all, democracy will not in itself make the United States a more equal, free, or just political space—except to the extent that democratic institutions, procedures, and norms support our everyday capacities[60] to embrace one another, despite the differences we believe divide us, as equal citizens and fellow humans.

Epilogue

Much of my life has been spent wondering about political chasms: what they mean, where they come from, and whether and how to bridge them. This has been an academic concern, but it has always been personal, too. The daughter of a devout conservative, I couldn't take "Because I said so" (in any form) for an answer from my father, but I also couldn't help but be troubled by the political impasses I acutely felt as a result. The helplessness I experienced with engaging him politically was never really resolved—he died of ALS before that could happen—but I have remained vexed as the same dynamics that hounded my relationship with my dad fuel the fires of political acrimony all over American politics.

Little did I know, my dad was vexed too. I didn't know it while he was alive, or even well into writing this book, but in the last months of his life, he too wondered a lot about the two of us. He felt, like me, that he had no answers when our conversations turned to deadlock. All he knew was that we persistently ended up on the opposite sides of any issue: "If I was right, you were left. If I was conservative, you were liberal," he would say. (And, true to the spirit of what my dad thought, I'd be incensed that he even dared to put me in the binary terms of his politics—*I would not be labeled by him as a liberal!*) But instead of grieving why we could never connect, my dad left a light on in the house of our relationship: as he said, I later learned, "we danced this dance over many years with neither of us knowing or understanding the depth of our relationship and connection."

We like to say that "actions speak louder than words," but when actions are so at odds with words, it's hard to really hear them. But despite what he said he believed in, my dad did pretty much everything he could to put me on a path where my beliefs couldn't help but come into conflict with his. He's the one who moved our family all over the country and, eventually, the world, instilling in us an appreciation for the new, the different, the unexpected, the contrarian. He's the one who pushed me to leave the conservative state of Indiana to pursue an Ivy League degree in liberal New England (an ironic reversal of him leaving the liberal city of Chicago to pursue his undergraduate degree at West Point). He's the one who ensured that, despite many blunders of youth that could have ended up in me having to give up on my PhD in Sociology at UC Berkeley, I would finish that degree and make good on my dreams of becoming a university professor. What my dad *said* taught me that I was a poster child for everything that conservatives reviled, but what my dad *did* taught me that it is possible to vehemently disagree with someone and still support them and their perseverance on a path you might not choose for yourself. My dad was showing me the ropes of civic grace, although I had no idea at the time.

My father cried when I got tenure, with just over a month left in his life. His soon-fatal struggle with ALS had made it physically difficult for him to speak, but over the three years of his illness, he managed to find a different voice than I had ever heard from him. Halted at the top of the career ladder because of his diagnosis, my dad left his corporate position and all the accolades attached to it. He mentioned several times that he wished he would have become a social worker; it was so contrary to everything that I had thought he stood for that I had a hard time, regretfully, believing that he really meant it. At one point he managed to communicate to my mother, in that last month before his death, that if he couldn't have pursued social work like he now wished he did, at least I did something along those lines. In a message my mom eventually relayed from my dad from that time, "you followed your North Star in pursuing what you were passionate about and what would have an impact. Thank you for making that decision, showing me what is really important." If only we could all have the perspective that death deals while still having plenty of life to make good on it.

In this book, I have struggled to make sense of our contemporary political divides and what they mean for American democracy. My conversations with gun sellers told me a lot about where we've been, where we are, and where we are going if we stay committed to our current political divides. But as I tried to envision a different kind of politics than the one we have now—one centered on civic grace, social vulnerability, and political equanimity—I realized that my own political imagination might have come from a source I hadn't expected.

ACKNOWLEDGMENTS

Authors often remark on the lonely pursuit of writing a book. This book was an especially lonely endeavor, conceived and written during the two most intensely isolated years of the pandemic (2020 and 2021). When I started developing this book project, I believed I was once again turning to writing as a way to make it through difficult times. But instead of giving me respite from the collapsing, chaotic, and confusing world, this book drove me deeper into it, requiring a degree of mental toughness that I hadn't realized I didn't have and that I would have to develop, again and again, every time I sat down to think, read, and write. At the same time, however, this book—and the research that undergirds it— *did* provide a way out of the loneliness and isolation precisely because this book made it impossible *not* to stay engaged—both with the world "out there" as well as with the friends and colleagues upon whom I relied to keep going. It turns out that no book—even a book that took shape during a global lockdown is ever really written alone.

First, I am grateful to the gun sellers in Arizona, California, Michigan, and Florida who were willing to pick up the phone and talk to me, despite your onerous schedules and your partisan apprehensions. From April to August 2020, your conversations kept my mind lit up and gave me a reason to wake up and stay focused, despite the deepening pandemic anomie. Not only did each of you give me your time, but you also gave me insights that—despite studying gun politics for more than a decade—I wouldn't have been able to grasp without your frank honesty, your sardonic humor, your passion for selling guns and promoting gun rights, and your willingness to try, along with me, to make sense of it all even as none of it made sense. I hope you read this book and find that it is written from a place of wanting to give all of us tools to understand,

and bridge, our political divides and that this book conveys my sincere belief that that endeavor necessarily requires not just that we speak our own political truths but that we listen—and engage with—the political truths of others as well.

Next, I am grateful to the graduate students who worked with me as I fielded interviews, analyzed data, and began to put the pieces together in the form of articles and a book. I have been exceedingly lucky to work with Madison Armstrong and Cat Burgess on this manuscript, both of whom have combed through it for readability and typographical errors. This manuscript benefitted enormously from Madie's rare blend of editorial acumen and sociological insight; her thoughtful engagement of the manuscript not only clarified but also elevated the argument. I am also very grateful to Cat for filling out much of the material that appears in the footnotes as well as for compiling the bibliography—a huge and unsung task. Finally, I especially thank Minyoung An and Elliot Ramo, both of whom worked as research assistants who provided crucial support at the early stages of the research by coordinating inter-views, compiling relevant literature, and assisting in data analysis. While I drafted the book manuscript, I also collaborated with An and Ramo on two co-authored articles published in *Social Problems* ("Politics at the Gun Counter: Examining Partisanship and Masculinity among Conservative Gun Sellers during the 2020 Gun Purchasing Surge" with An) and *Social Forces* ("'I'm not a Conspiracy Theorist, But . . .': Knowl-edge and Conservative Politics in Unsettled Times" with Ramo). Note that because I relied on book material, drafted independently of these collaborations, for portions of my contributions to these co-authored articles, there are overlaps between these articles with chapters 2 and 3. Any unattributed overlapping material represents my own thoughts and work; the insights that reflect our collaborative work are acknowledged and attributed accordingly.

None of this—the interviews with gun sellers, nor the research as-sistance from graduate students—would have been possible without the support of the School of Sociology at the University of Arizona (for the first period of data collection) and the National Science Foundation (for data collection after July 1 and subsequent analysis). I had been approved to begin a study on gun violence survivors, funded by the NSF, when the pandemic disrupted life in March 2020. I am grateful that not only did the NSF provide me with the support to pivot my research but they did so in a way that would expand training for graduate students, who were rendered particularly precarious by the pandemic. Further, no acknowledgment of funding support would be complete without applauding the staff who managed it. I am grateful to Raquel Fareio and Lauren Jacobson for ensuring that our School of Sociology ran smoothly throughout the pandemic and its ongoing aftermath. Lacee Gonzalez painstakingly ensured that my research agenda—and really, research across the University of Arizona's College of Social and Behavior Sciences—could move forward despite the dizzying array of pandemic-era restrictions and red tape. Thank you, Lacee.

As I shifted from data collection and analysis to writing, I relied on colleagues and mentors who kept me engaged with my own work. Each of them turned what felt at times to be an insurmountable task into something that was not just doable but also worth doing. In the early stages of book development, Abigail Andrews provided feedback, accountability, and a reminder that the book—despite what I may have felt in the lonely dredges of writing—was moving forward. After the book was drafted, I was grateful to have engaged readers who managed, despite the chaos and constraints of pandemic times, to provide insightful and astute feedback on the book. I am endlessly grateful to Kathleen Cavanaugh and Kimberly Hoang, who organized a workshop on the book manuscript at the University of Chicago's Pozen Center for Human Rights, and to Marco Garrido, Aziz Huq, and Laura Beth Nielsen, alongside Kathleen and Kimberly, for providing crucial feedback that improved the cogency of the manuscript in too many ways to enumerate.

This book would not have taken shape without the enthusiasm and engagement of Princeton University Press. My editor, Meagan Levinson, understood the vision from the start and painstakingly coached me through the writing process. I am a better writer, a better thinker, and a better sociologist from having worked with Meagan on this project— and I only wish that every author has the chance to develop their writing in this way. Likewise, I am grateful to Katie Stileman and Kate Hensley, both of whom have worked ingeniously to find ways to make my work speak to audiences within and beyond academia. I am grateful to the often unseen labor of the production team led by the redoubtable Terri O'Prey, especially Karen Verde's work in polishing and perfecting the final manuscript. From copyedits to book design, I am overwhelmed by the care taken with this manuscript.

Finally, I am grateful to my family, who encouraged me, supported me, and inspired me. They believed in what I was doing—even when I wasn't sure I did. Thank you Mom for celebrating every big and small step of this project. Thank you siblings Chris and Brittany for cheering me up and talking me down as I struggled with writing. Thank you Dad who, while not physically here, was nevertheless with me as I wrote every word. And thank you Jeremy, my husband, best friend, and partner, for standing by my side every day, whether or not the world fell apart around us. I only had to look up from my writing to know that I was never, ever, really alone.

REFLECTIONS ON METHODOLOGY

This book primarily draws on interviews with gun sellers. These interviews were conducted across Arizona, California, Florida, and Michigan, starting in April 2020 and concluding in August 2020. With the permission of the interviewee, most interviews were recorded; for the handful of interviewees who chose not to have their interviews recorded, I took notes and later reconstructed them into a narrative. Although some interviews lasted one to two hours, a typical interview was 30 minutes, as gun sellers were frequently too busy to spend additional time given the surge in their business activity. Interviews addressed six major topics: the social construction of coronavirus; the gun purchasing surge; gun purchaser demographics; motivations behind purchasing; the impact of coronavirus on the appeal of gun rights and the future of gun politics; and general attitudes about American society and American politics. As interviews were semi-structured and open-ended, interviewees raised relevant topics as they emerged in real time, including conspiracist explanations of COVID-19, the surge in #BlackLivesMatter protests in spring and summer of 2020, and an increasing focus on the presidential election in the summer of 2020. I transcribed all interviews, anonymized them, and analyzed them with the support of Atlas.ti. All names are pseudonyms, and small details have been changed to preserved the anonymity of interviewees. To put the interview data into conversation with gun rights discourse more broadly, I also draw throughout this book on pro-gun media outlets, including the top two most visited online gun news outlets, *The Truth About Guns* and *Ammoland*, as well as the legislative alerts from the leader of the gun lobby, the National Rifle Association. From these sources, I compiled a database of stories on coronavirus, Black Lives Matter, and the 2020 US elections running from March 2020 to the inauguration of Joe Biden on January 20, 2021. These news and opinion data allowed me to follow "the long 2020," using sociologist Sarah Quinn's phrasing,[1] from the first mentions of coronavirus in early 2020 through the thirteenth month of 2020—January 2021. My analysis of these news and opinion data followed—both analytically and temporally—my analysis of the interview data. Following an abductive approach, my first phase of analysis involved iteratively moving between interview data and existing scholarship to develop a preliminary analytical framework that emphasized armed individualism, conspiracism, and partisanship as civic tools. Adopting this abductive approach[2] to the data meant following new literatures down the proverbial rabbit hole, especially with respect to scholarship on knowledge, science, and politics, on the one hand, and democratic instability and authoritarianism, on the other. The second phase of analysis brought this preliminary analytical framework, developed through coding and memo-writing with respect to the interview data, to bear on the news and opinion data, which allowed me an opportunity to broaden the analytical framework and ensure that it captured civic phenomena beyond the sample of gun sellers I interviewed. The third and final phase—writing the book and revising it with the help of keen reviewers and colleagues—allowed me to sharpen my analytical framework, engage adjacent literatures, and ultimately craft an argument that speaks to urgent questions of politics and democracy in the United States.

———

Perhaps that is where the description of my data collection and data analysis process should stop; it is adequate in a scholastic sense in that it explains the basic parameters of the study that undergirds this book. However, it fails to capture just how—as the cliché now goes—2020 upended qualitative research, compelling a different relationship not only between myself and my methodology, but also between myself and my interview subjects. It also forced me to grapple with time—as a variable in my research design, and as a fulcrum for harnessing sociological insight—more explicitly than ever before. I learned more in the process of researching and writing this manuscript than I could have imagined at its onset—and not just in terms of the "what" of my book's argument but also with regard to the "how" of developing that argument.

Looking back, I realize that rethinking the "how" of research and writing began as soon as I picked up my phone to dial in my first interviewee.

Defetishizing the In-Person Interview

Qualitative work seems to always come with the risk of methodological fetishization. This risk is often palpable among ethnographers—especially in the expectations that ethnographers be willing to do whatever it takes to "get the data," whether putting themselves in harm's way, playing loose with their ethics and morals, or reproducing relations of exploitation between themselves and those they study. Interviewers have often slid out of the room when these arguments explode, leaving the ethnographers to duke it out among themselves. But interviewers harbor their own brands of methodological fetishism: like their ethnographer cousins, they tend to overvalue the data obtained by in-person interviews as superior to interview data obtained otherwise by virtue of the je ne sais quoi of rapport, but unlike the ethnographers, they tend to fetishize their own distance from their research subjects by recourse to their interview guides, their sampling structure, and their rigorously reasoned-out positionality vis-à-vis the object of study and the social dynamics that object will presumably illuminate.

Going into 2020, I too fetishized the in-person interview as the "gold standard."[3] I had long advised against students using remote interviews as the basis for their dissertations as I saw it necessarily compromising the quality of their data and also representing a lost opportunity for building the skills of in-person interviewing. In my own research leading up to this project, I had crisscrossed the states of Arizona, California, and Michigan, driving hours to remote locations to secure in-person interviews with firearms instructors, gun carriers, and police chiefs. When I added up travel time, the interview itself, and the time taken for transcription, each interview transcript easily took five to ten hours to produce. For some groups of interviewees, this process was essential to executing the research project; I don't think, for example, police chiefs would have been willing to talk to me over the phone, at such length and with such candor, had they not been able to meet me, sit down with me, and judge me as someone trustworthy enough to engage in the interview.

But as 2020 unfolded, I recognized that navigating this was not an inherent dynamic of the interview process but rather a dynamic unique to the population under study—especially with respect to that population's presumptions regarding research conducted by outsiders. Universalizing this valuation of the in-person interview necessarily overlooked the fact that not only are remote interviews *not worse* than in-person interviews, but depending on the group being studied, they may actually be much, much better. While the pomp and circumstance of a scheduled, in-person interview may appeal to certain populations, this may be altogether off-putting to other groups. Striving to fill our quotas of interview subjects, researchers can too easily forget how overscheduled people's lives are, and how intrusive and time-intensive interviews may be. That's not to say that interviews aren't often enjoyable or illuminating experiences for people—they are—but even things we enjoy exact a certain cost. Remote interviews allow people much more flexibility in terms of when they are interviewed. For example, gun sellers, who experienced a great deal of time shortage and time uncertainty throughout 2020, at times scoffed at trying to schedule a time in a future they felt they could hardly predict, but they were often willing to "chat for a few minutes right now." The few minutes often mushroomed into a half hour or an hour as business unexpectedly lulled; if not for the flexibility of remote interviewing, many of these interviews might have never happened.

Likewise, remote interviews allow interviewees more flexibility about not just *when* but also *where* they interview. Had I conducted these interviews in person, I would have been able to see the kind of stores these gun sellers operate, beyond the online footprint I could ascertain remotely. I would have been able to see whether or not they had Trump paraphernalia loudly displayed; whether they traded in ATF-stamped items (full autos and silencers, for example) or made their business by focusing on a niche item, such as competitive rifles; and what kinds of people they hired to work their counters. Many of these elements, of course, would be disclosed to me during the interviews anyway, but I would have liked to see for myself, first-hand. But this cost came with its own reward. Not being physically present during the interviews meant that gun sellers could take me anywhere their phones could go. In person, I may or may not have been invited to the backroom vaults of any given gun store, but remotely, I could hear gun sellers shuffling through their paperwork in their back offices as they pulled up the latest data on their sales figures and product stock. Likewise, every time I was put on hold because "I got a customer, hang on!" I knew that there was a good chance that that customer—purchasing as they were in the midst of the very gun surge about which I was interviewing the gun seller—would evoke something worthy of note for the gun seller to report back upon return.

And while I was not in a position to instruct gun sellers on where to take my call given the time pressures of interviewing, I can easily imagine remote interviews in which such a deliberation—"Think about doing this interview in a place that is evocative to you"—might be not only appropriate but also rapport-building. Such a request may well serve the interests of the interviewee much more than asking that the interview take place in a facetiously "impartial" place of the interviewee's choosing, like a coffee shop, a personal residence, or the interviewer's office.

Remote interviewing may also better serve the needs of the interviewer—and not just in terms of getting "better" data. Though we might convince ourselves otherwise, in-person interviews can easily exhaust, unnerve, and even endanger interviewers—and with no clear pay-off, other than keeping our methodological fetishism intact. During my remote interviews, I could focus on managing the conversation while letting my expressive face do what it does—without fear of jeopardizing rapport. (Being able to snuggle with my cat didn't hurt, either.) But remote interviews aren't just about increasing the comfort of interviewers. The insights that Rebecca Hanson and Patricia Richards offer in *Harassed* on the embodied endangerment of ethnographers during fieldwork[4] likewise apply to interviewing (even if, because the interaction is often shorter and because the interviewer has more control over the parameters of the interview itself, such perils may be somewhat lessened for interviewers). For example, during my 2010 interviews with gun carriers for *Citizen-Protectors*, I most certainly felt that, because I was the researcher calling the shots, I was in control of the situation. I didn't allow myself to feel unsettled by the sheer firepower that accompanied me at every step of my fieldwork (indeed, I eventually carried a gun too—as described in *Citizen-Protectors*), nor did I allow myself to play out in my mind the possible happenstances that could occur by virtue of constantly being around so many guns. My point is not that there was some danger awaiting me with the people I was studying—to be very clear, there wasn't—but rather that I should have at least considered the possibility given that I was entering a new social world. But the stakes were too high—I had to finish my *dissertation*! Perhaps my advisors at UC Berkeley worried about my safety, but I didn't. It wasn't until someone at a conference asked me the obvious question— "weren't you scared being around so many people with so many guns?"— that I realized it was something I should have been at least *nominally* concerned with. I realized I hadn't let my feelings matter—because all that mattered was "getting the data."

Thinking back on that fieldwork, I can't help but think that that naïve audacity had a whole lot to do with my own positionality: an able-bodied, cisgender white girl from the suburbs inhabited just the right blend of innocence and entitlement to feel invulnerable in a situation that others might well have deemed viscerally, irreconcilably dangerous. Of course, I understood very early on that the narrow conditions of possibility for the kind of fieldwork that I did for *Citizen-Protectors* and *Policing the Second Amendment* depended on the particular intersection of my race, gender, class, and age status; what I didn't realize was that I colluded with these narrow conditions by fetishizing in-person interviews and discounting remote interviews as not "real" data collection. The truth is that in-person interviews may simply ask too much of people who are already disparately disadvantaged in academia: people with disabilities; people who are marginalized by virtue of race or gender; people who don't have the time or funding to go on extended road trips chasing interviews across the country. Fetishizing the in-person interview cuts too many people out of the methodological fold out of hand, biasing the method from the inside out—and for this reason alone, I won't defend it as a "gold standard" any longer. Remote interviewing does not do away with inequality in social positionality, but it does shake up the playing field in a way that allows the chips to fall a little differently, with perhaps a bit more equity.

The Politics of Rapport

Some scholars—by virtue of their object of study, or perhaps the status they claim in the hierarchy of knowledge production—may be tempted to opt out of considering the political valence of their work at some (or even all) stages of the research process. At the very least, qualitative researchers are often encouraged to adopt an unbiased, objective stance as we go about amassing our data in the form of fieldnotes and interview transcripts. While ethnographers have interrogated the possibility, let alone the desirability, of such a relationship between the researcher and the researched, interviewers seem a bit more swayed by the lure of objectivity   after all, the interview itself is often designed precisely to harness its utility to produce data that can lead to theoretically rich and generalizable insights. The underlying presumption here is not just that objectivity maximized is better than objectivity discarded but also that *there is a choice to be made about objectivity at all*. But a yearning for objectivity in itself does not allow anyone to opt out of the politics of knowledge production—and most certainly not at the stage of data collection. Put simply, researchers don't get to opt out of the society in which they are embedded by virtue of donning the cap and gown of scholarly bookishness.

While academics may have entertained such tenants, gun sellers quickly instructed me otherwise. Reflecting long-standing features of gun politics described elsewhere in this book, gun sellers were already steeped in trenchant apprehension regarding the motivations of university professors—and I received entertainingly articulate declinations that attested to this apprehension. My scholarly record and my online footprint were crucial elements in recruitment that allowed me to thread a delicate needle: I had the receipts to show that I was a scholar motivated to understand, rather than condemn, the social life of gun rights, and I was willing to cross some thresholds—own a gun, carry it, even become an NRA-certified instructor, all activities undertaken as part of my research for *Citizen-Protectors*—in pursuit of that end. This approach and background were crucial to building rapport in the context I was researching (one of heightened political animosity) and in the format of data collection I was using (that is, remote interviews). And as with *Citizen-Protectors*, my identity as a white cisgender woman who sounded young (a handful of gun sellers commented on my presumed age) likely also worked to make the interview a nonthreatening space for the largely white, middle-aged men who comprised the interviewees. Remarkably, 53 gun sellers agreed to participate in the study, offering up data ranging from mind-boggling sales numbers to impromptu political philosophizing. My final sample for analysis was 50 gun sellers; three of the interviewees, while agreeing to participate, resulted in interviews that were too short and curt to yield the kind of rich data necessary for qualitative analysis. While I have checked my findings against those three interviews for robustness, I focused on the final sample of 50 in-depth interviews to generate my analysis and to justify my claims throughout the book. Table 1 profiles the demographics of these 50 interviewees. (Note that while I include more nuanced descriptors when introducing interviewees, for the purposes of this table I categorize interviewees by their primary racial identification; a gun seller who identifies as "white with a touch of Mexican" would be included in the "white" category, while a gun seller who describes themselves as "biracial" would be in the "racialized minority" category.)

I have always found gun people a fascinating bunch with whom to converse, and those who participated in this study did not disappoint. Though my interviews with gun sellers would bear some striking differences from my research for *Citizen-Protectors* (more on that, below), that

TABLE 1. Interviewee Demographics

N = 50		
Age (mean)		49 years
Race	White	90%
	Racialized Minority	10%
Gender	Male	88%
	Female	12%
Politics	Right-Leaning	84%
	Independent	8%
	Left-Leaning	6%
	Centrist	2%

earlier research gave me the capacity to engage in the kind of gun talk necessary to build rapport once interviewees were on board to talk to me—dropping in firearms jargon; knowing which touchstone event, court case, or ideological cue to mention in passing; framing questions in ways that eased interviewees and avoided eliciting a beginner's lecture on the Second Amendment. While the process of building rapport is a full-body experience in the context of in-person research, my words had to bear the entire weight during these remote interviews. Sociologists are not therapists, but our toolkits necessarily overlap when the former's goal is to facilitate an interview space conducive to focused conversation. But rather than creating a safe zone for interviewees to spill their deep-seated "truths" (as a therapist might), my goal was to forge enough connection that interviewees would let their guard down and allow me to peer into the dynamism of their political reasoning: what sense they made of the bewildering circumstances of 2020 and—crucially—*how* they made that sense.

From *Citizen-Protectors*, I knew going in that guns—and the armed individualism they facilitated—were going to be crucial linchpins for political sense-making. Accordingly, I had prepared my interview guide attendant to what I thought were the kinds of prompts that would incite gun sellers to give me some insight into how they understood guns, and the broader politics in which they were embedded, at this particular moment. But my interview guide could only be so long, so rigid, and so formal, given the felt dynamism of the American political landscape throughout 2020. While I may have desired, as an objective researcher, that my interviews probed the life histories of gun sellers for hours at a time, circumstances dictated to me, a researcher embedded in the same dynamism that baffled my interviewees, otherwise: my interviews would be snapshots of meaning-making and institution-navigating at a highly volatile time—a biographical instant and a historical moment capriciously melded into a conversation.

Rather than sticking to a strict script, I followed the prescient strategy of attending to slippages, uncertainties, and innuendos in order to cull what interviewees were saying and with what objectives. Interviewers should always do this, of course, but in the context of the world-historical events of a pandemic, anti-racist uprisings, and US democratic instability, this strategy folded in on itself, or rather folded in on *me*: I found myself at various moments not simply the interviewer but also the co-navigator of circumstances beyond both of our—mine and the interviewee's—control and comprehension. And accepting that I was, on some level, trying to make sense of this strange new world *with* my interviewees forced a peculiar mix of urgency and humility. And interviewees recognized this as well: perhaps using the interview as a vehicle to sharpen their own clarity, several turned the questions back at me, wondering what I made of all of it. In those moments, I was not the university professor who descended from the ivory tower to tell the world what it couldn't possibly know otherwise, nor were interviewees the salt-of-the-earth types who had, by virtue of their grit, all the answers that the pleasantries of the professoriate couldn't possibly fathom. Rather, we were people caught off guard by what history had in store for us—and were both grappling to figure out how to navigate it, albeit with very different tools at our disposal. In addition to my own background knowledge on guns and gun politics, then, it was this basic assertion of mutuality—that we were all in the same boat of uncertainty—that seemed paramount to building rapport well beyond anything lost by virtue of the interviews being conducted remotely.

Time in Unsettled Times

If there is a single lesson to be learned from so-called pandemic field-work for qualitative researchers, it is that research, like the social world, is messy. From the curious whims that often mark its beginning to its ultimate dissemination, research is at once bewildering and ser-endipitous. Research always entails the emergence of unanticipated dynamics, even in so-called settled contexts. But in "unsettled" contexts like 2020,[5] the process of data collection is all the more uneven and unexpected. In March 2020, as I began to lay the groundwork for this study, I could have barely fathomed where the pandemic would take us, let alone grasped the uprisings against white supremacy and anti-Black racism spurred by the police murder of George Floyd or the riots and insurrectionist protests instigated by Trump's unfounded claims of elec-tion fraud that would come by the end of 2020 and into 2021.

Mocking my attempts to impose order and structure on the research process, time became a strange companion during these "unsettled" times. Abductive analysis, however, was crucial in taming time. Empha-sizing comparisons within and across data, abductive analysis allowed me not only to move back and forth *within* my dataset of gun sellers to suss out puzzling data points that emerged along the axis of time. It also attuned me to puzzling data by juxtaposing my 2020 fieldwork with gun sellers with my 2010 fieldwork with gun carriers and gun instructors. The differences in political tenor across these two bands of fieldwork, separated by a decade, were striking. Gun rights advocates in 2010 took democratic process for granted; they didn't espouse conspiracist thinking; they were disgruntled at liberals, leftists, and Democrats but hardly subjected them to the kind of rancor that I heard in 2020. Abduc-tive reasoning—not just moving between data and existing scholarship, but also between different time periods of data—helped me begin to make sense of 2020.

While "site revisits" are often deemed costly research endeavors un-likely to yield advancements in knowledge adequate enough to justify their undertaking, I nevertheless came to understand my 2020 fieldwork as a "site revisit" of a kind. Most certainly, I had not returned to the same research participants, nor had I returned to the same research site (although Michigan figures in both studies). Rather, both studies pivot around the same basic question, strategically explored in a context chosen for its potential to yield rich insight: how does social upheaval shape the appeal of guns—and with what consequences? In 2010, social upheaval was defined by a faltering economy and a divested state; hardly "upheaval" by 2020's standards. Fielding back and forth between my 2010 findings and my 2020 observations was an abductive exercise in culling the historical changes that my data evidenced between the two time periods. Indeed, without my 2010 findings, perhaps I might have tried to explain away the rampant conspiracism and partisan rancor I saw in 2020 as the expected attributes of conservatism—a "paranoid style" endemic to conservatism. But my 2010 fieldwork, which largely lacked the skepticism for science and disdain for democracy that became nearly unremarkable by the end of 2020, made such easy "just so" explanations untenable and, instead, pointed to the ways in which gun politics, gun markets, and gun culture were dynamic terrains as Americans continued to turn to them out for order, for control, for safety, and security. Bringing into focus the coordinates of the analysis that I develop in this book, time served as an axis of unsettledness *within* a process of data collection and an indicator of historical shifts *across* fieldwork.

In centering time as an analytical praxis that could assist in navigating particularly unsettled research contexts, my goal is not to suggest that we only study that which we already have a "history" with (so to speak), nor is it to suggest that we should all try to build in comparisons within our projects not just *across* categories of analysis but also *across time as well*. While there are exemplar instances of such an approach (Lynne Haney's masterpiece *Offending Women*[6] immediately comes to mind), my emphasis here is a bit more heuristic: that we must keep history—including recent history—within the purview of how we do sociology, not just for context but as an analytical device that helps us gain traction on the contemporary conditions that we hope to illuminate.

———

To try to make sense of history in the making—living history—is easily a fool's errand. And yet what else is there to do but to try? This is the lesson of humility that 2020-onward has ultimately imparted to everyday people, to politicians, and to academics from virologists to sociologists. For my part, this project has humbled me with respect to a variety of methodological touchstones—what I've explored here as defetishizing the in-person interview, the politics of rapport, and time in unsettled times. Humility is a quiet kind of power: it gives us the strength to let go of the habits that no longer serve us, and it reorients us to other stakes that we might instead prioritize. As we stand grasping for the "new normal" and wondering whether we shall remake our worlds anew or hold onto our old habits hoping to just survive, this is the power that I hope will guide us—as citizens, surely, and also as researchers.

NOTES

Introduction: Democracy Disarmed

1. Note that all names are pseudonyms, and small details have been changed to preserve the anonymity of interviewees.

2. Grisales (2022).

3. Lucas (2022).

4. Lindsay (2020).

5. Reed (2021).

6. Popli and Zorthian (2022).

7. Gerstein (2021); Kanno-Youngs, Tavernise, and Cochraine (2021).

8. Two other police officers at the riot—Jeffrey Smith and Howard Liebengood—died by suicide within the week. See Healy (2021).

9. Schmidt and Broadwater (2021).

10. Hall et al. (2022). Figures reflect charges as of July 25, 2022; note that this database continues to be updated with additional arrests.

11. In a YouGov poll taken on the afternoon of January 6, 2021, 45% of Republicans said they strongly or somewhat support the "storming of the Capitol Building" (Sanders, Smith, and Ballard 2021).

12. A YouGov poll taken shortly after the riot found that 43% of Republicans surveyed described the actions of rioters as "patriotic," and 50% saw those actions as "defending freedom." See Blake (2021). Note that in April 2020, a Pew survey found that Republicans were much more likely to express confidence in a fair and free election as compared to Democrats (Gramlich 2020), but by January 2021, 88% of very conservative and 77% of conservative voters felt that Trump either definitely or probably won the election despite the ballot results (Pew Research Center 2021).

13. National Shooting Sports Foundation (2021a).

14. Savidge and Cartaya (2021).

15. Lacombe (2021: 18).

16. See also Yamane et al. (2020).

17. Lacombe (2021: 29).

18. Although they have largely been rallied on behalf of White, able-bodied, and property-owning men throughout American history, gun rights are not inherently conservative or liberal—as attest the broad appeal of guns past and present, the spread of pro-gun organizations across the political spectrum in the contemporary US context, and the diversity of societies

with meaningful—if less dominant, as compared to the United States—gun cultures, including, as examples, Georgia, India, South Africa, and Yemen. See Carlson (2014); Heinze (2014); Light and Slonimerov (2020).

19. Schutten et al. (2021); see also Haney-López (2014).

20. Lacombe (2021).

21. Whitehead, Schnabel, and Perry (2018).

22. Lacombe (2021).

23. Alexander (2010); Forman (2017); Hinton (2021); see also Metzl (2010).

24. Alexander (2010).

25. See chapter 1 in Carlson (2020).

26. By 2020, roughly three-quarters would oppose a handgun ban. Gallup (2020).

27. See chapter 1 in Carlson (2015).

28. Russell-Brown (2009).

29. See Carlson (2015; 2020).

30. Leonardatos (1999).

31. Lacombe (2021: 144).

32. Achenbach, Higham, and Horwitz (2013).

33. Achenbach et al. (2013).

34. Carlson (2015).

35. Lacombe (2021).

36. Carlson (2020).

37. Lacombe (2021: 237).

38. Writing of the rhetorical affinity across gun rights advocacy and evangelical Christianity, Dawson (2019: 1) notes that "the National Rifle Association (NRA) has capitalized on the religious nationalism that arose in the late 1970s alongside the Moral Majority and has increasingly used religious language to shape the discourse surrounding the Second Amendment." Further illuminating this connection, Whitehead et al. (2018) identified Christian nationalism as a top predictor of opposition to federal gun control, trailing only political orientation.

39. Du Mez (2020).

40. Sokol (2008).

41. The modern conservative movement could not have cohered without the coordinating work of media activists and national politicians (alongside leading organizations like the NRA). As early as the 1950s, media activists provided the foundation for conservative activism and organization by developing a network of conservative talk radio, right-leaning newspapers and publishing houses, and, much later, conservative cable networks (Hemmer 2016). Circumventing the presumed liberal bias of mainstream media and promoting messages of free market capitalism, social traditionalism, and white supremacy, these media outlets proclaimed "the rise of liberalism as a great betrayal of the American creed" (Hemmer 2016: 179) and beckoned their conservative audience as the "authentic moral core" (Peck 2019: 86) of American society. Meanwhile, right-wing politicians, starting with George Wallace, Barry Goldwater, and Richard Nixon in the 1960s, rallied against liberal policies, politicians, and pundits in government, media, and education. In doing so, they "kindled," as Carter (2000: 370) writes of Wallace, "the deep discontents of an embittered national political minority." To do so, they deployed what

Haney-López (2014) has defined as "strategic racism." The so-called Southern Strategy (which targeted whites within *and* beyond the South; see Haney-López [2014: 27]), the political galvanization of the "Silent Majority" and the "Moral Majority" as voting blocks, and the proliferation of conspiracy theories pathologizing Civil Rights activists, liberal elites, and left-leaning movements allowed politicians to exploit racial animus to win elections, all without the stigma of explicit or overt racism.

42. Peck (2019: 90).

43. Haney-López (2014: 29). As Peck (2019: 231), writing about Fox News, notes, "the coalescing function of rhetorically taking on 'the elite' is performed by outlets across the entire conservative media establishment."

44. Braunstein (2017: 111–112).

45. As Hemmer (2016: 162) notes, "denunciations of bipartisan politics almost invariably came paired with criticisms of the media establishment that conservatives felt supported it."

46. Peck (2019: 89).

47. As media scholars Phillips and Milner (2021: 42) note, conservative thinking by the second half of the twentieth century "naturally transformed anyone who opposed its policies into an enemy—and a spiritual enemy at that . . . moderates did not have a seat at that table. You were either with us or in league with the devil."

48. Haney-López (2014: 29). Hence, Reagan's inaugural adage, "government is not the solution to our problem, government is the problem."

49. Brewer and Stonecash (2001); Junn and Masuoka (2020); Kaufmann and Petrocik (1999); Knuckey (2005); Zingher (2018). For its part, the Democratic Party has attempted to build multiracial, gender-progressive, and cross-class alliances even as the party remained dominated by racial, class, and gender elites.

50. Hochschild (2018); Skocpol and Williamson (2011); White (2018).

51. Butler (2021: 130).

52. The apparent exceptions—celebrated politicians of color on the Right, such as Herman Cain or Ben Carson—seemed to prove the rule. As the sociologist Corey Fields (2016) notes, while Black Republicans are far from "racial sellouts" or "Uncle Toms" (as liberal critics might put it), conservative whites often take them as token examples to claim racial inclusion and avoid the burden of deeply wrestling with the politics of race. This "love it or leave" attitude allows white Republican leaders and adherents to cherry-pick the kinds of racial critiques they are willing to entertain—and treat the rest as examples of divisive "race-baiting."

53. Even at the height of segregationist resistance to the Civil Rights movement, many whites believed, however naïvely, that they were primarily engaged in "a defense of their own liberties, rather than a denial of others"; see Kruse (2013: 9).

54. Haney-López (2014: 5).

55. This phrase, used by Sokol (2008: 14) to describe white Southerners during the Civil Rights movement, echoes the findings of Bonilla-Silva in his study of white racial attitudes in his foundational study, *Racism without Racists* (2006).

56. See, e.g., Frenkel and Karnie (2020); Gray (2017).

57. Roy (2020).

58. See Bonilla-Silva (2006) on "honorary whiteness."

59. On efforts to legislatively restrict voting, see Hicks et al. (2015) and Piven and Cloward (2000); on efforts to microtarget voters via social media (whether to demobilize or mobilize them), see Laterza (2021) and Pybus (2019).

60. Lacombe (2021); see also Melzer (2018).

61. Jilani (2016).

62. Lacombe (2021: 174).

63. Goss (2010).

64. But see Burbick (2006) and DeBrabander (2015).

65. DellaPosta (2020).

66. In other words, this book adopts an understanding of liberal democracy as premised upon an inclusive, engaged, and consensual social contract, recognizing—following Mills (1997)—that that contract, historically, has also been a *racial* contract—a tool of white supremacy—insofar as classic Western social contract theory is fundamentally premised on a racist understanding of *which* people are capable of consent.

67. Omi and Winant (2014).

68. Perrin, Roos, and Gauchat (2014).

69. In *Democracy in America,* De Tocqueville acknowledged a pervasive embrace of equality as crucial to the American project of democracy while also worrying about the potential threat of the tyranny of the majority to exclude and repress minorities as well as the long-term consequences of American materialism and its cult of the individual.

70. Bellah et al. (1985: 26).

71. As Perrin (2009: 19) notes, they are "citizenship goods *independent* of any particular activities they may inspire."

72. Perrin (2009: 2).

73. Braunstein (2017: 11) similarly describes the concept as "an understanding of how democracy ought to work and the role of active citizens (like them) within it."

74. Braunstein (2017: 188).

75. Schradie (2019).

76. Eliasoph (1998).

77. See, e.g., Eliasoph (1998) and Zhelnina (2020) on apathy as a sociopolitical achievement.

78. See, e.g., Bonilla-Silva (2006) on color-blindness.

79. Eliasoph (1998).

80. Putnam (2000).

81. As Fraser (2019: 21) writes, "earthquake finally struck in the 2015–16 election season, as long-simmering discontent suddenly shapeshifted into a full-bore crisis of political authority." See Brown (2017) for an extended analysis of how neoliberalism has undermined the political sensibilities and civic capacities necessary for democratic praxis.

82. Mills (1997).

83. Thomas, Gabbatt, and Barr (2020).

84. Perrin et al. (2014: 287); see also Kozlowski (2021).

85. French (2020).

86. Frum (2021).

87. As Riley (2019: xxxi) notes, "the key task for the left is to lead a democratic revolution while avoiding the technocratic project of 'defending existing institutions,' which are to a large degree antidemocratic."

88. Müller (2021).

89. Riley (2019).

90. Mann (2005).

91. Schradie (2019: 157).

92. Braunstein (2017: 56).

93. Opening up the concept of democracy in this way leads to some uneasy conclusions, including the controversial claim that political regimes that are genocidally rigid in their construction of "the people" and that bypass electoral politics for a more collectively effervescent representation of the will of the people—that is, fascist regimes—may well be considered democratic in nature. See Riley (2019).

94. To illustrate, consider how gun politics, gun culture, and gun markets are stitched together through gun law. To start, shall-issue concealed carry legislation represents one of the major shifts in gun laws across the United States in the last half-century. These new laws transformed and expanded what it means to practice gun rights by bringing guns into everyday life on the hips of Americans as tools of safety and security as seemingly commonplace (at least to their bearers) as a wallet or cell phone. Further, these laws deepened self-defense as a hallmark of American gun culture, and they invigorated the gun industry by creating new consumer demand for defensive handguns and accessories. See Carlson (2015). Or consider the immunity laws that protect gun manufacturers and sellers from lawsuits, including the federal Protection of Lawful Commerce in Arms Act, which have a threefold impact: they directly protect the gun industry; they undermine attempts by gun control advocates to curtail gun rights by means of court action; and in turn, they reinforce the vaulted cultural status of guns and gun makers as compared to other industries. See Stolberg (2005); Center for American Progress (2016). Finally, consider state-level firearms preemption laws, which curtail the capacity of localities to pass more restrictive gun laws than those that bind the state; these laws are a boon for Second Amendment supporters, gun enthusiasts, and firearms sellers alike, as they protect people's legal ability to own, use, *and* sell firearms. See Simon (2020).

95. Habermas (1991).

96. Habermas (1991).

97. Habermas (1991).

98. Indeed, scholars studying cases as distinct as the fascist movements of 1930s Europe to the Tea Party movement of twenty-first-century North Carolina find that right-wing movements not only survive but even thrive amid a vibrant civil life; see Riley (2019) and Schradie (2019).

99. As another seeming exception, I interviewed a woman who had inherited a business: a gun store. A self-identified conservative, she nevertheless admitted that she was not interested in bringing politics to the store. But that didn't mean politics weren't in the mix: she clarified that while she's focused on running the business, another relative—who also works at the store—is the one who brings the politics into the shop.

100. At the end of each interview, I asked interviewees to explicitly label themselves politically in an open-ended question. These percentages reflect the answer to that question, rather

than my assessment of their overall politics, which may have veered from their labels. Also, note that these percentages do not add up to 100% because gun sellers often used multiple labels to describe themselves and their politics.

101. Swidler (1986); see also Carlson and Ramo (2022).

102. Quinn (2021).

103. E.g., Yamane, De Deyne, and Méndez (2020) and Yamane (2021).

104. See, e.g., Perrin (2009).

Armed Individualism

1. Obert and Schultz (2020: 236).

2. McCarthy (2014).

3. Schram (2018); Mintz (2021).

4. Though she does not develop this term in detail, Liebell at one point uses the term "armed individualism" in her 2021 essay on Protests, Insurrection, and the Second Amendment as a means of capturing the linkage between the emphasis on private initiative and insurrectionist ideology within contemporary gun rights advocacy. I take up this term to encompass these aspects of Liebell's usage while also expanding it to address how gun politics intersect with state withdrawal—as developed in my book on gun carriers, *Citizen-Protectors* (2015).

5. Lott and Wang (2021).

6. Gallup (2020).

7. Carlson (2015).

8. See chapter 1 in Carlson (2020) on the links between state prerogatives and private gun use.

9. Carlson (2015).

10. The list of people of color killed wantonly, and typically without accountability, by public law enforcement and private armed citizens continues to egregiously grow. The following high-profile killings occurred in just the first six months of 2020 alone.

On February 23, 2020, 25-year-old Ahmaud Arbery was out jogging when he was followed, shot, and killed by Travis and Gregory McMichael, two white residents of a neighborhood in southern Georgia. Claiming self-defense and "suspicion" of Arbery's presence in their neighborhood, the two men who stalked and ultimately shot Arbery did not face legal repercussions for months after the murder. The case first began to receive media attention when footage of the shooting was released. This footage—taken by William Bryan, who was present at the time of the murder—sparked outrage across the nation, as it became clear that McMichaels's claims of self-defense were entirely fabricated. Exacerbating the nationwide cry for justice was the knowledge of Travis McMichael's former law enforcement ties, which brought into focus the connections between systemic racism, gun violence, and policing in the United States. Travis McMichael, Gregory McMichael, and William Bryan ultimately all faced charges, and all three were convicted of a federal hate crime and attempted kidnapping. See Fausset (2021); Mzezewa, Burch, and Fausset (2022).

On March 13, 2020, Breonna Taylor was asleep when three Louisville police officers used a battering ram to enter her home as a part of a narcotics investigation under a "no-knock" warrant. Acting in self-defense and unaware that the intruders were police, Taylor's boyfriend

Kenneth Walker fired his gun in self-defense. The police officers responded with gunfire, firing blindly into the apartment and killing Breonna Taylor. Described in the media as a "botched-raid," this murder sparked outrage at the deadly repercussions of police incompetence, as well as lack of accountability for the violence. As of July 2022, no officers have been held accountable for the death of Breonna Taylor; only one officer faced charges for endangering neighbors by firing his gun into Taylor's apartment, and he was found not guilty in March 2022. See Lovan (2022); Oppel, Jr., Taylor, and Bogel-Burroughs (2021).

On May 25, 2020, George Floyd was murdered by a group of police officers led by Minneapolis police officer Derek Chauvin, who handcuffed Floyd and knelt on his neck for nine and a half minutes while Floyd exclaimed that he couldn't breathe. Footage of the murder spread quickly across the nation and spurred some of the largest nationwide protests against police brutality in US history. Across the country, chants of "I Can't Breathe" could be heard in the streets as protestors demanded accountability for the police murder and change to the broader racism and brutality that form the cornerstones of policing of Black Americans. Chauvin was found guilty of second-degree murder, third-degree murder, and second-degree manslaughter and sentenced to 21 years in prison; the other officers—J. Alexander Keung, Thomas Lane, and Tou Thao—have also been sentenced to prison time. See Arango et al. (2021); Kummer and Bogel-Burroughs (2022).

On May 25, 2020, Dion Johnson was shot and killed by George Cervantes, an Arizona Department of Public Safety trooper. Cervantes shot and killed Johnson during an attempted arrest on the side of the freeway, where Johnson's car was parked. Although there is neither bodycam nor dashcam footage to corroborate his claims, Cervantes says he shot and killed Johnson in self-defense after Johnson attempted to grab his service pistol. Johnson was unarmed at the time of the shooting. Cervantes faces no charges for the murder of Dion Johnson. See L. Gómez (2020).

On May 27, 2020, Tony McDade, a transgender man, was shot and killed by Tallahassee police. McDade's death sparked protest from supporters of #BlackLivesMatter as well as LGBTQ+ advocates and heightened the importance of intersectionality in conversations about police brutality and its disparate impacts. Because Tallahassee police claim that the officer who shot McDade is themselves a victim of crime after being "threatened" by McDade, their identity remains anonymous and protected under Florida's 2018 victim-rights' amendment. See Dickson (2020); Thompson (2020).

On June 12, 2020, Rayshard Brooks was shot and killed by Garrett Rolfe, an Atlanta police officer who was responding to complaints of Brooks sleeping in his car in the drive-through lane of a fast-food restaurant. Brooks was shot in the back while fleeing the two officers who responded to the call: Garrett Rolfe and Devin Brosnan. The protests and outcry following Brooks's murder prompted the resignation of the Atlanta police chief Erika Shields and resulted in charges against Brosnan and Rolfe. In the immediate aftermath, Brosnan was placed on administrative leave; Rolfe was fired. However, in an apparent about-face (the result of procedural errors in his firing, according to police officials), in 2021 Rolfe was reinstated onto the force and put on administrative leave until pending charges are resolved. See Danner (2020); Sullivan and Bowman (2021).

Special thanks to Catherine Burgess for compiling this endnote.

11. Johnson (2014); Light (2017); McCaughey (1997).

Chapter 1: Viral Gun Rights

1. According to the NSSF, "Regardless of economic conditions across the country, our industry has grown and created over 176,000 new, well-paying jobs since the middle of the Great Recession in 2008" (National Shooting Sports Foundation 2021a: 1).

2. National Shooting Sports Foundation (2021a: 6).

3. National Shooting Sports Foundation (2021a: 1).

4. Bureau of Alcohol, Tobacco, Firearms, and Explosives (2021).

5. National Shooting Sports Foundation (2021b).

6. Federal Bureau of Investigation (2021).

7. For example, more than one firearm can be purchased on a single background check; background checks are required for certain non-firearms items (such as a concealed pistol license or the purchase of a silencer); and, due to private sales, not every firearm purchased requires a background check.

8. National Shooting Sports Foundation (2020a).

9. Hersh (2020).

10. NRA-ILA (2020i).

11. Cepaluni, Dorsch, and Branyicki (2020). Had I looked for this tension elsewhere (for example, among racialized minorities rather than conservative white gun sellers), it's likely that it would have taken a markedly different form (e.g., the underpolicing/overpolicing paradox) that would compel a very different set of solutions, perhaps including but almost certainly expanding far beyond individual gun rights. See Rios (2011) and Soss and Weaver (2017).

12. Cepaluni et al. (2020).

13. NRA (2020).

14. Liebell (2021: 1).

15. Liebell (2021: 4, 2).

16. See, e.g., Kruse (2013) and Sokol (2008).

17. Boch (2020b).

18. Hurricane Katrina provided a crucial stepping stone—ideologically, politically, and legally—that would update and reinvigorate the significance of guns as crucial to states of emergency alongside their more quotidian marking as instruments of personal protection. In August 2005, Hurricane Katrina tore through the Gulf Coast and wreaked particular havoc on the city of New Orleans—a natural disaster turned human-made catastrophe. Evacuation measures dragged on for weeks as first responders patrolled the city's rooftops for trapped survivors. By early September, officials began preparing for forced evacuations, and New Orleans Police Superintendent Edwin P. Compass III declared that "only law enforcement are allowed to have weapons." All told, the disaster lead to the deaths of over 1,800 people and up to $160 billion in damage. For Second Amendment advocates, however, the primary lesson was not about public infrastructure, structural racism, or government incompetence but about the tyranny that Hurricane Katrina had unleashed: as the headline of an NRA story summarized ten years later, "A Decade Later, Remember New Orleans . . . Gun Confiscation Can (and Has) Happened in America." The NRA was right: guns were indeed confiscated, although the scale varies widely depending on the source. Some estimate gun confiscation in the thousands; the official count

by New Orleans police is 552. The underlying motivations of the policy are also subject to dispute; while a disarmed population is certainly easier to forcibly evacuate, others suggest that police, short on firepower themselves, were not enforcing gun confiscation as much as begging for additional firepower to aid in emergency response. Soon after Hurricane Katrina, the Disaster Recovery Personal Protection Act of 2006, which became an amendment to the 2007 Department of Homeland Security Appropriations Act, was passed with bipartisan support and signed by then-President George W. Bush. The Act forbids government authorities from seizing and confiscating lawfully possessed guns during a government-declared state of emergency. According to the NRA's count in late 2019, 33 other states have also passed their own laws prohibiting confiscation and seizure of lawful firearms during states of emergency, with Hurricane Katrina as a rallying point. Many of these state-level equivalents address not just gun possession and confiscation but also gun sales and transfers—as became consequential in the lockdown orders that proliferated as the coronavirus spread in March 2020. See NRA-ILA (2019); NRA-ILA (2015); Hutchinson and Masson (2007); Weinstein (2015); Martel (2015); NRA-ILA (2006); America's 1st Freedom (2019).

19. As Harcourt (2004: 653) writes, "Say the words 'gun registration' to many Americans— especially pro-gun Americans . . . and you are likely to hear about Adolf Hitler, Nazi gun laws, gun confiscation, and the Holocaust. More specifically, you are likely to hear that one of the first things that Hitler did when he seized power was to impose strict gun registration requirements that enabled him to identify gun owners and then to confiscate all guns, effectively disarming his opponents and paving the way for the genocide of the Jewish population."

20. Codrea (2020a).

21. Early in the pandemic, the idea of a government-led "door-to-door" campaign might have seemed far-fetched, especially considering the nation's uncertainty about coronavirus contagions. Gun rights activists and others on the Right began seriously considering a door-to-door threat to their firearms only in mid-2021, when the Biden administration undertook knock campaigns to encourage vaccination in some cities. GOP Representative Madison Cawthorn, for example, publicly speculated that these same techniques could be used to take citizens' guns or Bibles. See Castronuovo (2021), Welch (2021).

22. Critical infrastructure is defined in the US Patriot Act as those "systems and assets, whether physical or virtual, so vital to the United States that their incapacitation or destruction would have a debilitating effect on security, national economic security, national public health or safety, or any combination thereof." While President Bill Clinton officially recognized "critical infrastructure" with the establishment of the Commission on Critical Infrastructure Protection by Executive Order No. 13010 in 1996, the broader concept of "critical infrastructure" in the United States reflects a jaunting history of American militarism, from the early days of violent settler-colonialism to the activation of Cold War pugnacity in the service of a War on Terror at the turn of the twentieth century, that often depended on private initiative alongside, or even in place of, state-sanctioned force. See USA Patriot Act (2001).

23. Michigan Executive Order 2020–21 (2020).

24. This devolution of state responsibility echoes the "frontline bureaucracy" that social workers and police confront as they interface with the public, often finding themselves not just navigating but also interpreting and implementing law. As compared to "frontline bureaucrats"

in the public sector (Lipsky 2010), though, such work in the private sector often involves the frontline regulation of consumption—a devolution of state prerogatives into private enforcement known as "sumptuary labor." Applied to the question of critical infrastructure, though, this sumptuary labor places a neoliberal spin on security, not just charging everyday individuals with defense of themselves and others but also levying on them the decision of whether and how to be part of this apparatus in the first place. See Sallaz and Wang (2016).

25. Peele and Salonga (2020).

26. This is in line with my own interviews with California police chiefs in 2015 and 2016; see Carlson (2020).

27. According to the *Los Angeles Times*, Los Angeles County Sheriff Alex "Villanueva said that the timing [of his removal as chief of emergency operations] suggests retaliation for his decision to close gun shops during the pandemic, viewing them as nonessential businesses." For details, see Tchekmedyian (2020).

28. Soon into the pandemic's breaking in March 2020, many states immediately and without hesitation designated gun stores as essential—or followed existing law to the same end. Arizona's executive order designated as essential "firearm and ammunition suppliers and retailers for purposes of safety and security," as did executive action in Georgia, Indiana, New Hampshire, South Carolina, Wisconsin, and several other states. Other states, such as Ohio, South Dakota, and Kansas, considered legislative action to explicitly protect gun stores and ranges, the validity of concealed pistol permits, and/or the purchase of ammunition. See NRA-ILA (2020a); NRA-ILA (2020c); NRA-ILA (2020d); NRA-ILA (2020e); NRA-ILA (2020f); NRA-ILA (2020g); NRA-ILA (2020h); NRA-ILA (2020j); NRA-ILA (2020l).

29. Stroud (2016).

30. Elcioglu (2020).

31. NRA-ILA (2020b).

32. Despite the fears of gun rights advocates, gun control has largely stalled at the federal level. That, however, doesn't stop gun buyers from acting on what they see as the writing on the wall: the potential for gun control raised by the specter of Democrats, on the one hand, and high-profile acts of egregious gun violence, on the other.

33. For an analysis of how the 2020 surge illuminates cultural toolkit theory, please see Carlson and Ramo (2022).

34. Lang and Lang (2021).

35. In 2016, when candidate Hillary Clinton appeared as the nearly inevitable successor to President Barack Obama, the firearms industry "bloated [inventory] after dealers incorrectly forecasted a Clinton election win and resulting demand surge," according to one industry analyst. Instead, Trump won—and share prices for Sturm, Ruger, and Smith and Wesson dropped more than 20% in the immediate aftermath of the surprise victory. By the end of 2019, many gun sellers found themselves in dire straits—if they survived at all. As Andrew, a California gun seller, recounted,

> Sadly, many stores did not survive the Trump Slump, and those that had, many of those—the nail in the coffin was the dead Christmas season [of 2019] . . . As a continuation of the Trump Slump . . . we had the worst holiday sales we've ever experienced in our near-decade of being in business. So slow in fact that there was no discernible bump off of the summer lull, which is our slowest season.

This was a dramatic shift from the gun industry's faring in anticipation of, and during, the Obama presidency. Some gun sellers labeled the Obama years the longest panic buy of all time; one economist documented a dramatic surge prior to the 2008 elections traceable to fears that Obama's election would lead to gun control, which was followed by sustained stockpiling. See Fritz (2017); Smith (2016); Depetris-Chauvin (2015).

36. Walsh (2022).

37. Simon (2010).

38. Waxman (2019).

39. Craven (1996).

40. Taylor (2020).

41. Anestis and Bryan (2021).

42. At least since the 1960s, these narratives have been powerful not only in shaping how racial unrest is imagined but also in galvanizing gun ownership as an appropriate and necessary response to social disorder. Such narratives, which frame urban disorder as racial threat, have also galvanized a robust and well-armed prepper subculture within the United States. See Belmont and Stroud (2020); Ford (2021); Foster (2016); Kelly (2020).

43. Chenoweth and Pressman (2020).

44. As Waldron (2020: 34–35) notes of the present-day context, "Black protest movements such as BLM are pathologized by those who choose to focus more on the looting and rioting that, at times, erupt during protests and rallies, than on the structurally rooted forms of racism that continues to plague law enforcement and harm Black communities."

45. Yamane (2021).

46. Lang and Lang (2021).

47. Khubchandani and Price (2021).

48. Anestis and Bryan (2021).

49. Vegter and Haider-Markel (forthcoming).

50. For preliminary coverage of this survey, see Tavernise (2021).

51. National Shooting Sports Foundation (2020a).

52. Spencer (2021).

53. Gutowski (2020)

54. National Shooting Sports Foundation (2021a).

55. One California gun seller reported to me that at some point early in the pandemic, "the ratio of firearms safety certificates issued to guns sold exploded to almost 1:1." As new gun owners are required to acquire a firearms safety certificate in California, this is a good indication—at least in the California context—that gun sales to new owners comprised a large faction of firearms sales.

56. Wintemute (2021).

57. Wertz et al. (2018); Yamane et al. (2021).

58. This articulation of diversity, empowerment, and gun ownership reveals that gun sellers are not simply "doing politics" but also "doing race" (Sims, Pirtle, and Johnson-Arnold 2020) and "doing gender" (West and Zimmerman 1987) as they navigate their perceptions of the new gun sellers of 2020. See An and Carlson (2022) on how gun sellers "do gender" as part of everyday partisanship.

59. Singh (2022).

60. Goss (2017); Schwartz (2021).

61. For example, White (2018: 139) describes the Tea Party as particularly impactful in terms of redefining the boundaries of femininity: "The Tea Party women explained aggression as a *feminine* quality—contrary to the typical rhetoric about female political candidates . . . by drawing on 'Mama Grizzly' rhetoric, the Tea Party women sought to be judged in relation to a *female* norm. . . . the term 'Mama Grizzly' makes the identity of mother a descriptor, not the noun— these women are more grizzly than mom."

62. For their part, a few gun sellers told me that they dealt with shortages by limiting, e.g., the number of boxes of ammunition purchasable per person. While no one admitted to price-gouging themselves, gun sellers accused other gun sellers of engaging in the practice amid the shortages.

63. Carlson (2015).

64. Hate crimes against Asian Americans and Pacific Islanders increased 73% in 2020 as compared to 2019 and then 339% in 2021 as compared to 2020. See Venkatraman (2021) and Yam (2022).

65. Andrew was eager to help the man buy a firearm for self-protection but had to explain that California law would still prohibit him from carrying his gun for self-defense—he had to have a carry permit for that.

66. Lah (2017).

67. Lah (2017).

68. Further, at least one incident of anti-Black violence perpetrated by Korean Americans, alongside LAPD police brutality, helped fuel the riots that would ignite in 1992. See Wong (2020).

69. Respectability politics represents a racial discourse that celebrates marginalized people who conform to white, middle-class values while denigrating those who don't, won't, or can't. For more on respectability politics and "the price of the ticket" during the Obama administration, see Harris (2012).

70. Lenthang (2021).

71. See Wintemute (2021) on the intersecting factors related to gun violence and gun sales. Analyzing the first months of the pandemic, Schleimer et al. (2021: 1), for example, find that while "the magnitude of the increase in purchasing was not associated with the magnitude of the increase in firearm violence," increased gun sales "may have contributed to" increases in domestic gun violence.

72. Abt, Bocanegra, and Tingirides (2022); Arango and Closson (2022)

73. To quote the famous phrase from Mao Zedong.

74. Zimmerman (2020b).

75. Goldblatt (2020).

76. Filipovic (2021).

77. Diaz (2016).

78. For insight on how gun sellers navigate their own politics vis-à-vis the gun regulatory apparatus they enforce in the Australian context, see Fay (2022).

79. Burbick (2006).

80. Cepaluni et al. (2020).

81. Bove and Di Leo (2020).

82. Buštíková and Baboš (2020).

83. Landman and Di Gennaro Splendore (2020).

84. Baldacchino (2021), summarizing Simpson (2020).

85. Toscano (2020: 390) goes on to note "the curious ideological chiasmus whereby the political bearers of some of the most concerning authoritarian trends in the present (Trump, Bolsonaro and their coteries) have been the least interested in turning a public health emergency into an occasion for the militarisation of everyday life."

86. Pozen and Scheppele (2020).

87. Pozen and Scheppele (2020: 609–610).

88. Pozen and Scheppele (2020: 614–615).

89. See Bialasiewicz and Eckes (2021).

90. National Shooting Sports Foundation (2020b).

91. NRA-ILA (2020k).

92. Feinblatt (2020).

93. Bellah et al. (1985: 23).

94. For more on how freedom is defined through the cult of individualism, see Bellah et al. (1985).

95. This embrace of guns as a practice of civic engagement is far from new. Historically, Americans, particularly white, property-owning men, have turned to guns to enforce sovereign prerogatives rooted in white supremacy against enslaved and indigenous peoples; to chase safety as a means of social order maintenance more broadly; to step in when government assurances fail; and to locate a modicum of safety and security in a hostile world. Within this historical landscape, marginalized Americans have also turned to guns for "that protection which the law refuses to give," in the words of anti-lynching activist Ida B. Wells (Johnson 2014: 81)—a sentiment reflected more recently in the motivations of Black gun buyers in the aftermath of the police murder of George Floyd in 2020 and the white supremacist attack on a Buffalo, NY, supermarket in a Black community in 2022 (Bunn, 2022). For a discussion on how the racial politics of guns shape who can exercise gun rights and on what terms, see Carlson (2020), especially chapter 5. Further, as described in the next chapter, it is worth noting that the individualist ethos attached to gun ownership and gun bearing is not inherent to guns themselves; gun politics may also be rallied for projects of collective empowerment and efficacy. See, e.g., Austin (2006); Bloom and Martin (2016); Johnson (2014).

96. See Stroud (2020); Belmont and Stroud (2020); Carlson (2015).

Conspiracism

1. Uscinski and Parent (2014).

2. Bailyn (2017).

3. Bailyn (2017: 144).

4. Bailyn (2017: 155).

5. Anderson (2021).

6. Bogus (1998).

7. Newton (1980); Hoerl and Ortiz (2015); Drabble (2008).

8. Robinson (2020).

9. Brackman (2000); Suber (1979).

10. While conspiracism most certainly can express and encourage the prerogatives of the powerful, conspiracist thinking has also long been prevalent among marginalized communities. Sociologist Anita Waters (1997) has explained the well-documented prevalence of conspiracist thinking among African Americans by approaching conspiracy theories as examples of "ethnosociologies." Instead of presuming conspiracist adherents as "paranoid and delusional" (113), Waters notes that "treating conspiracy theories as mistaken is unrealistic in societies where concerted and secretly planned social action is an everyday accomplishment of industries and government agencies" (122), particularly as this social action often negatively impacts those who are disadvantaged by these systems. As another analysis of conspiracist thinking among marginalized communities, see Thornton and Reich (2022) on vaccine refusal among Black mothers.

11. Gauchat (2012; 2015).

12. Brenan (2020).

13. Parker (2019).

14. Pew Research Center (2019a).

15. Hagen (2019: 1235).

16. Rosenblum and Muirhead (2020).

17. IPSOS/NPR Poll (2020).

Chapter 2: Conspiracism for the People

1. Novak (2020).

2. Lewis (2021).

3. Milman (2020).

4. Pew Research Center (2020).

5. Tyson (2020).

6. Pew Research Center (2020).

7. Pew Research Center (2020).

8. Glatter (2020).

9. Spring (2020).

10. Saslow (2020).

11. Mazziotta (2020).

12. Salazar (2020).

13. Novak (2020).

14. Lewis (2021).

15. Mazziotta (2020).

16. Roose (2021).

17. Hofstadter (1964).

18. Lynch (2021).

19. Hofstadter (1964); Miller, Saunders, and Farhart (2016).

20. Fenster (2008: 90).

21. Fenster (2008: 87). See also LaClau and Mouffe (2014).

22. Fenster (2008: 87).

23. Fenster (2008: 89).

24. Brewer (2016: 258).

25. Brewer (2016: 252).

26. Stelter (2021).

27. Bouie (2020).

28. Phillips and Milner (2021: 18).

29. As Peck (2019: 4) notes, "One of the long-standing political narratives of the conservative movement has focused on how 'overeducated elites' use government power to both expropriate the wealth of 'producing' Americans and impose non-traditional cultural values on them."

30. Peck (2019: 15).

31. As Hemmer (2016: xv) describes the early conservative media movement, "Unlike most groups excluded from power, these conservative activists had extensive resources to challenge their exclusion. This blend of populism and power helps explain the tremendous success of a movement that began on the fringes of American politics, as well as the right's ability to maintain an outsider identity in the face of that success."

32. Hemmer (2016: 71).

33. Peck (2019: 25).

34. Hemmer (2016: 275) notes that "truthiness signified a world in which certainty was valued over inquisitiveness, emotion over information. . . . [it] had become a dominant mode of communication [by the mid-2000s] within conservative and Republican circles, and it was interfering in the party's policymaking as well as its electioneering." Gun sellers' epistemological stances resonated with some aspects of this definition of "truthiness," especially its implicit emphasis on personal experience, but as illustrated below, they were markedly more invested in inquisitiveness than certainty.

35. Peck (2019: 185).

36. I follow interviewees' designation of what constitutes "mainstream" media. When specifying particular outlets, interviewees designated cable news networks (such as CNN or MSNBC) in this category; some also included Fox News, while others designated this network as outside of "mainstream" networks, as indicated in the quotations excerpted above.

37. I want to thank Elliot Ramo for the pithy formulation of this insight; see Carlson and Ramo (2022).

38. See also Merlan (2019).

39. See Braunstein (2017); Schradie (2019); Tripodi (2018). As Schradie (2019: 275) writes, "post-election studies . . . have found that pro-Trump/anti-Clinton stories identified as fake news were read and shared on social media at a rate almost three times as much as stories whose veracity could be verified. Such statistics have been seized on by progressives as evidence that conservatives are easier to dupe, or just plain dumb. However . . . it is more plausible that this gap is the result of conservatives more motivated to share their 'Truth', or at least content that fits their view of the truth."

40. Ray (2021).

41. Tripodi (2018). As another example of this synergy, recall Dawson's (2019: 1) finding that the NRA has used religious language to transform "the Second Amendment from an important Constitutional amendment to an article of faith in religious nationalism"; see also Whitehead,

Schnabel, and Perry (2018) on the strong link between Christian nationalism and opposition to federal gun laws.

42. Tripodi (2018: 18).

43. Perhaps the most well-documented campaigns acting to delegitimize scientific consensus are those led by oil corporations, with five major oil corporations in the United States spending more than $3.6 billion on advertisement in the last three decades (Holden 2020; Rust 2019). Frequently at odds with scientific recommendations, and often in legal battles involving breaches of protective environmental code, corporations have used such public campaigns to delegitimize the scientific research that opposes them, often positioning themselves as victims of a purposeful and personal attack by governmental agencies. For more on the use of corporate campaigns as means of encouraging the general public to call into question scientific findings, research, and information from politically opposing news sources, see Nichols (2017).

44. As Tripodi (2018: 6–7) notes, "A quest for truth may start in good faith, but . . . bad actors looking to exploit an audience disillusioned with mainstream media are taking advantage of this intellectual exploration." Gauchat (2012) finds that right-leaning Americans are more likely to distrust scientific elites, oppose government funding of science, and resist the use of scientific findings to support government policy. On issues as diverse as climate change, stem cell research, or gun policy, conservatives are more likely to doubt scientific expertise than their liberal counterparts—and they are also more likely to doubt the scientists themselves. Mann and Schleifer (2020) find that anti-science attitudes among conservatives are driven by a distaste for scientists rather than science itself. Indeed, while liberals may have applauded the efforts of experts to "March for Science" in 2017 amid the threat that Trump posed to scientific consensus, many conservatives found the same show of support as reason to doubt the intentions of scientists— and consider them untrustworthy. See Motta (2018).

45. White (2018: 31).

46. White (2018), studying the portrayal of the Tea Party in news media, shows that conservative news media have proactively worked to associate mainstream media with liberal bias. Tea Party coverage by conservative media included "descriptors [that] connote a widespread belief that all media outlets and workers have inherent ideological biases that affect their content," for example, "Liberal Media and the NAACP condemn Tea Party as racist; Left-Wingers in the media and Democrats; Media and elite universities; Media and our domestic enemies" (White 2018: 162).

47. Sulzberger (2019); Basu (2019).

48. According to Rosenblum and Muirhead (2020), classical conspiracism rallies a complicated, often convoluted though nevertheless logic-minded collection of insights and suspicious facts and quasi-facts, truths, and half-truths to point to an alternative explanation of events and trends that contradicts official or authoritative accounts. Its goal is to peel back the veneer to get at the "real" reality.

49. Ong, Zhang, and Shaw (2021); Reny and Barreto (2020).

50. Rosenblum and Muirhead (2020).

51. In her study of online anti-lockdown groups, Tripodi (2021: 6) found "frequent analogies between public health measures and both slavery and Nazi Germany." Beyond COVID, the use of Nazi imagery (as implied by "immunization camps") as well as communist symbology to bolster conservative critiques of liberals, progressives, and Democrats is commonplace, as

discussed in more detail in chapter 4. For a discussion of the use of Nazi imagery (as implied by "immunization camps") in conservative critiques of gun control, see Harcourt (2004). Relatedly, for insight on anti-science campaigns and Trump's role in bolstering this thinking, see Krauss (2016).

52. I want to thank Abigail Andrews and Elliot Ramo for developing this point in conversation and in collaboration; see Carlson and Ramo (2022). As Peck (2019: 95) notes, "in the mold of talk show legend Oprah Winfrey, Fox News' top hosts consistently personalize discussion topics by framing them in relation to their own biographies and current personal relationships." See also Tripodi (2018) on "scriptural inference."

53. Its teen producer, Darnella Frazier, was awarded a Pulitzer Prize Special Citation for her courage in reporting. See Hauck (2021).

54. Skolnick (2002).

55. Hinton (2021).

56. Niedzwiadek (2020).

57. Sokol (2008: 86).

58. Silverstein (2019).

59. This executive order never went into effect, as Trump lost his bid for re-election. See Guynn (2021). However, several states have subsequently moved to pass restrictions on speech within the workplace, especially in education.

60. Klepper and Hinnant (2020).

61. Bump (2020).

62. Budryk (2020).

63. Censky (2020).

64. Braunstein (2017: 147) found a similar tendency among the conservative group she studied, who understood political power fundamentally in terms of "individuals acting together" rather than agency on behalf of a collective or community.

65. This move echoes historian Sokol's (2008: 86) analysis of how whites used conspiracist thinking to make sense of, and justify their opposition to, the Civil Rights movement in the 1960s; as he put it, conspiracism "helped whites to make sense of black rebellion."

66. Seflle (2020).

67. Butler (2021: 41), for example, discusses how evangelical Christians associated evilness with Civil Rights advocates: "many black activists working for civil rights were called communists . . . the linkage of communism with civil rights work—combined with evangelicals' fear of the end times and the Antichrist—instilled fear and determination in evangelists and evangelical listeners alike." See also Phillips and Milner (2021) on "enemy within" narratives.

68. Grewal (2017). In this way, conspiracist thinking surrounding Black Lives Matter can function as an example of "dog whistle politics" by bringing "race into the conversation through thinly veiled references to threatening nonwhites," though without "any direct reference to a racial group or any use of an epithet" other than the protest itself, to use Haney-López's (2014: 4) formulation.

69. In this regard, conspiracism is an epistemological mechanism that may aggravate the "racial empathy gap." Scholars have introduced this concept to capture a troubling pattern: people are less likely to recognize, understand, and acknowledge pain experienced by people of color as opposed to white people (Gutsell and Inzlicht 2012; Silverstein 2013). The racial

empathy gap helps illuminate why African Americans experience disproportionately poorer health outcomes—as their reports of pain and discomfort are disproportionately dismissed by medical professionals; why punishment for African Americans outpaces that for whites—as African Americans are viewed as inured to the punishments that would otherwise be appropriate (implicitly, to whites); and why African American interests continue to be marginalized in key arenas of politics and policy making—as the suffering African Americans endure is treated as less urgent than the harms befalling whites. The racial empathy gap, further, is not simply a declination to acknowledge another's pain as real; it is also a declination to acknowledge another as capable of knowing their own pain—a curtailment of agency.

70. Liebell (2021: 5).

71. Note that "The Truth About Guns" is the name of one of the most popular online gun news sources; I borrow their clever title for this section but suggest that any "truth about guns" goes beyond adjudicating whether certain claims are true or false to also entail an orientation to truth—an epistemology, if you will—that reinforces armed individualism.

72. Williams (2021).

73. Litke (2020).

74. Associated Press (2020). Trump took the same tack in extending Rittenhouse the benefit of the doubt: had he himself not killed others first, "he probably would have been killed." See Crisp (2020).

75. Guardian Staff (2020).

76. As conservative commentator and "Never Trumper" David French (2021) wrote for *The Atlantic*, "the narrow nature of the self-defense inquiry is one reason people can escape responsibility for killings that are deeply wrongful in every *moral* sense."

77. French (2021).

78. See, e.g., Glaser's (2021) interview with Kathleen Belew.

79. Regarding the significance of conservative politics, particularly authoritarianism and libertarianism, in shaping contemporary gun culture, see Kahan and Braman (2003) on the cultural theory of risk and Lacombe (2021) on the National Rifle Association.

80. This reminds us that conspiracism is at once psychological and political in its appeal. See Miller et al. (2016).

81. For a fusion of the two, consider the Black Panthers, which forwarded conspiracist claims regarding government surveillance and persecution that were later vindicated with the disclosure of the FBI's COINTEL-PRO initiative. Rather than use conspiracist claims to celebrate individualism, the Black Panthers instead advocated for collective empowerment through the community-led organization of social services, from health care to policing, independent from white power structures. See Galloway (2020); Waters (1997).

82. Smallpage, Enders, and Uscinski (2017: 2).

83. Peck (2019: 146) developed this phrase from his analysis of Fox News.

84. van der Linden, Panagopoulos, and Jost (2020).

85. Writing on the presidential campaigns of Bernie Sanders and Donald Trump, Oliver and Rahn (2016: 202) note, "Despite this year's attacks on economic elites and Sanders's trade nationalism, the American Left cannot credibly assemble 'the people' so essential for a successful populist movement given its dependence on minorities and the more cosmopolitan and well

educated. American populism in the twenty-first century has a conservative tinge and is felt most acutely in the political turmoil of the Republican Party."

Partisanship

1. Pew Research Center (2019d).
2. Pew Research Center (2019f).
3. Pew Research Center (2019e).
4. Mordecai and Connaughton (2020).
5. Pew Research Center (2020).
6. Pew Research Center (2020).
7. Pew Research Center (2017).
8. Parker, Horowitz, and Anderson (2020).
9. Clement and Balz (2020).
10. Thomas and Horowitz (2020).
11. Deane and Gramlich (2020).
12. Pew Research Center (2019d).
13. Note that demographics regarding gun attitudes are structured somewhat differently than demographics on gun ownership; for the latter, gender is key.

Chapter 3: America Unmasked

1. Larosiere (2020a).
2. Larosiere (2020a).
3. Yamane et al. (2020).
4. Lacombe (2021).
5. Yamane et al. (2020).
6. See Lacombe (2021); Spitzer (2020).
7. Mills (1958).
8. As Hemmer (2016: 162) notes, "Denunciations of bipartisan politics almost invariably came paired with criticisms of the media establishment that conservatives felt supported it."
9. Hemmer (2016: 161).
10. Pew Research Center (2019c).
11. Martherus et al. (2021).
12. Phoenix (2019).
13. Pew Research Center (2019c). Indeed, media scholar Reece Peck (2019: 44) notes that the political impact of conservative media such as Fox News on partisanship lies, in part, in the capacity of these news outlets to "exploit . . . class differences based on taste and education [and] . . . *partisanize* such differences."
14. DellaPosta, Shi, and Macy (2015).
15. Zengerle (2021).
16. Abbate (2020).
17. Kornfield (2020).

18. Starbucks (2022).

19. Kornfield (2020).

20. DellaPosta, Shi, and Macy (2015).

21. Bishop (2009).

22. See also DellaPosta (2020).

23. Bishop (2009: 153).

24. See also DellaPosta (2020). Further, speaking of information siloes that shape people's political views, Phillips and Milner (2021: 3) note, "the problem . . . isn't merely polarization itself; it's the fact that polarization emerges from the world around us."

25. Sunstein (2002; 2009).

26. Doherty et al. (2015).

27. See Schradie (2019) and Tripodi (2018) on conservative approaches to social media; see Bail (2021) on online political polarization.

28. Bishop (2009: 36).

29. French (2020: 69)

30. Pew Research Center (2016).

31. Pew Research Center (2019c). Note that alongside ideology, these dynamics are inflected by gender, race, and religion—an alignment that reflects the uniquely intractable nature of political polarization in the United States as compared to other countries. See Carothers and O'Donohue (2019).

32. French (2020: 69–70).

33. V. Gómez (2020).

34. In her analysis of *PragerU*, Tripodi (2018) finds a similar narrative depicting liberals, the Left, and the Democratic Party as opportunistic and intolerant extremists who use social justice terminology as a self-interested effort to delegitimize the Right and advance their access to political power. Accordingly, conservatives in her study worry about being treated "unfairly" or even "silenced" in the college classroom or on social media due to the putative intolerance of liberals.

35. Hutchison (2020). And shortly before Biden took office as president, the outlet likewise posed, "Here's the question for Mr. Biden and his supporters: How many innocent, patriotic gun owners are you willing to kill or incarcerate, in a futile effort to slightly reduce the use of firearms by violent criminals?" See Knox (2021).

36. BBC News (2016). For an analysis of racist humor, see Pérez (2022).

37. For more on dehumanization in the context of the War on Crime, the War on Terror, the Bathroom Wars, and US Migration Policy, see Owusu-Bempah (2016); Steuter and Wills (2010); Jorge (2021); and Ames (2019), respectively.

38. Abramowitz and McCoy (2019).

39. Martherus et al. (2021); see also Cassese (2021).

40. Martherus et al. (2021: 535).

41. Martherus (2021: 523).

42. Cramer (2016).

43. Phillips and Milner (2021: 51).

44. See Callcut et al. (2019). Using California data, they find that since 2011, gun sales have increased in the aftermath of active shootings, and since 2012, gun sales have increased

immediately prior to the implementation of gun restrictions in the state. See also Liu and Wiebe (2019). Using background check data, they find that gun purchasing increased specifically after mass shootings that received heightened media attention.

45. Belmont and Stroud (2020). For an extended analysis of how gender shapes these gun sellers' expressions of partisanship, see An and Carlson (2022). Specifically, this article examines how "doing partisanship" serves as a means of "doing masculinity" for conservative gun sellers; they mobilized partisanship not just to assert themselves vis-à-vis other men but also to forward gendered critiques of the state as overbearing and encroaching.

46. For example, an article in *The Truth About Guns* entitled "America's Preppers Are Finally Getting a Little Respect" noted that gun owners avoid the stereotypes of irrational and paranoid "preppers" that circulate in the media: "Most preppers say they are about self-reliance and common sense and are quick to distance themselves from the 'doomsday preppers' who are depicted on television shows awaiting the day most of the world's population is wiped off the map." See Seewer (2020).

47. Belmont and Stroud (2020).

48. The will to pass gun control among federal lawmakers, however, has largely not matched the imaginations of gun rights advocates.

49. An *Ammoland* article makes a similarly sardonic point with a humorous June 2020 headline: "Sage Advice from 'Deadly-Force Expert' Joe Biden." In addition to disparaging leading Democrats as lax and lazy (e.g., "Sleepy Joe"), this *Ammoland* article notes the legal and physical dangers of following their advice on armed self-defense: "Imagine his surprise when an untrained gun owner, but who has taken Sleepy Joe's advice, belatedly discovers that shooting for the legs is still 'deadly force,' and that such a false strategy does nothing to reduce his legal jeopardy, much less his physical jeopardy." See Farnam (2020b).

50. On the gendered dynamics of partisanship among gun sellers, see An and Carlson (2022). On masculinist protection, in general and among gun carriers, see Young (2003) and Carlson (2015), respectively.

51. Of course, political affiliation and demographic characteristics are connected on multiple levels; people of color are much more likely to support liberal policies and the Democratic Party as compared to whites, especially white men, and the Democratic Party itself is associated with efforts at building multiracial coalitions, even if these efforts ultimately fail to actually benefit marginalized Americans—especially African Americans. See Harris (2012).

52. Wintemute (2021).

53. Wertz et al. (2018); Yamane et al. (2021).

54. Vegter and Haider-Markel (forthcoming); Tavernise (2021).

55. The Truth About Guns (2020b); see also The Truth About Guns (2020a).

56. Bartozzi (2020).

57. Johnson (2020b).

58. Boch (2020e). Interestingly, some gun rights advocates have acknowledged that they share this concern with gun control advocates. For example, Tim Schmidt of USCCA skewers the latter's worries as a partisan dismissal of gun owners, saying "Perhaps not surprising in a world where seemingly everything is politicized, particularly when it comes to firearms, anti-gun groups and politicians have predicted that rising gun sales, coupled with schools being closed, will lead to more accidental shootings and deaths." Yet, he acknowledges that "making

the decision to carry a firearm, or even to simply keep a gun for home defense, is where the real responsibility begins . . . we need to remember that education, training and safety must remain the uncompromisable tenets on which we all stand." See Johnson (2020a).

59. In this regard, we can consider gun sellers as "street-level bureaucrats" (Lipsky 2010) operating within the marketplace to enforce gun laws (Sallaz and Wang 2016). See Fay (2022) on gun sellers in Australia in this regard.

60. Note that this is not the only context in which "responsibility" is used by conservatives to draw lines around deserving and undeserving citizens. In current pro-life discourse, for example, restrictions on abortion are justified as a means of dissuading "irresponsible" sexual behavior. I thank Madison Armstrong for noting this parallel.

61. Inacker (2020); see also Zimmerman (2020a).

62. Chwick and Eisen (2020a).

63. Keane (2020).

64. Peck (2019: 26).

65. Hemmer (2016: 275).

66. Reflecting scholarship showing that affective partisanship is driven by popular tropes of extremism rather than "average" counter-partisans (e.g., Bail 2021), Ron admits that he doesn't know many liberals first-hand: "I'm in a pretty conservative area, so I don't really have too many liberals that I come across, um, that project to be liberal, or come out and say they are liberal."

67. These interview excerpts resonate with Tripodi's (2018) analysis of conservative media literacy; she finds this narrative connection between liberal ideology and disregard for facts proactively promulgated by conservative outlets like *PragerU* and conservative figureheads like Ben Shapiro.

68. See Schradie (2019); Tripodi (2018).

69. Riehl (2020b).

70. As *The Truth About Guns* straightforwardly noted, "In less than a week, Versacarry has switched their focus and production and will be shipping face masks and face shields shortly. With weekly output expected at 20,000+ of each item, these will be sent to the front line of this pandemic war and into the hands of hospital personnel, EMT, police officers, firefighters and others facing the COVID-19 virus on a daily basis." See The Truth About Guns (2020c).

71. Carlson (2015).

72. As he told me, "Now I can't walk into Wal-Mart without getting the stink eye if I'm not wearing a mask. You know? And my wife made a very good comment a couple of weeks ago, she said—*Right now it's masks, but when they tell you to get on the train because it's for your safety, are you going to get on the train?* You know, harkening back to World War II and the Nazis. The government has already proven that they can pretty much get you to do what they say. Where does it stop, when you finally realize—*hey, this is an overreach?*"

73. These claims also circulated in gun news outlets as part of, for example, Democrat "zealotry" in response to the coronavirus pandemic. See Codrea (2021).

74. TrueJKDAcademy (2020).

75. Ware (2020).

76. Tripodi (2021: 7) documents these trends in her analysis of The ReOpen the States Movement aimed at denying and/or minimizing COVID as a public health threat.

77. However, at least one gun shop owner in Florida *did* ban masks in his store; see Larosiere (2020b).

78. While none of the gun sellers I interviewed discussed the legal intersections of wearing a mask while holstering a firearm, gun news outlets addressed—and, for the most part, dispelled—rumors that mask mandates could place gun carriers into a legal gray zone under the presumption that gun bearers were not allowed to be masked while carrying a firearm. See Grant (2020); Codrea (2020b); Crump (2020).

79. Ware (2020).

80. Morse (2020a).

81. Kalmoe and Mason (2019).

82. Kalmoe and Mason (2019). Reflecting as much as reinforcing partisanship, the propensity for violence among liberals and leftists is a common refrain among gun rights advocates. For example, one *Ammoland* story covering the 2020 elections collected a set of statements by Democrats, liberals, and leftists endorsing the sentiment that their political opponents should "just die"; the story was instigated by comedian Trevor Noah "posting a GIF of the Star Wars Death Star destroying Florida in retaliation for President Donald Trump winning the state." See Codrea (2020c). In another story, *The Truth About Guns* provided a cautionary warning about the threat armed liberals posed to freedom when one armed man named Todd Ghoulston shot someone for not wearing a mask: "to throw one's carry license and gun rights away by pretending you're the mask police seems especially short-sighted and ill-considered. But then again, carrying a gun isn't for everyone. . . . Ghoulston will have a long time to contemplate the silliness of engaging a third party over their personal choices when it comes to wearing masks in public." See Boch (2020g).

83. Wintemute (2021).

84. Wertz et al. (2018); Yamane et al. (2021).

Democracy

1. Isakhan and Stockwell (2011).

2. See Crick (2002) for a summary of Western philosophical approaches to democracy.

3. See Mills (1997) on Thomas Jefferson.

4. Mills (1997).

5. Du Bois (2016).

6. Jahanbegloo (2015).

7. See the September 15, 2021, *NYTimes* Mini Crossword Puzzle. As sociologist Mo Torres (2021) quips on Twitter, "'Democracy' is such a weak ideal in the United States that the word is essentially synonymous with the ballot box. Still, it's incredible to see such a crystal clear demonstration of this point."

8. Crick (2002: 92).

9. Klarman (2020).

10. Klarman (2020: 18).

11. Klarman (2020: 19).

12. Bump (2021).

13. Gómez and Doherty (2021).

14. Hartig (2021).

15. Gómez and Doherty (2021).

16. Hartig (2021).

17. As Haney-López (2014: 160) remarks, "the campaign against voting fraud is intimately connected with dog whistle concerns."

18. Dionne (2021).

19. Kuznia, Ortega, and Tolan (2021).

20. Klein (2021).

Chapter 4: At the Edge of Democracy

1. Fichera (2021); Creitz (2020).

2. Kraychik (2021).

3. Bergengruen (2021); Ferré-Sadurní and McKinley (2020).

4. For example, in September 2020 the CDC issued a moratorium on residential evictions. Wolfe and Conlin (2021).

5. Bandler et al. (2020).

6. Halon (2020).

7. Fox News (2021).

8. Hamel et al. (2020).

9. Simmons-Duffin (2021).

10. Sun and Achenbach (2020).

11. Chwick and Eisen (2020b).

12. Moyer (2017).

13. Jamieson (2013).

14. Throughout the twentieth century and into the twenty-first, conservatives have lambasted the criminal justice system for coddling criminals; decried the Environmental Protection Agency for undermining free enterprise and inordinately hampering business; and vigorously opposed the welfare apparatus, public health care, and public education for unjustly redistributing wealth, in one way or another, to those designated as undeserving. As Metzl (2019) shows in *Dying of Whiteness*, conservatives are not unaware that they might personally suffer if their own policy preferences were put into place, but that may further the point: to oppose entitlements means embracing a kind of freedom *from* the state rather than *through* the state.

15. With this anti-statist sentiment resplendent on the Right, it is easy to forget that calls to freedom throughout American history and certainly in the present day, vociferously on the Right *but also* on the Left, have traded on an anti-statist ethos that tends toward deep suspicion of the American state's ability to provide for, and protect, the foundational structures of a free, fair, and just society.

16. Mauger and Leblanc (2020).

17. Carlson (2015).

18. Carlson (2015).

19. Stroud (2016: 127, 14).

20. Metzl (2019).

21. As discussed in more detail in the conclusion, Ross (2021: 2) notes that the January 6 rioters in particular "had assigned [a] tyrannical label" to "American republicanism itself."

22. Perrin et al. (2014); see also Kozlowski (2021).

23. To illustrate this, recall that right-leaning gun sellers used a variety of labels to define themselves politically: Republican, conservative, libertarian, constitutionalist, Christian.

24. As he noted, "there's this perception that one side wants to control our uteruses and the other side wants to control our freedoms, and there's just this power struggle of control which [we've] always had since the beginning of time, but now it's pervasive."

25. As Peter told me, "It's really given me the opportunity lately to reach across [the political aisle], and get them to look at [the idea that] 'Hey, your vote matters, and you keep voting for these same people that keep killing people's rights.' Whether it's your rights, everybody's rights—it doesn't matter! [Because] if you keep doing this [supporting politicians who undermine people's rights], you are not even going to be able to have the ability to protect yourself."

26. Pence (2020).

27. Boch (2020d).

28. Though "Karen" serves on the Left as "a symbol of racism and white privilege" (Goldblatt 2020), within gun rights discourse "Karen" is also used to label the kinds of people described by Ben—those who would call on the power of the state to police fellow citizens for minor infractions. As a story in *The Truth About Guns* rails, "America has edged closer to tyranny this year. . . . the Karens, in the age of the ChiCom [Chinese Communist] virus, have gone from obnoxious to dangerous. The Karens are the ones calling the police because someone took their kid to the park, and the Karens are on social media demanding that pastors be arrested for holding church services." See Boch (2020h).

29. It is important to recognize that US libertarianism often entails outspoken critiques of police, including anti-Black police violence. One story in *The Truth About Guns* called for "solace in the knowledge that Derek Chauvin has been fired, arrested, and indicted for the murder of George Floyd. Chauvin will ultimately be judged by a jury of his peers. The voices of peaceful resistance have been heard. Justice will be served," while an *Ammoland* writer designated the shots fired from Breonna Taylor's apartment upon the police's no-knock raid as an example of "Another No-Knock Raid Legitimately Resisted by Armed Force." As this latter excerpt suggests, in favoring private initiative over collective social change, libertarianism forwards a different solution to racial injustice than, say, activists affiliated with Black Lives Matter. See Jacobson (2020); Weingarten (2020).

Note that this critical stance on police, on the one hand, helps to justify private gun ownership as an alternative to public law enforcement, but on the other hand, it also speaks to the historical reality that American policing has always entailed a blend of private and public initiative. In other words, the contemporary division between private and public force is more a reflection of contemporary politics than an intrinsic aspect of policing; some of the earliest examples of policing in the United States include individual citizens "deputized" by their whiteness to police disorderly or vagrant people, especially people of African descent, as well as organized private citizens aimed at enforcing class and racial orders (e.g., night watches, vigilante committees, and slave patrols). Since their institutionalization in the mid-nineteenth century as a public organization, American public law enforcement have relied upon the initiatives of private civilians and have borrowed from their tactics, which helps explain commonalities, e.g., across slave patrols and Southern law enforcement. See chapter 1 in Carlson (2020).

30. See Anderson (2021). I summarized color-blind discourse in pro-gun sentiment in *Citizen-Protectors* (2015: 76) by noting, "Eclipsing other explanations of crime (for example, the structural forces that marginalize, incarcerate, and disenfranchise predominantly poor men of color), this discourse individualizes the problem of criminal behavior and moves killing—in some circumstances—from an immoral act to a moral act." Echoing this individualizing approach to social problems, Ben similarly presents individual rights as an effective and upstanding response to collective problems (e.g., racial injustice).

31. One author writing for *The Truth About Guns* illustrates this aspect: "I've come to believe that a person who considers homosexual behavior a sin can still support gay rights. Likewise, he can abstain from drugs, while contending for another's right to use them, and never himself own a firearm, but advocate for those who do. . . . our personal choices don't need to align with the personal choices of our neighbors in order for us to value our neighbors' liberty to choose . . . We can rejoice that, in contradistinction to many brutal regimes and nations of times past and present, a great number of our countrymen still value liberty, limited government, self-reliance, equal rights under the law, and toleration of diverse personal beliefs and habits, save for when those infringe on the rights of others." See McMillan (2020).

32. As a July *Ammoland* story observed, "People around the nation are getting fed up and are buying guns, getting trained, and are preparing to protect what they have worked hard to achieve. We've seen people wake up and take responsibility for themselves and their property like never before." While this article clearly drew boundaries around upstanding and depraved Americans (after all, it was written in response to civil unrest and headlined "You Loot, We Shoot!"—a devaluation of human life as interchangeable with private property). Nevertheless, it stipulated the "people" as a sleeping giant, waking up "like never before." See Hammer (2020).

33. Riehl (2020a).

34. Wingfield and Feagin (2012).

35. Recall Harcourt's (2004: 653) summary of this phenomenon from note 19 in chapter 1: "Say the words 'gun registration' to many Americans—especially pro-gun Americans . . . and you are likely to hear about Adolf Hitler, Nazi gun laws, gun confiscation, and the Holocaust. More specifically, you are likely to hear that one of the first things that Hitler did when he seized power was to impose strict gun registration requirements that enabled him to identify gun owners and then to confiscate all guns, effectively disarming his opponents and paving the way for the genocide of the Jewish population."

36. Wingfield and Feagin (2012).

37. During 2020, *Ammoland* and *The Truth About Guns* likewise ran headlines that publicized instances of illegitimate violence perpetrated by leftists, liberals, and progressives; consider, e.g., "Angry Leftist Brings Rifle to Lubbock George Floyd Protest to 'Off Racists and MAGA People'" (*The Truth About Guns*); "Pennsylvania Doctor and School Board Member Threatens to Shoot Anyone Not Wearing a Mask" (*The Truth About Guns*); and "The Political Left's Lust for Violence and the Control of Guns" (*Ammoland*). See Boch (2020c); Zimmerman (2020c); Wos (2020).

38. This sentiment was not confined to Eli; an *Ammoland* piece entitled "America Burning, We Now Know What to Expect If Trump Wins in November" told readers "be prepared to vote. And as always stay heavily armed, trained, dangerous, and prepared to defend our way of life and our Constitution. God bless the USA! We are going to need it." See Riehl (2020a).

39. See Phillips and Milner (2021) on the "Deep State" narrative and its predecessors; see also Carter (2000), Du Mez (2020), and Sokol (2008) on the conservative framing of the Civil Rights movement as a communist threat.

40. Eli thus put forward "a conceptualization of the public sphere [that] is fundamentally 'illiberal'" (as media scholar Reece Peck [2019: 89] describes Fox News) insofar as he eschewed pluralism in favor of defending a singular political identity (the "Real Americans") who are imagined as beleaguered outsiders in American politics. As Peck (2019: 89) notes, this stance fundamentally distinguishes left-wing from right-wing versions of partisanship; despite its pervasiveness across the political spectrum, partisanship on the Left still values political pluralism, as will be seen below with regard to self-identified liberal and Democrat gun sellers.

41. Ben-Ghiat (2020).

42. Dorf (2021: 4).

43. Ben-Ghiat (2020).

44. Note that this strikingly contrasts with the libertarian imagination; see endnote 29 in this chapter.

45. Consider, for example, the FBI's approach to the Black Power movement of the 1960s as an existential threat to the fabric of white American society, which helped justify aggressive government repression of dissident groups. See Austin (2006); Bloom and Martin (2016).

46. *Ammoland* similarly used the term "treason" to discuss the Seattle police-free zone. See Farnam (2020a).

47. Boch (2020a).

48. Boch (2020f).

49. Katz (2020).

50. As he told me, "I liked a lot of the things that he said were going to happen, [and] I think he's made good on a lot of the promises that he made."

51. A few gun sellers I interviewed emphasized racism as a pressing contemporary issue. Many condemned racism in the abstract, and many also intimated that racial injustice had, at some point, been a problem in the United States. Some even outright condemned the killing of George Floyd, as Oliver described, as a "tragedy." But only a handful—largely the handful who identified as Democrat, liberal, or progressive—recognized racism, racial oppression, and racial injustice as ongoing issues and acknowledged the eruptions of protests as sincere responses to those issues.

52. This is not to say that racial ideologies do not inform their views—we know, for example, that liberals and conservatives are not so different in *that* they harbor racializing, and racist, attitudes and practices, but rather in *how* they do so. See Bonilla-Silva (2006); Hughey (2020); Zamudio and Rios (2006); Wodtke (2016).

53. SSRS (2021).

54. Morse (2020b).

55. Braunstein (2017: 185).

Conclusion: The Democracy We Deserve

1. Müller (2021).

2. In the 1970s, according to Joslyn (2020: 53), the gap between the proportion of gun owners versus non gun owners voting Republican in presidential elections was as low as 9 percentage points; by the 2016 US presidential election, the gap had widened to 31 points.

3. Joslyn (2020).

4. Lacombe (2021: 6).

5. Mak (2021).

6. Pro-gun media disavowed an explicit connection or endorsement; see, e.g., Marbut (2021).

7. See Dorf (2021: 1). Further, similar events occurring in places with less restrictive gun laws than DC's have showcased firearms as vehicles of protests; consider the armed protests in Lansing, Michigan, that took place in the Spring of 2020.

8. Healy (2021). As noted in the introduction, two police officers completed suicide in the days that followed.

9. Cochrane and Broadwater (2021).

10. Zimmerman (2020d).

11. Hall et al. (2022). Figures reflect charges as of July 25, 2022; note that this database continues to be updated with additional arrests.

12. Müller (2021).

13. Riehl (2021).

14. Mogelson (2021).

15. Huq (2021: 3). Huq (2021: 7) notes, however, that the same texts that are used to justify right-wing insurrectionism—for example, Machiavelli's oeuvre—also speak to the concerns more prevalent on the Left, including passages by Machiavelli that "describe . . . a conflict internal to the republic between the people and the *grandi*, or well-off, as a precursor to contemporary concerns about economic inequality and the concentrated power of wealthy elites."

16. Brewster (2021).

17. See Brewster (2021); Cox (2021); Dickson (2021).

18. Lenthung (2021); Thebault and Rindler (2021); Wintemute (2021). Whether gun availability helped drive this jump or gun purchasing was simply a response to a growing sense of insecurity that ran parallel to, but did not drive, the increase in violence remains unclear.

19. DeBrabander (2015).

20. Blocher and Siegel (2021: 3, 5).

21. Blocher and Siegel (2021: 4).

22. Burbick (2006: 186).

23. Anderson (2016).

24. Recall this observation from Ross (2021: 2): "The U.S. Capitol insurrectionists came armed, ready to resist America's core governing principle to which they had assigned that tyrannical label: the transfer of power through a fair and legitimate election. In other words, the tyranny was American republicanism itself."

25. Braunstein (2017).

26. Hochschild (2018).

27. Skocpol and Williamson (2011).

28. For example, consider Levitsky and Ziblatt (2018).

29. Horncastle (2020).

30. Overton (2022).

31. Philips (2021).

32. Roosevelt (2021).

33. Bellah et al. (1985: 287).

34. Perrin (2014).

35. I especially recommend *Zen and the Art of Saving the Planet*, *Radical Dharma*, and *Grieving While Black* for further reading and enrichment.

36. As Müller (2021) reminds us, certainty of political outcomes is the stuff of authoritarianism, not democracy.

37. Braunstein (2017: 188).

38. Butler (2021: 147).

39. Bellah et al. (1985: 194).

40. See Gordon (2015: 70) for a discussion of this dimension of Fanon's writing in *Black Skin, White Masks* (2008).

41. Wade (2021: 1).

42. As bell hooks (2014: 215) notes, "what connects us [is] our awareness that we know it [pain], have known it, or will know it again."

43. Wade (2021: 16).

44. Wade (2021).

45. Butler (2021: 111).

46. See, e.g., Butler (2018); Carter and Rossi (2019); Forgiarini, Gallucci, and Maravita (2011); Johnson (2008); Trawalter, Hoffman, and Waytz (2012).

47. Cullors (2018).

48. Williamson (2022).

49. As Phillips and Milner (2021: 201) observe, "too many people fixate on their own freedoms *from*, burying their responsibility to cultivate freedoms *for*."

50. hooks (2014: 215).

51. Winfrey and Perry (2021).

52. Brown (2012).

53. hooks (1994: 298).

54. Ross (2021: 3).

55. Du Bois (2016: 28).

56. As just one example, see Murakawa (2014) on the liberal justification of mass incarceration.

57. As James Baldwin wrote in 1963, "this is the crime of which I accuse my country and my countrymen, and for which neither I nor time nor history will ever forgive them, that they have destroyed and are destroying hundreds of thousands of lives and do not know it and do not want to know it. . . . But it is not permissible that the authors of devastation should also be innocent. It is the innocence which constitutes the crime." See Baldwin (2013: 5–6).

58. Müller (2021).

59. For scholarship on gun owners, such as liberal gun owners, who might bridge these divides, see Combs (2021); McCaughey (1997); Yamane et al. (2001). In contrast, note that a working paper from political scientists Matthew Lacombe, Matthew Simonson, Jon Green, and James Druckman finds that people who became gun owners in 2020 were more likely to ascribe to "strong conspiracy and anti-system beliefs" than long-standing gun owners. See Lacombe et al. (2022).

60. This emphasis on civil society organizations as the crucial glue between the state and the citizen—insofar as civil society shapes the citizens' cultural capacities on behalf of the public good—is of course indebted to De Tocqueville's analysis of American democracy.

Reflections on Methodology

1. Quinn (2021).

2. Tavory and Timmermans (2014).

3. Gerson and Damaske (2020).

4. Hanson and Richards (2019).

5. Please see Carlson and Ramo (2022) for an extended discussion of 2020 as "unsettled" times.

6. Haney (2010).

BIBLIOGRAPHY

Abbate, L. (2020). Why a Maine Couple Opened a Trump-Themed Coffee Shop in Rockland. *Bangor Daily News*. Accessed September 16, 2021. https://bangordailynews.com/2020/02/28/news/why-a-maine-couple-opened-a-trump-themed-coffee-shop-in-rockland/.

Abramowitz, A. and McCoy, J. (2019). United States: Racial Resentment, Negative Partisanship, and Polarization in Trump's America. *ANNALS of the American Academy of Political and Social Science*, 681(1), 137–156.

Abt, T., Bocanegra, E., and Tingirides, E. (2022). Violent Crime in the US Is Surging. But We Know What to Do About It. *Time Magazine*. Accessed April 18, 2022. https://time.com/6138650/violent-crime-us-surging-what-to-do/.

Achenbach, J., Higham, S., and Horwitz, S. (2013). How NRA's True Believers Converted a Marksmanship Group into a Mighty Gun Lobby. *Washington Post*. Accessed July 14, 2021. https://www.washingtonpost.com/politics/how-nras-true-believers-converted-a-marksmanship-group-into-a-mighty-gun-lobby/2013/01/12/51c62288-59b9-11e2-88d0-c4cf65c3ad15_story.html?hpid=z1.

Alexander, M. (2010). *The New Jim Crow*. New Press.

America's 1st Freedom. (2019). Highlights from NRA-ILA's History of Achievements. *America's 1st Freedom*. Accessed August 2, 2021. https://www.americas1stfreedom.org/articles/2019/11/25/highlights-from-nra-ila-s-history-of-achievements.

Ames, B. C. (2019). The Dehumanization of Immigrants and the Rise of the Extreme Right. *AICGS*. Accessed September 16, 2021. https://www.aicgs.org/publication/the-dehumanization-of-immigrants-and-the-rise-of-the-extreme-right/.

An, M. and Carlson, J. (2022). Politics at the Gun Counter: Examining Partisanship and Masculinity among Conservative Gun Sellers During the 2020 Gun Purchasing Surge. *Social Problems*. doi: https://doi.org/socpro/spac046.

Anderson, C. (2016). *White Rage: The Unspoken Truth of Our Racial Divide*. Bloomsbury Publishing.

Anderson, C. (2021). *The Second: Race and Guns in a Fatally Unequal America*. Bloomsbury Publishing.

Anderson, J. (2021). The Extraordinary Ethics of Self-Defence: Embodied Vulnerability and Gun Rights among Transgender Shooters in the United States. *Ethnos*, 1–18.

Anestis, M. D. and Bryan, C. J. (2021). Threat Perceptions and the Intention to Acquire Firearms. *Journal of Psychiatric Research*, 133, 113–118.

Arango, T., Bogel-Burroughs, N., Burch, A.D.S., Cramer, M., Eligon, J., Fernandez, M., Hauser, C., MacFarquhar, N., Opam, K., Taylor, D. B., Tompkins, L., and Vigdor, N. (2021). How

George Floyd Died, and What Happened Next. *New York Times*. Accessed July 15, 2021. https://www.nytimes.com/article/george-floyd.html.

Arango, T. and Closson, T. (2022). "We Can't Endure This": Surge in US Shootings Shows No Signs of Easing. *New York Times*. Accessed April 18, 2022. https://www.nytimes.com/2022/03/23/us/shooting-gun-violence.html.

Associated Press. (2020). Patriots or Instigators? Americans Divided Over Armed Civilians Who Flock to Protests. *Penn Live*. Accessed August 16, 2021. https://www.pennlive.com/nation-world/2020/09/patriots-or-instigators-americans-divided-over-armed-civilians-who-flock-to-protests.html.

Austin, C. J. (2006). *Up Against the Wall: Violence in the Making and Unmaking of the Black Panther Party*. University of Arkansas Press.

Bail, C. (2021). *Breaking the Social Media Prism: How to Make Our Platforms Less Polarizing*. Princeton University Press.

Bailyn, B. (2017). *The Ideological Origins of the American Revolution*. Harvard University Press.

Baldacchino, G. (2021). Extra-Territorial Quarantine in Pandemic Times. *Political Geography*, 85(1). doi: https://doi.org/10.1016/j.polgeo.2020.102302.

Baldwin, J. (2013). *The Fire Next Time*. Vintage.

Bandler, J., Callahan, P., Rotella, S., and Berg, K. (2020). Inside the Fall of the CDC. *ProPublica*. Accessed October 22, 2021. https://www.propublica.org/article/inside-the-fall-of-the-cdc.

Bartozzi, J. (2020). Guns Are Selling, But Gun Safety Is Priceless. *National Shooting Sports Foundation*. Accessed September 19, 2021. https://www.nssf.org/articles/guns-are-selling-but-gun-safety-is-priceless/.

Basu, Z. (2019). The 24 Times Trump Has Accused Somebody of "Treason." *Axios*. Accessed August 12, 2021. https://www.axios.com/trump-treason-russia-investigation-new-york-times-e1660029-c73c-4809-8bd5-8988f1ed4fda.html.

BBC News. (2016). Michelle Obama "Ape in Heels" Post Causes Outrage. Accessed September 16, 2021. https://www.bbc.com/news/election-us-2016-37985967.

Bellah, R. N., Madsen, R., Sullivan, W. M., Swidler, A., and Tipton, S. M. (1985). *Habits of the Heart: Individualism and Commitment in American Life*. University of California Press.

Belmont, C. and Stroud, A. (2020). Bugging Out: Apocalyptic Masculinity and Disaster Consumerism in Offgrid Magazine. *Feminist Studies*, 46(2), 431–458.

Ben-Ghiat, R. (2020). *Strongmen: Mussolini to the Present*. W. W. Norton.

Bergengruen, V. (2021). How "America's Frontline Doctors" Sold Access to Bogus COVID-19 Treatments—and Left Patients in the Lurch. *TIME*. Accessed October 22, 2021. https://time.com/6092368/americas-frontline-doctors-covid-19-misinformation/.

Bialasiewicz, L. and Eckes, C. (2021). "Individual Sovereignty" in Pandemic Times—A Contradiction in Terms? *Political Geography*, 85(1). doi: https://doi.org/10.1016/j.polgeo.2020.102277.

Bishop, B. (2009). *The Big Sort: Why the Clustering of Like-minded America Is Tearing Us Apart*. Houghton Mifflin Harcourt.

Blake, A. (2021). Many Republicans Sympathize with Those Who Stormed the Capitol. *Washington Post*. Accessed October 19, 2021. https://www.washingtonpost.com/politics/2021/01/13/lurking-beneath-surface-gop-plenty-sympathy-those-who-stormed-capitol/.

Blee, K. M. and Creasap, K. A. (2010). Conservative and Right-Wing Movements. *Annual Review of Sociology*, 36, 269–286.

Blocher, J. and Siegal, R. (2021). Guns and Democracy. *The Brennan Center for Justice*. Accessed October 27, 2021. https://www.brennancenter.org/sites/default/files/2021-06/Blocher-Siegel_final.pdf.

Bloom, J. and Martin, W. E. (2016). *Black Against Empire: The History and Politics of the Black Panther Party*. University of California Press.

Boch, J. (2020a). Americans Growing Impatient with Heavy-Handed Authoritarianism. *The Truth About Guns*. Accessed October 24, 2021. https://www.thetruthaboutguns.com/americans-growing-impatient-with-heavy-handed-authoritarianism/.

Boch, J. (2020b). Emergency Preparedness: How Much Is Enough? *The Truth About Guns*. Accessed August 2, 2021. https://www.thetruthaboutguns.com/preparedness-much-enough/.

Boch, J. (2020c). FEDS: Angry Leftist Brings Rifle to Lubbock George Floyd Protest to "Off Racists and MAGA People." *The Truth About Guns*. Accessed October 24, 2021. https://www.thetruthaboutguns.com/feds-angry-leftist-brings-rifle-to-lubbock-george-floyd-protest-to-off-racists-and-maga-people/.

Boch, J. (2020d). Gun Owners: Be Goodwill Ambassadors to Your Neighbors, Community. *The Truth About Guns*. Accessed October 24, 2021. https://www.thetruthaboutguns.com/gun-owners-be-goodwill-ambassadors-with-neighbors-community/.

Boch, J. (2020e). How Do You Handle People Who Suddenly Want to Borrow a Gun? *The Truth About Guns*. Accessed September 17, 2021. https://www.thetruthaboutguns.com/how-would you handle people-who-suddenly-want-to-borrow-a-gun/.

Boch, J. (2020f). If Police Won't Stop the Violence and Looting, America's Gun Owners Will. *The Truth About Guns*. Accessed October 24, 2021. https://www.thetruthaboutguns.com/if-police-wont-stop-the-violence-and-looting-americas-gun-owners-will/.

Boch, J. (2020g). Licensed Carrier Forfeits His Gun Rights by Drawing on a Man for Not Wearing a Mask. *The Truth About Guns*. Accessed September 20, 2021. https://www.thetruthaboutguns.com/licensed-carrier-forfeits-his-gun-rights-drawing-on-a-man-for-not-wearing-a-mask/.

Boch, J. (2020h). Tyranny of the Snitches: If "Karens" Will Snitch on You for Playing in a Park, They'll Definitely Do It Over Your Guns. *The Truth About Guns*. Accessed October 24, 2021. https://www.thetruthaboutguns.com/tyranny-of-the-snitches-if-karens-will-snitch-on-you-for-playing-in-a-park-theyll-definitely-do-it-for-your-guns/.

Bogus, C. T. (1998). The Hidden History of the Second Amendment. *UC Davis Law Review*, 31 309.

Bonilla-Silva, E. (2006). *Racism without Racists: Color-Blind Racism and the Persistence of Racial Inequality in the United States*. Rowman & Littlefield.

Bouie, J. (2020). The Conspiracist in Chief Will Save Us All. *New York Times*. Accessed July 19, 2021. https://www.nytimes.com/2020/09/04/opinion/the-conspiracist-in-chief-will-save-us-all.html.

Bove, V. and Di Leo, R. (2020). COVID-19, Security Threats and Public Opinions. *Peace Economics, Peace Science and Public Policy*, 26(3). doi: https://doi.org/10.1515/peps-2020-033.

Brackman, H. D. (2000). The Attack on Jewish Hollywood: A Chapter in the History of Modern American Anti-Semitism. *Modern Judaism*, 20(1), 1–19.

Braunstein, R. (2017). *Prophets and Patriots.* University of California Press.

Brenan, M. (2020). Americans Remain Distrustful of Mass Media. *Gallup.* Accessed July 19, 2021. https://news.gallup.com/poll/321116/americans-remain-distrustful-mass-media.aspx.

Brewer, M. (2016). Populism in American Politics. *The Forum,* 14(3), 249–264.

Brewer, M. D. and Stonecash, J. M. (2001). Class, Race Issues, and Declining White Support for the Democratic Party in the South. *Political Behavior,* 23(2), 131–155.

Brewster, J. (2021). Nearly Half of Republican Voters Call January 6 Riot "Legitimate Protest," Poll Finds. *Forbes.* Accessed October 19, 2021. https://www.forbes.com/sites/jackbrewster/2021/06/17/nearly-half-of-republican-voters-call-jan-6-riot-legitimate-protest-poll-finds/?sh=59b066586ce4.

Brown, B. (2012). *Daring Greatly: How the Courage to be Vulnerable Transforms the Way We Live, Love, Parent, and Lead.* Penguin.

Brown, W. (2017). *Undoing the Demos: Neoliberalism's Stealth Revolution.* Zone Books.

Budryk, Z. (2020). Head of CrossFit to Staff: "We're Not Mourning for George Floyd." *The Hill.* Accessed August 12, 2021. https://thehill.com/blogs/blog-briefing-room/news/501947-head-of-crossfit-told-staff-were-not-mourning-for-george-floyd.

Bump, P. (2020). Trump Sides with Deranged Conspiracy Theories over Black Lives Matter Protestors. *Washington Post.* Accessed August 12, 2021. https://www.washingtonpost.com/politics/2020/06/09/trump-sides-with-deranged-conspiracy-theories-over-black-lives-matter-protesters/.

Bump, P. (2021). Approval of the Jan. 6 Capitol Riot Is More Deeply Embedded Than You Might Think. *Washington Post.* Accessed October 19, 2021. https://www.washingtonpost.com/politics/2021/07/21/approval-jan-6-capitol-riot-is-more-deeply-embedded-than-you-might-think/.

Bunn, C. (2022). Why More Black People Are Looking for Safety in Gun Ownership. *NBC News.* Accessed July 27, 2022. https://www.nbcnews.com/news/nbcblk/black-people-are-looking-safety-gun-ownership-rcna32150

Burbick, J. (2006). *Gun Show Nation: Gun Culture and American Democracy.* The New Press.

Bureau of Alcohol, Tobacco, Firearms and Explosives. (2021). Firearms in the United States: Annual Statistical Update 2021. US Department of Justice. Accessed July 19, 2022. https://www.atf.gov/firearms/docs/report/2021-firearms-commerce-report/download.

Buštíková, L. and Baboš, P. (2020). Best in Covid: Populists in the Time of Pandemic. *Politics and Governance,* 8(4), 496–508.

Butler, A. (2021). *White Evangelical Racism: The Politics of Morality in America.* UNC Press Books.

Butler, P. (2018). *Chokehold: Policing Black Men.* The New Press.

Callcut, R. A., Robles, A. M., Kornblith, L. Z., Plevin, R. E., and Mell, M. W. (2019). Effect of Mass Shootings on Gun Sales—A 20-year Perspective. *Journal of Trauma and Acute Care Surgery,* 87(3), 531.

Carlson, J. (2014). States, Subjects and Sovereign Power: Lessons from Global Gun Cultures. *Theoretical Criminology,* 18(3), 335–353.

Carlson, J. (2015). *Citizen-Protectors: The Everyday Politics of Guns in an Age of Decline.* Oxford University Press.

Carlson, J. (2020). *Policing the Second Amendment: Guns, Law Enforcement, and the Politics of Race.* Princeton University Press.

Carlson, J. and Ramo, E. (2022). "I'm Not a Conspiracist, But . . .": Knowledge and Conservative Politics in Unsettled Times. *Social Forces*. doi: https://doi.org/10.1093/sf/soac082.

Carothers, T. and O'Donohue, A. (Eds.). (2019). *Democracies Divided: The Global Challenge of Political Polarization*. Brookings Institution Press.

Carter, D. T. (2000). *The Politics of Rage: George Wallace, the Origins of the New Conservatism, and the Transformation of American Politics*. LSU Press.

Carter, L. and Rossi, A. (2019). Embodying Strength: The Origin, Representations, and Socialization of the Strong Black Woman Ideal and Its Effect on Black Women's Mental Health. *Women & Therapy*, 42(3–4), 289–300.

Cassese, E. C. (2021). Partisan Dehumanization in American Politics. *Political Behavior*, 43(1), 29–50.

Castronuovo, C. (2021). Cawthorn: Biden Door-to-Door Vaccine Strategy Could Be Used to "Take" Guns, Bibles. *The Hill*. Accessed August 2, 2021. https://thehill.com/homenews/house/562372-cawthorn-biden-door-to-door-vaccine-strategy-could-be-used-to-take-guns-bibles.

Censky, A. (2020). Heavily Armed Protestors Gather Again at Michigan Capitol to Decry Stay-at-Home Order. *NPR*. Accessed August 16, 2021. https://www.npr.org/2020/05/14/855918852/heavily-armed-protesters-gather-again-at-michigans-capitol-denouncing-home-order.

Center for American Progress. (2016). Immunizing the Gun Industry: The Harmful Effect of the Protection of Lawful Commerce in Arms Act. Accessed July 19, 2021. https://www.americanprogress.org/issues/guns-crime/reports/2016/01/15/128949/immunizing-the-gun-industry-the-harmful-effect-of-the-protection-of-lawful-commerce-in-arms-act/.

Cepaluni, G., Dorsch, M., and Branyiczki, R. (2020). Political Regimes and Deaths in the Early Stages of the COVID-19 Pandemic. *SSRN*. Accessed August 2, 2021. https://ssrn.com/abstract=3586767.

Chalabi, M. (2021). Tim Scott Says "America Is Not a Racist Country"—The Data Says Otherwise. *The Guardian*. Accessed August 16, 2021. https://www.theguardian.com/news/datablog/2021/may/06/tim-scott-america-racist-data-racial-disparities.

Chenoweth, E. and Pressman, J. (2020). This Summer's Black Lives Matter Protesters Were Overwhelmingly Peaceful, Our Research Finds. Accessed May 4, 2022. *Washington Post*. https://www.washingtonpost.com/politics/2020/10/16/this-summers-black-lives-matter-protesters-were-overwhelming-peaceful-our-research-finds/.

Chwick, A. J. and Eisen, J. D. (2020a). Second Amendment Supporters Welcome the 2020 Class of New Gun Owners! *Ammoland*. Accessed September 20, 2021. https://www.ammoland.com/2020/07/second-amendment-supporters-welcome-2020-class-new-gun-owners/#axzz761alXA5q.

Chwick, A. J. and Eisen, J. D. (2020b). Lies About Hydroxychloroquine, Just Like Lies About Guns. *Ammoland*. Accessed October 22, 2021. https://www.ammoland.com/2020/05/lies-about-hydroxychloroquine-like-lies-about-guns/#axzz796VlZDQa.

Clement, S. and Balz, D. (2020). Big Majorities Support Protests Over Floyd Killing and Say Police Need to Change, Poll Finds. *Washington Post*. Accessed October 30, 2021.

https://www.washingtonpost.com/politics/big-majorities-support-protests-over-floyd
-killing-and-say-police-need-to-change-poll-finds/2020/06/08/6742d52c-a9b9-11ea
-9063-e69bd6520940_story.html.

Cochrane, E. and Broadwater, L. (2021). Capitol Riot Costs Will Exceed $30 Million, Official Tells Congress. *New York Times.* Accessed October 25, 2021. https://www.nytimes.com /2021/02/24/us/politics/capitol-riot-damage.html.

Codrea, D. (2020a). Coronavirus Hysteria Raises Legitimate Gun and Freedom Concerns. *Ammoland.* Accessed August 2, 2021. https://www.ammoland.com/2020/03/coronavirus -hysteria-raises-legitimate-gun-and-freedom-concerns/#axzz72Prka095.

Codrea, D. (2020b). ISP's Weak "Assurances" on Masked Concealed Carry Offer No Guarantees. *Ammoland.* Accessed September 20, 2021. https://www.ammoland.com/2020/05/isps -weak-assurances-on-masked-concealed-carry-offer-no-guarantees/#axzz76xaeNbvg.

Codrea, D. (2020c). Trevor Noah Tweet Makes Mass Death "Joke" Many Gun Prohibitionists Agree With. *Ammoland.* Accessed September 20, 2021. https://www.ammoland.com/2020 /11/trevor-noah-tweet-makes-mass-death-joke-many-gun-prohibitionists-agree-with /#axzz761alXA5q.

Codrea, D. (2021). NY Democrat Citizen Disarmament Zealot Proposes Covid "Detention Centers." *Ammoland.* Accessed September 20, 2021. https://www.ammoland.com/2021/01 /ny-democrat-citizen-disarmament-zealot-proposes-covid-detention-centers /#axzz761alXA5q.

Combs, T. P. (2021). Queers with Guns? Against the LGBT Grain. *Sociological Perspectives,* 65(1), 77–96.

Cox, D. (2021). After the Ballots Are Counted: Conspiracies, Political Violence, and American Exceptionalism. *Survey Center on American Life.* October 26, 2021. https://www .americansurveycenter.org/research/after-the-ballots-are-counted-conspiracies-political -violence-and-american-exceptionalism/.

Cramer, K. J. (2016). *The Politics of Resentment: Rural Consciousness in Wisconsin and the Rise of Scott Walker.* University of Chicago Press.

Craven, W. (Director). (1996). *Scream* [Film]. Woods Entertainment.

Creitz, C. (2020). Minnesota Doctor Blasts 'Ridiculous' CDC Coronavirus Death Count Guidelines. *Fox News.* Accessed October 22, 2021. https://www.foxnews.com/media /physician-blasts-cdc-coronavirus-death-count-guidelines.

Crick, B. (2002). *Democracy: A Very Short Introduction.* Oxford University Press.

Crisp, E. (2020). Trump on Teen Accused in Wisconsin Killings: "He Probably Would Have Been Killed." *Newsweek.* Accessed August 16, 2021. https://www.newsweek.com/trump-teen -accused-wisconsin-killings-he-probably-would-have-been-killed-1528801.

Crump, J. (2020). Wearing a Mask While Legally Carrying a Gun in Virginia. *Ammoland.* Accessed September 20, 2021. https://www.ammoland.com/2020/06/wearing-a-mask-while -legally-carrying-a-gun-in-virginia/#axzz761alXA5q.

Cullors, P. (2018). *When They Call You a Terrorist: A Black Lives Matter Memoir.* St. Martin's Press.

Danner, C. (2020). Everything We Know About the Killing of Rayshard Brooks by Atlanta Police. *New York Magazine.* Accessed July 15, 2021. https://nymag.com/intelligencer/2020 /06/what-we-know-about-the-killing-of-rayshard-brooks.html.

Dawson, J. (2019). Shall Not Be Infringed: How the NRA Used Religious Language to Transform the Meaning of the Second Amendment. *Palgrave Communications*, 5(1), 1–13.

De Tocqueville, A. (1835). *Democracy in America.*

Deane, C. and Gramlich, J. (2020). 2020 Election Reveals Two Broad Voting Coalitions Fundamentally at Odds. *Pew Research Center.* Accessed July 19, 2021. https://www.pewresearch .org/fact-tank/2020/11/06/2020-election-reveals-two-broad-voting-coalitions -fundamentally-at-odds/.

DeBrabander, F. (2015). *Do Guns Make Us Free?.* Yale University Press.

DellaPosta, D. (2020). Pluralistic Collapse: The "Oil Spill" Model of Mass Opinion Polarization. *American Sociological Review*, 85(3), 507–536.

DellaPosta, D., Shi, Y., and Macy, M. (2015). Why Do Liberals Drink Lattes?. *American Journal of Sociology*, 120(5), 1473–1511.

Depetris-Chauvin, E. (2015). Fear of Obama: An Empirical Study of the Demand for Guns and the US 2008 Presidential Election. *Journal of Public Economics*, 130, 66–79.

Diaz, Daniella. (2016). Trump Calls Clinton "a Nasty Woman." CNN.com. Accessed November 23, 2021. https://www.cnn.com/2016/10/19/politics/donald-trump-hillary-clinton -nasty-woman/index.html.

Dickson, C. (2021). Poll: Two-Thirds of Republicans Still Think the 2020 Election Was Rigged. *Yahoo!News.* Accessed October 26, 2021. https://news.yahoo.com/poll-two-thirds-of -republicans-still-think-the-2020-election-was-rigged-165934695.html.

Dickson, E. J. (2020). Another Black Man, Tony McDade, Was Shot and Killed by Police Last Week. *Rolling Stone.* Accessed July 15, 2021. https://www.rollingstone.com/culture/culture -news/tony-mcdade-shooting-death-tallahassee-1008433/.

Dionne, E. J., Jr. (2021). A Make-or-Break Moment for Our Democracy. *Washington Post.* Accessed October 19, 2021. https://www.washingtonpost.com/opinions/2021/09/12/make -or-break-moment-our-democracy/.

Doherty, C., Kiley, J., Tyson, A., and Jameson, B. (2015). Beyond Distrust: How Americans View Their Government. *Pew Research Center.* Accessed July 12, 2021. https://www.pewresearch .org/politics/2015/11/23/beyond-distrust-how-americans-view-their-government/.

Dorf, M. (2021). Disaggregating Political Violence. *The Brennan Center for Justice.* Accessed October 27, 2021. https://www.brennancenter.org/sites/default/files/2021-06/Dorf_final.pdf.

Drabble, J. (2008). Fighting Black Power-New Left Coalitions: Covert FBI Media Campaigns and American Cultural Discourse, 1967–1971. *European Journal of American Culture*, 27, 65–91.

Du Bois, W. E. B. (2016). *Darkwater.* Verso.

Du Mez, K. K. (2020). *Jesus and John Wayne: How White Evangelicals Corrupted a Faith and Fractured a Nation.* Liveright Publishing.

Elcioglu, E. F. (2020). *Divided by the Wall: Progressive and Conservative Immigration Politics at the U.S.-Mexico Border.* University of California Press.

Eliasoph, N. (1998). *Avoiding Politics: How Americans Produce Apathy in Everyday Life.* Cambridge University Press.

Fanon, F. (2008). *Black Skin, White Masks.* Grove Press.

Farnam, J. (2020a). ANTIFA Thugs Perpetrating Treason in City of Seattle. *Ammoland.* Accessed October 24, 2021. https://www.ammoland.com/2020/06/antifa-thugs-perpetrating -treason-in-take-over-of-city-of-seattle-portion-video/#axzz7AF6S7xmY.

Farnam, J. (2020b). Sage Advice from "Deadly-Force Expert" Joe Biden. *Ammoland.* Accessed September 17, 2021. https://www.ammoland.com/2020/06/sage-advice-from-deadly-force -expert-joe-biden/#axzz761alXA5q.

Fausset, R. (2021). What We Know About the Shooting Death of Ahmaud Arbery. *New York Times.* Accessed July 15, 2021. https://www.nytimes.com/article/ahmaud-arbery-shooting -georgia.html.

Fay, S. (2022). Gun Dealer Motivations for Complying with the Law: Lessons from the Australian Experience of Gun Control. *Sociological Perspectives,* 65(1): 154–176.

Federal Bureau of Investigation. (2021). NICS Firearm Checks: Month/Year. *FBI.* Accessed August 2, 2021. https://www.fbi.gov/file-repository/nics_firearm_checks_-_month_year .pdf/view.

Feinblatt, J. (2020). Deeming Gun Stores Essential Is Unfair—and Unsafe. CNN. Accessed August 5, 2021. https://www.cnn.com/2020/04/07/opinions/gun-stores-open-covid-19 -unsafe-feinblatt/index.html

Fenster, M. (2008). *Conspiracy Theories: Secrecy and Power in American Culture.* University of Minnesota Press.

Ferré-Sadurní, L. and McKinley, J. (2020). Alex Jones Is Told to Stop Selling Sham Anti-Coronavirus Toothpaste. *New York Times.* Accessed October 22, 2021. https://www.nytimes .com/2020/03/13/nyregion/alex-jones-coronavirus-cure.html.

Fichera, A. (2021). Flawed Report Fuels Erroneous Claims About COVID-19 Death Toll. *Fact-Check.* Accessed October 22, 2021. https://www.factcheck.org/2021/04/scicheck-flawed -study-fuels-erroneous-claims-about-covid-19-death-toll/.

Fields, C. (2016). *Black Elephants in the Room: The Unexpected Politics of African American Republicans.* University of California Press.

Filipovic, J. (2021). Nancy Pelosi: A Study in Power. *Washington Post.* Accessed November 23, 2021. https://www.cnn.com/2016/10/19/politics/donald-trump-hillary-clinton-nasty -woman/index.html.

Ford, A. E. (2021). "They Will Be Like a Swarm of Locusts": Race, Rurality, and Settler Colonialism in American Prepping Culture. *Rural Sociology,* 86(3), 469–493.

Forgiarini, M., Gallucci, M., and Maravita, A. (2011). Racism and the Empathy for Pain on Our Skin. *Frontiers in Psychology,* 2, 108.

Forman, Jr., J. (2017). *Locking Up Our Own: Crime and Punishment in Black America.* Farrar, Straus and Giroux.

Foster, G. A. (2016). Consuming the Apocalypse, Marketing Bunker Materiality. *Quarterly Review of Film and Video,* 33(4), 285–302.

Fox News. (2021). Laura Ingraham on CDC Updating Mask Guidance for Vaccinated Americans. Accessed October 22, 2021. https://www.foxnews.com/transcript/laura-ingraham-on -cdc-mask-guidance.

Fraser, N. (2019). *The Old Is Dying and the New Cannot Be Born: From Progressive Neoliberalism to Trump and Beyond.* Verso Books.

French, D. (2020). *Divided We Fall: America's Secession Threat and How to Restore Our Nation.* St. Martin's Publishing Group.

French, D. (2021). Kyle Rittenhouse's Acquittal Does Not Make Him a Hero. *The Atlantic*. Accessed December 2, 2021. https://www.theatlantic.com/ideas/archive/2021/11/kyle-rittenhouse-right-self-defense-role-model/620715/.

Frenkel, S. and Karnie, A. (2021). Proud Boys Celebrate Trump's "Stand By" Remark About Them at the Debate. *New York Times*. Accessed May 9, 2022. https://www.nytimes.com/2020/09/29/us/trump-proud-boys-biden.html.

Fritz, M. (2017). Sure Shot: Analyst Initiates American Outdoor Brands with a Buy as Dealers Recover from Betting on Clinton Presidency. *Bezinga*. Accessed August 3, 2021. https://sports.yahoo.com/sure-shot-analyst-initiates-american-134347339.html.

Frum, D. (2021). There's a Word for What Trumpism Is Becoming. *The Atlantic*. Accessed August 18, 2021. https://www.theatlantic.com/ideas/archive/2021/07/theres-word-what-trumpism-becoming/619418/.

Galloway, L.F.E. (2020). "A Conspiracy of the Nation": Case Study of Stokely Carmichael's and H. Rap Brown's Arguments in Support of Black Power. *Journal of Black Studies*, 51(1), 83–102.

Gallup. (2020). Do you think there should or should not be a law that would ban the possession of handguns, except by the police and other authorized persons? *Gallup*. Accessed July 14, 2021. https://news.gallup.com/poll/1645/guns.aspx.

Gauchat, G. (2012). Politicization of Science in the Public Sphere: A Study of Public Trust in the United States, 1974 to 2010. *American Sociological Review*, 77(2), 167–187.

Gauchat, G. (2015). The Political Context of Science in the United States: Public Acceptance of Evidence-Based Policy and Science Funding. *Social Forces*, 94(2), 723–746.

Gerson, K. and Damaske, S. (2020). *The Science and Art of Interviewing*. Oxford University Press.

Gerstein, J. (2021). Officers Calmly Pose for Selfies and Appeared to Open Gates for Protesters During the Madness of the Capitol Building Insurrection. *Business Insider*. Accessed July 18, 2022. https://www.yahoo.com/video/officers-calmly-posed-selfies-appeared-043437603.html

Glaser, A. (2021). A Historian of White Power Reacts to the Rittenhouse Verdict: "A Bonanza for the Far-Right." *The Guardian*. Accessed April 21, 2022. https://www.theguardian.com/us-news/2021/nov/24/historian-white-power-reacts-kyle-rittenhouse-verdict-far-right.

Glatter, R. (2020). Here's Why You Shouldn't Go to a "Covid Party." *Forbes*. Accessed August 10, 2021. https://www.forbes.com/sites/robertglatter/2020/07/12/covid-parties-should-you-go-to-one/?sh=7850c36e2249.

Goldblatt, H. (2020). A Brief History of "Karen." *New York Times*. Accessed October 24, 2021. https://www.nytimes.com/2020/07/31/style/karen-name-meme-history.html?.?mc=aud_dev&ad-keywords=auddevgate&gclid=Cj0KCQjw5JSLBhCxARIsAHgO2SclVWaM_hVZVK0sA6JzO0Mxup6OWaHm02HEjofNTQ7iFW6zVFqMskAaAoe5EALw_wcB&gclsrc=aw.ds.

Gómez, L. (2020). No Charges for Trooper in Dion Johnson's Death, Family Will File Civil Suit. *Arizona Mirror*. Accessed July 15, 2021. https://www.azmirror.com/2020/09/22/no-charges-for-trooper-in-dion-johnsons-death-family-will-file-civil-suit/.

Gómez, V. (2020). Democrats More Optimistic than Republicans that Partisan Relations in Washington Will Improve in 2021. *Pew Research Center*. Accessed September 16, 2021.

https://www.pewresearch.org/fact-tank/2020/12/01/democrats-more-optimistic-than
-republicans-that-partisan-relations-in-washington-will-improve-in-2021/

Gómez, V. and Doherty, C. (2021). Wide Partisan Divide on Whether Voting Is a Fundamental Right or a Privilege with Responsibilities. *Pew Research Center.* Accessed October 19, 2021. https://www.pewresearch.org/fact-tank/2021/07/22/wide-partisan-divide-on-whether -voting-is-a-fundamental-right-or-a-privilege-with-responsibilities/.

Gordon, L. R. (2015). *What Fanon Said.* Fordham University Press.

Goss, K. (2010). Disarmed. In *Disarmed.* Princeton University Press.

Goss, K. (2017). The Socialization of Conflict and Its Limits: Gender and Gun Politics in America. *Social Science Quarterly,* 98(2), 455–470.

Gramlich, J. (2020). Americans' Expectations about Voting in 2020 Presidential Election Are Colored by Partisan Differences. *Pew Research.* Accessed October 19, 2021. https://www .pewresearch.org/fact-tank/2020/09/08/americans-expectations-about-voting-in-2020 -presidential-election-are-colored-by-partisan-differences/.

Grant, J. (2020). MCRGO: Carrying While Wearing a Mask in Michigan Not Illegal. *Ammoland.* Accessed September 20, 2021. https://www.ammoland.com/2020/07/mcrgo-carrying -while-wearing-a-mask-in-michigan-not-illegal/#axzz76xaeNbvg.

Gray, R. (2017). Trump Defends White Nationalist Protesters: "Some Very Fine People on Both Sides." *The Atlantic.* Accessed May 9, 2022. https://www.theatlantic.com/politics/archive /2017/08/trump-defends-white-nationalist-protesters-some-very-fine-people-on-both -sides/537012/.

Grewal, D. (2017). The "Black Is Bad" Effect. *Scientific American.* Accessed April 20, 2022. https://www.scientificamerican.com/article/the-bad-is-black-effect/.

Grisales, C. (2022). Jan. 6 Panel Says It Has Evidence Trump Broke Law in Trying to Overturn the Election. NPR. Accessed April 15, 2022. https://www.npr.org/2022/03/02/1084098799 /trump-select-committee-capitol-insurrection-conspiracy.

Guardian Staff. (2020). Tucker Carlson Defends Actions of Teen Charged in Killings of Kenosha Protesters. *The Guardian.* Accessed August 16, 2021. https://www.theguardian.com/media /2020/aug/26/tucker-carlson-kenosha-shooting-teen-kyle-rittenhouse.

Gutowski, S. (2020). African American Gun Group Saw Membership Surge After George Floyd Killing. *Washington Free Beacon.* Accessed April 18, 2022. https://freebeacon.com/issues /african-american-gun-group-saw-membership-surge-after-george-floyd-killing/.

Gutsell, J. N. and Inzlicht, M. (2012). Intergroup Differences in the Sharing of Emotive States: Neural Evidence of an Empathy Gap. *Social Cognitive and Affective Neuroscience,* 7(5), 596–603.

Guynn, J. (2021). President Joe Biden Rescinds Donald Trump Ban on Diversity Training About Systemic Racism. *USA Today.* Accessed August 12, 2021. https://www.usatoday.com/story /money/2021/01/20/biden-executive-order-overturns-trump-diversity-training-ban /4236891001/.

Habermas, J. (1991). *The Structural Transformation of the Public Sphere: An Inquiry into a Category of Bourgeois Society.* MIT Press.

Hagen, R. (2019). Collisions Between Institutional and Populist Risk Imaginaries: The "Dark Side" of Negative Asymmetric Thinking. *Sociological Forum,* 34(1), 1235–1250.

Hall, M., Gould, S., Harrington, R., Shamsian, J., Haroun, A., Ardrey, T., and Snodgrass, E. (2022). At Least 884 People Have Been Charged in the Capitol Insurrection So Far. *Insider*. Accessed July 25, 2022. https://www.insider.com/all-the-us-capitol-pro-trump-riot-arrests -charges-names-2021-1.

Halon, Y. (2020). Tucker Carlson Responds to CDC after Agency Critiques Commentary about Mask-Wearing. Fox News. Accessed October 22, 2021. https://www.foxnews.com /media/tucker-carlson-responds-cdc-mask-wearing.

Hamel, L., Kearney, A., Kirzinger, A., Lopes, L., Muñana, C., and Brodie, M. (2020). KFF Health Tracking Poll—September 2020: Top Issues in 2020 Election, The Role of Misinformation, and Views on a Potential Coronavirus Vaccine. *KFF*. Accessed October 22, 2021. https:// www.kff.org/coronavirus-covid-19/report/kff-health-tracking-poll-september-2020/.

Hammer, M. P. (2020). The Record-Breaking American Arms Race of 2020 Means One Thing: You Loot, We Shoot! *Ammoland*. Accessed October 24, 2021. https://www.ammoland .com/2020/07/recordbreaking-american-arms-race-2020-you-loot-we-shoot/#axzz 796VlZDQa.

Haney, L. (2010). *Offending Women: Power, Punishment, and the Regulation of Desire*. University of California Press.

Haney-López, I. (2014). *Dog Whistle Politics: How Coded Racial Appeals Have Reinvented Racism and Wrecked the Middle Class*. Oxford University Press.

Hanh, Thich Nhat. (2021). *Zen and the Art of Saving the Planet*. Random House.

Hanson, R. and Richards, P. (2019). *Harassed: Gender, Bodies, and Ethnographic Research*. University of California Press.

Harcourt, B. E. (2004). On Gun Registration, the NRA, Adolf Hitler, and Nazi Gun Laws: Exploding the Gun Culture Wars. *Fordham Law Review*, 73(1), 653.

Harris, F. (2012). *The Price of the Ticket: Barack Obama and Rise and Decline of Black Politics*. Oxford University Press.

Hartig, H. (2021). Share of Republicans Saying "Everything Possible" Should Be Done to Make Voting Easy Declines Sharply. *Pew Research Center*. Accessed October 19, 2021. https://www .pewresearch.org/fact-tank/2021/04/01/share-of-republicans-saying-everything-possible -should-be-done-to-make-voting-easy-declines-sharply/.

Hauck, G. (2021). Darnella Frazier, Teen Who Recorded George Floyd's Murder, Awarded Pulitzer Prize Special Citation. *USA Today*. Accessed August 12, 2021. https://www.usatoday .com/story/news/nation/2021/06/11/darnella-frazier-pulitzer-prize-citation-george -floyd-video/7656851002/.

Healy, J. (2021). These Are the 5 People Who Died in the Capitol Riot. *New York Times*. Accessed October 25, 2021. https://www.nytimes.com/2021/01/11/us/who-died-in-capitol-building -attack.html.

Heinze, M. C. (2014). On "Gun Culture" and "Civil Statehood" in Yemen. *Journal of Arabian Studies*, 4(1), 70–95.

Hemmer, N. (2016). *Messengers of the Right*. University of Pennsylvania Press.

Hersh, J. (2020). Gun Lovers Are Claiming a Huge "I Told You So" Moment with the Coronavirus Outbreak. *Vice News*. Accessed August 2, 2021. https://www.vice.com/en/article/k7ejga/gun -lovers-are-having-a-huge-i-told-you-so-moment-with-the-coronavirus-outbreak.

Hicks, W. D., McKee, S. C., Sellers, M. D., and Smith, D. A. (2015). A Principle or a Strategy? Voter Identification Laws and Partisan Competition in the American States. *Political Research Quarterly*, 68(1), 18–33.

Hinton, E. (2021). *America on Fire: The Untold History of Police Violence and Black Rebellion Since the 1960s.* Liveright.

Hochschild, A. R. (2018). *Strangers in Their Own Land: Anger and Mourning on the American Right.* The New Press.

Hoerl, K. and Ortiz, E. (2015). Organizational Secrecy and the FBI's COINTELPRO—Black Nationalist Hate Groups Program, 1967–1971. *Management Communication Quarterly*, 29(4), 590–615.

Hofstadter, R. (1964). The Paranoid Style in American Politics. *Harper's Magazine.* Accessed July 15, 2021. https://harpers.org/archive/1964/11/the-paranoid-style-in-american-politics/.

Holden, E. (2020). How the Oil Industry Has Spent Billions to Control the Climate Change Conversation. *The Guardian.* Accessed August 12, 2021. https://www.theguardian.com /business/2020/jan/08/oil-companies-climate-crisis-pr-spending.

hooks, b. (1994). *Outlaw Culture.* Routledge.

hooks, b. (2014). *Yearning: Race, Gender and Cultural Politics.* Routledge.

Horncastle, W. (2020). Ten Years On, the Legacy of Citizens United Still Threatens Representative Democracy in the United States. *LSE United States Politics and Policy Blog.* Accessed January 7, 2022. https://blogs.lse.ac.uk/usappblog/2020/01/21/ten-years-on-the-legacy-of -citizens-united-still-threatens-representative-democracy-in-the-united-states/.

Hughey, M. (2020). *White Bound: Nationalists, Antiracists, and the Shared Meanings of Race.* Stanford University Press.

Huq, A. (2021). On the Origins of Republican Violence. *The Brennan Center for Justice.* Accessed October 27, 2021. https://www.brennancenter.org/sites/default/files/2021-06/Huq_final.pdf.

Hutchinson, G. and Masson, T. (2007). *The Great New Orleans Gun Grab: Descent into Anarchy.* Louisiana Publishing.

Hutchison, H. (2020). Just What Penance Does Warnock Want Gun Owners to Do? *Ammoland.* Accessed September 16, 2021. https://www.ammoland.com/2020/11/just-what-penance -does-warnock-want-gun-owners-to-do/#axzz76l alXA5q.

Inacker, T. (2020). Welcome All the New Gun Owners Who Are Now Buying Firearms . . . But . . . *The Truth About Guns.* Accessed September 16, 2021. https://www.thetruthaboutguns .com/welcome-all-the-new-gun-owners-who-are-now-buying-firearms-but/.

IPSOS/NPR Poll. (2020). More Than 1 in 3 Americans Believe a "Deep State" Is Working to Undermine Trump. *IPSOS.* Accessed July 19, 2021. https://www.ipsos.com/en-us/news -polls/npr-misinformation-123020.

Isakhan, B., and Stockwell, S. (Eds.). (2011). *The Secret History of Democracy.* Palgrave Macmillan.

Jackson, J. (2021). The False Republican Mantra: "America Is Not a Racist Country." *Chicago Sun Times.* Accessed August 16, 2021. https://chicago.suntimes.com/columnists/2021/5/4 /22419646/republican-party-american-racism-slavery-jim-crow-jesse-jackson.

Jacobson, J. (2020). Is America Losing the Rule of Law? *The Truth About Guns.* Accessed October 24, 2021. https://www.thetruthaboutguns.com/is-america-losing-the-rule-of-law/.

Jahanbegloo, R. (2015). The Gandhian Vision of Democracy. *Democratic Theory*, 2(2): 59–70.

Jamieson, C. (2013). Gun Violence Research: History of the Federal Funding Freeze. *American Psychological Association*. Accessed October 22, 2021. https://www.apa.org/science/about/psa/2013/02/gun-violence.

Jilani, Z. (2016). Donald Trump in 2000: "I Support the Ban on Assault Weapons." *The Intercept*. Accessed May 9, 2022. https://theintercept.com/2016/01/27/donald-trump-in-2000-i-support-the-ban-on-assault-weapons/.

Johnson, D. (2008). Racial Prejudice, Perceived Injustice, and the Black-White Gap in Punitive Attitudes. *Journal of Criminal Justice*, 36(2): 198–206.

Johnson, D. (2020a). USCCA Op-Ed on the Importance of Education and Training as Gun Sales Rise. *Ammoland*. Accessed September 17, 2021. https://www.ammoland.com/2020/05/uscca-op-ed-on-the-importance-of-education-and-training-as-gun-sales-rise/#axzz761alXA5q.

Johnson, D. (2020b). USCCA Emphasizes Training and Responsible Gun Ownership, Now More Than Ever. *Ammoland*. Accessed September 19, 2021. https://www.ammoland.com/2020/03/uscca-emphasizes-training-responsible-gun-ownership-now-more-than-ever/#axzz761alXA5q.

Johnson, N. (2014). *Negroes and the Gun*. Prometheus Books.

Jorge, K. (2021). Nashville DA: Transgender Bathroom Law "Dehumanizing," Won't Enforce Despite Pressure. Fox News. https://fox17.com/news/local/nashville-da-transgender-bathroom-bill-dehumanizing-wont-enforce-despite-pressure-multiperson-restroom-glenn-funk-lgbtq-politics-legislature.

Joslyn, M. R. (2020). *The Gun Gap: The Influence of Gun Ownership on Political Behavior and Attitudes*. Oxford University Press.

Junn, J. and Masuoka, N. (2020). The Gender Gap Is a Race Gap: Women Voters in US Presidential Elections. *Perspectives on Politics*, 18(4), 1135–1145.

Jurkowitz, M., Mitchell, A., Shearer, E., and Oliphant, J. B. (2020). Before Trump Tested Positive for Coronavirus, Republicans' Attention to Pandemic Had Sharply Declined. *Pew Research Center*. Accessed July 19, 2021. https://www.journalism.org/2020/10/07/before-trump-tested-positive-for-coronavirus-republicans-attention-to-pandemic-had-sharply-declined/.

Kahan, D. M. and Braman, D. (2003). More Statistics, Less Persuasion: A Cultural Theory of Gun-Risk Perceptions. *University of Pennsylvania Law Review*, 151(4), 1291–1327.

Kalmoe, N. P. and Mason, L. (2019). Lethal Mass Partisanship: Prevalence, Correlates, and Electoral Contingencies. In *Prepared for Presentation at the January 2019 NCAPSA American Politics Meeting*. Accessed September 20, 2021. https://www.dannyhayes.org/uploads/6/9/8/5/69858539/kalmoe____mason_ncapsa_2019_-_lethal_partisanship_-_final_lmedit.pdf.

Kanno-Youngs, Z., Tavernise, S., and Cochrane, E. (2021). As House Was Breached, a Fear "We'd Have to Fight" to Get Out. *New York Times*. Accessed July 12, 2021. https://www.nytimes.com/2021/01/06/us/politics/capitol-breach-trump-protests.html.

Katz, R. (2020). Seditious U.S. Press Appeases China but Attacks Trump. *Ammoland*. Accessed October 24, 2021. https://www.ammoland.com/2020/04/seditious-u-s-press-appeases-china-but-attacks-trump/#axzz796PBmhRj.

Kaufmann, K. M. and Petrocik, J. R. (1999). The Changing Politics of American Men: Understanding the Sources of the Gender Gap. *American Journal of Political Science*, 864–887.

Keane, L. (2020). Nothing Makes Gun Grabbers Angrier Than Hundreds of Thousands of New American Gun Owners. *The Truth About Guns*. Accessed September 20, 2021. https://www.thetruthaboutguns.com/nothing-makes-gun-grabbers-angrier-than-hundreds-of-thousands-of-new-american-gun-owners/.

Kelly, C. R. (2020). *Apocalypse Man: The Death Drive and the Rhetoric of White Masculine Victimhood*. The Ohio State University Press.

Khubchandani, J. and Price, J. H. (2021). Public Perspectives on Firearm Sales in the United States during the COVID-19 Pandemic. *Journal of the American College of Emergency Physicians Open*, 2(1). doi: https://doi.org/10.1002/emp2.12293.

Klarman, M. J. (2020). Foreword: The Degradation of American Democracy—and the Court. *Harvard Law Review*, 134(1), 1–264.

Klein, E. (2021). The Rest of the World Is Worried About America. *New York Times*. Accessed October 19, 2021. https://www.nytimes.com/2021/07/01/opinion/us-democracy-erosion.html?searchResultPosition=13.

Klepper, D. and Hinnant, L. (2020). George Soros Conspiracy Theories Surge as Protests Sweep US. *AP News*. Accessed August 12, 2021. https://apnews.com/article/ap-top-news-racial-injustice-mn-state-wire-united-states-us-news-f01f3c405985f4e3477e4e4ac27986e5.

Knox, J. (2021). Biden Pledges to "Beat the NRA . . ." But He Can Not Beat the Citizen Gun Lobby. *Ammoland*. Accessed September 16, 2021. https://www.ammoland.com/2021/01/biden-pledges-to-beat-the-nra-cannot-beat-citizen-gun-lobby/#axzz761alXA5q.

Knuckey, J. (2005). Racial Resentment and the Changing Partisanship of Southern Whites. *Party Politics*, 11(1), 5–28.

Kornfield, M. (2020). This Trump-Themed Coffee Shop Mocks Liberals But Still Wants to Serve Them. *Washington Post*. Accessed September 16, 2021. https://www.washingtonpost.com/nation/2020/02/29/conservative-grounds-coffee-shop/.

Kozlowski, A. C. (2021). How Conservatives Lost Confidence in Science: The Role of Ideological Alignment in Political Polarization. *Social Forces*.

Kummer, J. and Bogel-Burroughs, N. (2022). Last 2 Officers Involved in George Floyd's Death are Sentenced to Prison. *New York Times*. Accessed July 27, 2022. https://www.nytimes.com/2022/07/27/us/george-floyd-j-alexander-kueng.html.

Krauss, L. M. (2016). Trump's Anti-Science Campaign. *New Yorker*. Accessed August 12, 2021. https://www.newyorker.com/news/news-desk/trumps-anti-science-campaign.

Kraychik, R. (2021). Rep. Greg Murphy: "Very concerning" for CDC to Float Vaccine Database. *Breitbart*. Accessed October 22, 2021. https://www.breitbart.com/radio/2021/07/29/rep-greg-murphy-very-concerning-for-cdc-to-float-vaccine-database/.

Kruse, K. M. (2013). *White Flight*. Princeton University Press.

Kuznia, R., Ortega, B., and Tolan, C. (2021). In the Wake of Trump's Attack on Democracy, Election Officials Fear for the Future of American Elections. CNN. Accessed October 19, 2021. https://www.cnn.com/2021/09/12/politics/trump-2020-future-presidential-elections-invs/index.html.

LaClau, E. and Mouffe, C. (2014). *Hegemony and Socialist Strategy: Towards a Radical Democratic Politics*. Verso Books.

Lacombe, M. J. (2021). *Firepower: How the NRA Turned Gun Owners Into a Political Force*. Princeton University Press.

Lacombe, M. J., Simonson, M., Green, J., and Druckman, J. (2022). Social Disruption, Gun Buying and Anti-System Beliefs. *Institute for Policy Research Working Paper Series*. Northwestern University. https://www.ipr.northwestern.edu/documents/working-papers/2022/wp-22-13.pdf

Lah, K. (2017). The LA Riots Were a Rude Awakening for Korean-Americans. CNN. Accessed April 18, 2022. https://www.cnn.com/2017/04/28/us/la-riots-korean-americans/index.html.

Lakoff, G. (2016). *Moral Politics: How Liberals and Conservatives Think*. University of Chicago Press.

Landman, T. and Di Gennaro Splendore, L. (2020). Pandemic Democracy: Elections and COVID-19. *Journal of Risk Research*, 23(7–8), 1060–1066.

Lang, B. J. and Lang, M. (2021). Pandemics, Protests, and Firearms. *American Journal of Health Economics*, 7(2), 131–163.

Larosiere, M. (2020a). Ammopocalypse Now! and other COVID19-Induced Hysteria. *The Truth About Guns*. Accessed September 16, 2021. https://www.thetruthaboutguns.com/ammopocalypse-now-and-other-covid19-induced-hysteria-video/.

Larosiere, M. (2020b). Florida Gun Shop Owner Bans Wearing Masks in His Store. *The Truth About Guns*. Accessed September 20, 2021. https://www.thetruthaboutguns.com/florida-gun-shop-bans-wearing-masks-in-their-store-video/?web=1&wdLOR=c2C6806CF-2CA7-524D-855C-3DAEC17B0CA5.

Laterza, V. (2021). Could Cambridge Analytica Have Delivered Donald Trump's 2016 Presidential Victory? An Anthropologist's Look at Big Data and Political Campaigning. *Public Anthropologist*, 3(1), 119–147.

Lenthung, M. (2021). Why Experts Say Gun Violence Rose in 2020, Amid Pandemic Lockdowns. ABC News. Accessed April 18, 2022. https://abcnews.go.com/US/experts-gun-violence-rose-2020-amid-pandemic-lockdowns/story?id=80466932.

Leonardatos, C. D. (1999). California's Attempts to Disarm the Black Panthers. *San Diego Law Review*, 36, 947.

Levitsky, S. and Ziblatt, D. (2018). *How Democracies Die*. Penguin Books.

Lewis, I. (2021). Ted Nugent Tests Positive for Coronavirus After Calling Pandemic a "Scam." *Independent*. Accessed August 10, 2021. https://www.independent.co.uk/arts-entertainment/music/news/ted-nugent-coronavirus-b1834274.html.

Liebell, S. (2021). BLM versus #BLM. *The Brennan Center for Justice*. Retrieved October 27, 2021. https://www.brennancenter.org/sites/default/files/2021-06/Liebell_final.pdf.

Light, C. E. (2017). *Stand Your Ground: A History of America's Love Affair with Lethal Self-Defense*. Beacon Press.

Light, M. and Slonimerov, E. (2020). How Gun Control Policies Evolve: Gun Culture, "Gunscapes" and Political Contingency in Post-Soviet Georgia. *Theoretical Criminology*, 24(4), 590–611.

Lindsay, J. M. (2020). The 2020 Election by the Numbers. *Council on Foreign Relations*. Accessed July 12, 2021. https://www.cfr.org/blog/2020-election-numbers.

Lipsky, M. (2010). *Street-Level Bureaucracy: Dilemmas of the Individual in Public Service*. Russell Sage Foundation.

Litke, E. (2020). Fact Check: Police Gave Kyle Rittenhouse Water and Thanked Him before Shooting. *USA Today*. Accessed August 16, 2021. https://www.usatoday.com/story/news/factcheck/2020/08/29/fact-check-video-police-thanked-kyle-rittenhouse-gave-him-water/5661804002/.

Liu, G. and Wiebe, D. J. (2019). A Time-Series Analysis of Firearm Purchasing after Mass Shooting Events in the United States. *JAMA Network Open*, 2(4). doi: https://doi.org/10.1001/jamanetworkopen.2019.1736.

Lott, J. R. and Wang, R. (2020). Concealed Carry Permit Holders Across the United States: 2021. *Report from the Crime Prevention Research Center*.

Lovan, D. (2022). Ex-Officer Cleared in Shooting During Breonna Taylor Raid. ABCNews. Accessed July 27, 2022. https://abcnews.go.com/US/wireStory/jurors-weigh-fate-officer-fired-breonna-taylor-raid-83229151.

Lucas, R. (2022). Where the Jan. 6 Insurrection Investigation Stands, One Year Later. NPR. Accessed May 6, 2022. https://www.npr.org/2022/01/06/1070736018/jan-6-anniversary-investigation-cases-defendants-justice.

Lynch, S. N. (2021). Exclusive: "QAnon Shaman" in Plea Negotiations after Mental Health Diagnosis. *Reuters*. Accessed August 10, 2021. https://www.reuters.com/world/us/exclusive-qanon-shaman-plea-negotiations-after-mental-health-diagnosis-lawyer-2021-07-23/.

Mak, T. (2021). Judge Dismisses NRA Bankruptcy Case, Heightening Risk for Dissolution of Group. NPR. Accessed July 25, 2022. https://www.npr.org/2021/05/11/995934682/judge-dismisses-nra-bankruptcy-case-heightening-risk-for-dissolution-of-group.

Mann, M. (2005). *The Dark Side of Democracy: Explaining Ethnic Cleansing*. Cambridge University Press.

Mann, M. and Schleifer, C. (2020). Love the Science, Hate the Scientists: Conservative Identity Protects Belief in Science and Undermines Trust in Scientists. *Social Forces*, 99(1), 305–332.

Marbut, G. (2021). Armed Rallies at State Capitols? Beware: Potential False Flag Event. *Ammoland*. Accessed October 25, 2021. https://www.ammoland.com/2021/01/armed-rallies-at-state-capitols-beware-false-flag-event/.

Martel, B. (2015). Katrina May Have Killed Thousands in New Orleans, Mayor Says. *Billings Gazette*. Accessed August 2, 2021. https://billingsgazette.com/news/national/katrina-may-have-killed-thousands-in-new-orleans-mayor-says/article_8635402d-ee24-5a89-98a9-5408cf21aa1d.amp.html.

Martherus, J. L., Martinez, A. G., Piff, P. K., and Theodoridis, A. G. (2021). Party Animals? Extreme Partisan Polarization and Dehumanization. *Political Behavior*, 43(2), 517–540.

Mauger, C. and Leblanc, B. (2020). Trump Tweets 'Liberate' Michigan, Two Other States with Dem Governors. Accessed April 27, 2022. *The Detroit News*. https://www.detroitnews.com/story/news/politics/2020/04/17/trump-tweets-liberate-michigan-other-states-democratic-governors/5152037002/.

Mazziotta, J. (2020). Man Who Called COVID a "Hoax" Feels Guilty After He and 13 Family Members Test Positive—and 2 Die. *People*. Accessed August 10, 2021. https://people.com/health/man-called-covid-hoax-feels-guilty-14-family-members-test-positive-2-die/.

McCarthy, J. (2014). More Than Six in 10 Americans Say Guns Make Homes Safer. *Gallup*. Accessed July 14, 2021. https://news.gallup.com/poll/179213/six-americans-say-guns-homes-safer.aspx.

McCaughey, M. (1997). *Real Knockouts: The Physical Feminism of Women's Self-Defense*. NYU Press.

McMillan, R. (2020). Modern Day 2A: Fighting the Gun Culture War in the Trenches. *The Truth About Guns*. Accessed October 24, 2021. https://www.thetruthaboutguns.com/modern-day -2a-fighting-the-gun-culture-war-in-the-trenches/.

Melzer, S. (2018). Fighting the Left and Leading the Right: NRA Politics and Power Through the 2016 Elections. Pp. 117–135 in *Gun Studies: Interdisciplinary Approaches to Politics, Policy, and Practice*. Routledge.

Merlan, A. (2019). *Republic of Lies: American Conspiracy Theorists and Their Surprising Rise to Power*. Metropolitan Books.

Metzl, J. M. (2010). *The Protest Psychosis: How Schizophrenia Became a Black Disease*. Beacon Press.

Metzl, J. M. (2019). *Dying of Whiteness: How the Politics of Racial Resentment Is Killing America's Heartland*. Basic Books.

Michigan Executive Order 2020–21. (2020). Accessed August 2, 2021. https://www.michigan .gov/whitmer/0,9309,7-387-90499_90705-522626—,00.html.

Micklethwait, J. and Wooldridge, A. (2004). *The Right Nation: Conservative Power in America*. Penguin.

Miller, J. M., Saunders, K. L., and Farhart, C. E. (2016). Conspiracy Endorsement as Motivated Reasoning: The Moderating Roles of Political Knowledge and Trust. *American Journal of Political Science*, 60(4), 824–844.

Mills, C. (1997). *The Racial Contract*. Cornell University Press.

Mills, C. W. (1958). The Structure of Power in American Society. *British Journal of Sociology*, 9(1), 29–41.

Milman, O. (2020). Seven of Donald Trump's Most Misleading Coronavirus Claims. *The Guardian*. Accessed August 10, 2021. https://www.theguardian.com/us-news/2020/mar/28 /trump-coronavirus-misleading-claims.

Mintz, B. (2021). Neoliberalism and the Crisis in Higher Education: The Cost of Ideology. *American Journal of Economics and Sociology*, 80(1), 79–112.

Mogelson, L. (2021). A Reporter's Video from Inside the Capitol Siege. *The New Yorker*. Accessed October 26, 2021. https://www.newyorker.com/video/watch/a-reporters-footage -from-inside-the-capitol-siege.

Mordecai, M. and Connaughton, A. (2020). Public Opinion About Coronavirus Is More Politically Divided in U.S. Than in Other Advanced Economies. *Pew Research Center*. Accessed July 19, 2021. https://www.pewresearch.org/fact-tank/2020/10/28/public-opinion-about -coronavirus-is-more-politically-divided-in-u-s-than-in-other-advanced-economies/.

Morse, R. (2020a). Should You Be a Slave to My Fears? *Ammoland*. Accessed September 20, 2021. https://www.ammoland.com/2020/05/should-you-be-a-slave-to-my-fears /#axzz76xaeNbvg.

Morse, R. (2020b). Yes, You Need a Gun During the Virus Scare . . . and After. *Ammoland*. Accessed October 24, 2021. https://www.ammoland.com/2020/03/yes-you-need-a-gun -during-the-virus-scare-and-after/#axzz796PBmhRj.

Motta, M. (2018). The Polarizing Effect of the March for Science on Attitudes toward Scientists. *Political Science & Politics*, 51(4), 782.

Moyer, M. W. (2017). More Guns Do Not Stop More Crimes, Evidence Shows. *Scientific American*. Accessed May 9, 2022. https://www.scientificamerican.com/article/more-guns-do-not-stop-more-crimes-evidence-shows/.

Müller, J. W. (2021). *Democracy Rules*. Farrar, Straus and Giroux.

Murakawa, N. (2014). *The First Civil Right: How Liberals Built Prison America*. Oxford University Press.

Mzezewa, T., Burch, A., and Fausset, R. (2022). Three Men are Found Guilty of Hate Crimes in Arbery Killing. *New York Times*. Accessed July 27, 2022. https://www.nytimes.com/2022/02/22/us/gregory-mcmichael-travis-mcmichael-william-bryan.html.

National Shooting Sports Foundation. (2020a). First-time Gun Buyers Grow to Nearly 5 Million in 2020. Accessed August 2, 2021. https://www.nssf.org/articles/first-time-gun-buyers-grow-to-nearly-5-million-in-2020/.

National Shooting Sports Foundation. (2020b). NSSF Thanks Trump Administration for Industry's Infrastructure Designation. Accessed August 4, 2021. https://www.nssf.org/articles/nssf-thanks-trump-administration-for-industrys-critical-infrastructure-designation/.

National Shooting Sports Foundation. (2021a). Firearm and Ammunition Industry Economic Impact Report 2021. Accessed August 2, 2021. https://www.nssf.org/wp-content/uploads/2021/03/2021-Firearm-Ammunition-Industry-Economic-Impact.pdf.

National Shooting Sports Foundation. (2021b). Firearm Freedoms Do Not End During Emergencies. Accessed August 2, 2021. https://www.nssf.org/wp-content/uploads/2021/03/NSSF-factsheet-Emergency-Powers.pdf.

Newton, H. P. (1980). War Against the Panthers: A Study of Repression in America (Doctoral dissertation, UC Santa Cruz). *Online University of the Left*. Accessed August 17, 2021. http://ouleft.org/wp-content/uploads/Huey-WATP.pdf.

Nichols, T. (2017). *The Death of Expertise: The Campaign Against Established Knowledge and Why It Matters*. Oxford University Press.

Niedzwiadek, N. (2020). Trump Goes After Black Lives Matter, "Toxic Propaganda" in Schools. *Politico*. Accessed August 12, 2021. https://www.politico.com/news/2020/09/17/trump-black-lives-matter-1619-project-417162.

Novak, M. (2020). Man Who Famously Died From Covid Says Covid Isn't Very Deadly. *Gizmodo*. Accessed August 10, 2021. https://gizmodo.com/man-who-famously-died-from-covid-says-covid-isnt-very-d-1844901909.

NRA. (2020). Disabled Woman Weak to Coronavirus Issues Message to Politicians Using Pandemic to Push Gun Control. YouTube. Accessed August 2, 2021. https://www.youtube.com/watch?v=z8fvDk4E5Pk.

NRA-ILA. (2006). Congress Passes NRA-backed "Disaster Recovery Personal Protection Act of 2006." Accessed August 2, 2021. https://www.nraila.org/articles/20061002/congress-passes-nra-backed-disaster.

NRA-ILA. (2015). A Decade Later, Remember New Orleans . . . Gun Confiscation Can (and Has) Happened in America. Accessed August 2, 2021. https://www.nraila.org/articles/20150821/a-decade-later-remember-new-orleans-gun-confiscation-can-and-has-happened-in-america.

NRA-ILA. (2019). Working Together to Save the Second Amendment Part II: State Success Stories. Accessed August 2, 2021. https://www.nraila.org/articles/20190521/working -together-to-save-the-second-amendment-part-ii-state-success-stories.

NRA-ILA. (2020a). Arizona: Second Amendment Rights Protected by Governor's Executive Order. Accessed August 2, 2021. https://www.nraila.org/articles/20200324/arizona-second -amendment-rights-protected-by-governor-s-executive-order.

NRA-ILA. (2020b). Cities Seek to Close Gun Stores, Claim Exercise of Second Amendment Rights "Non-Essential." Accessed August 3, 2021. https://www.nraila.org/articles/20200320 /cities-seek-to-close-gun-stores-claim-exercise-of-second-amendment-rights-non-essential ?utm_campaign=InSight%20Newlsetters&utm_source=hs_email&utm_medium=email& _hsenc=p2ANqtz-8X4NfvTAnhEAS_mvJHyjzjuDN31WxggJM-H5FP0qume_pLzCd 9Ve6Md71HarjUe0zB_WPA.

NRA-ILA. (2020c). Georgia: Gov. Kemp Protects Second Amendment—Gun Stores to Remain Open. Accessed August 2, 2021. https://www.nraila.org/articles/20200403/georgia -gov-kemp-protects-second-amendment-gun-stores-to-remain-open.

NRA-ILA. (2020d). Indiana: Attorney General Opinion Protects Second Amendment. Accessed August 2, 2021. https://www.nraila.org/articles/20200402/indiana-attorney-general -opinion-protects-second-amendment.

NRA-ILA. (2020e). Kansas: Legislature Passes Emergency Powers Legislation and Adjourns from Special Session. Accessed August 2, 2021. https://www.nraila.org/articles/20200605 /kansas-legislature-passes-emergency-powers-legislation-and-adjourns-from-special -session.

NRA-ILA. (2020f). New Hampshire: Gov. Sununu Protects Second Amendment—Gun Stores Remain Open. Accessed August 2, 2021. https://www.nraila.org/articles/20200327/new -hampshire-gov-sununu-protects-second-amendment-gun-stores-remain-open.

NRA-ILA. (2020g). NRA Applauds Protection of Rights During Disasters in South Dakota. Accessed August 2, 2021. https://www.nraila.org/articles/20200331/nra-applauds -protection-of-rights-during-disasters-in-south-dakota.

NRA-ILA. (2020h). Ohio: Emergency Powers Legislation Scheduled for House Committee Hearing Tomorrow. Accessed August 2, 2021. https://www.nraila.org/articles/20201207 /ohio-emergency-powers-legislation-scheduled-for-house-committee-hearing-tomorrow.

NRA-ILA. (2020i). Pandemic Engenders Appreciation for Second Amendment Rights. Accessed August 2, 2021. https://www.nraila.org/articles/20200320/pandemic-engenders -appreciation-for-second-amendment-rights.

NRA-ILA. (2020j). South Carolina: Gov. McMaster Protects Second Amendment Rights. Accessed August 2, 2021. https://www.nraila.org/articles/20200407/south-carolina-gov -mcmaster-protects-second-amendment-rights.

NRA-ILA. (2020k). U.S. Senators Use COVID-19 to Push Longtime Gun Control Agenda. Accessed August 4, 2021. https://www.nraila.org/articles/20200420/us-senators-use-covid -19-to-push-longtime-gun-control-agenda.

NRA-ILA. (2020l). Wisconsin: Second Amendment Rights Protected by Governor's Emergency Order. Accessed August 2, 2021. https://www.nraila.org/articles/20200324 /wisconsin-second-amendment-rights-protected-by-governors-emergency-order.

Obert, J. and Schultz, E. (2020). Right Wing Militias, Guns, and the Technics of State Power. *Law, Culture, and the Humanities*, 16(2), 236–249.

Oliver, J. E. and Rahn, W. M. (2016). Rise of the *Trumpenvolk:* Populism in the 2016 Election. *The ANNALS of the American Academy of Political and Social Science*, 667(1), 189–206.

Omi, M. and Winant, H. (2014). *Racial Formation in the United States*. Routledge.

Ong, C., Zhang, A., and Shaw, V. (2021). Asian American, Asian Immigrant, and Pacific Islander Businesses and Workers During COVID-19 Recovery, Resilience, and Loss. *Report from the National Hazards Center*.

Oppel Jr., R. A., Taylor, D. B., and Bogel-Burroughs, N. (2021). What to Know About Breonna Taylor's Death. *New York Times*. Accessed July 15, 2021. https://www.nytimes.com/article/breonna-taylor-police.html.

Overton, S. (2022). Jan. 6 Attack on Multiracial Democracy Requires Senate to Protect Freedom to Vote. *The Hill*. Accessed January 7, 2022. https://thehill.com/opinion/campaign/588534-jan-6-attack-on-multiracial-democracy-requires-senate-to-protect-freedom-to.

Owusu-Bempah, A. (2016). Race and Policing in Historical Context: Dehumanization and the Policing of Black People in the 21st Century. *Theoretical Criminology*, 21(1), 23–34.

Parker, K. (2019). The Growing Partisan Divide in Views of Higher Education. *Pew Research Center*. Accessed July 19, 2021. https://www.pewresearch.org/social-trends/2019/08/19/the-growing-partisan-divide-in-views-of-higher-education-2/.

Parker, K., Horowitz, J. M., and Anderson, M. (2020). Amid Protests, Majorities Across Racial and Ethnic Groups Express Support for Black Lives Matter. *Pew Research Center*. Accessed July 21, 2022. https://www.pewresearch.org/social-trends/2020/06/12/amid-protests-majorities-across-racial-and-ethnic-groups-express-support-for-the-black-lives-matter-movement/.

Peck, R. (2019). *Fox Populism: Branding Conservatism as Working Class*. Cambridge University Press.

Peele, T. and Salonga, R. (2020). Coronavirus: Are Gun Stores Essential? Governor Newsom Sidesteps That Question, Leaves It to the Counties. *Mercury News*. Accessed August 2, 2021. https://www.mercurynews.com/2020/03/25/coronavirus-are-gun-stores-essential-governor-sidesteps-that-question-leaves-it-to-the-counties/.

Pence, C. (2020). Guns, Germs and Government: Why Americans Love Liberty More Than Safety. *The Truth About Guns*. Accessed October 24, 2021. https://www.thetruthaboutguns.com/guns-germs-and-government-why-americans-love-liberty-more-than-safety/.

Pérez, R. (2022). *The Souls of White Jokes*. Stanford University Press.

Perrin, A. J. (2009). *Citizen Speak*. University of Chicago Press.

Perrin, A. J. (2014). *American Democracy*. Polity Press.

Perrin, A., Roos, J., and Gauchat, G. (2014). From Coalition to Constraint: Modes of Thought in Contemporary American Conservatism. *Sociological Forum*, 29(2), 285–300.

Pew Research Center. (2016). Partisanship and Political Animosity in 2016. Accessed September 16, 2021. https://www.pewresearch.org/politics/2016/06/22/partisanship-and-political-animosity-in-2016/.

Pew Research Center. (2017). Race, Immigration and Discrimination. Accessed July 19, 2021. https://www.pewresearch.org/politics/2017/10/05/4-race-immigration-and-discrimination/.

Pew Research Center. (2019a). Americans' Struggles with Truth, Accuracy and Accountability. Accessed July 15, 2021. https://www.pewresearch.org/politics/2019/07/22/americans -struggles-with-truth-accuracy-and-accountability/.

Pew Research Center. (2019b). How Americans See Problems of Trust. Accessed July 15, 2021. https://www.pewresearch.org/politics/2019/07/22/how-americans-see-problems-of-trust/.

Pew Research Center. (2019c). How Partisans View Each Other. Accessed September 16, 2021. https://www.pewresearch.org/politics/2019/10/10/how-partisans-view-each-other/.

Pew Research Center. (2019d). In a Politically Polarized Era, Sharp Divides in Both Partisan Coalitions. Accessed July 19, 2021. https://www.pewresearch.org/politics/2019/12/17/in -a-politically-polarized-era-sharp-divides-in-both-partisan-coalitions/.

Pew Research Center. (2019e). The State of Personal Trust. Accessed July 15, 2021. https://www .pewresearch.org/politics/2019/07/22/the-state-of-personal-trust/.

Pew Research Center. (2019f). Partisan Antipathy: More Intense, More Personal. Accessed July 21, 2022. https://www.pewresearch.org/politics/2019/10/10/partisan-antipathy-more -intense-more-personal/.

Pew Research Center. (2020). Republicans, Democrats Move Even Further Apart in Corona-virus Concerns. Accessed July 19, 2021. https://www.pewresearch.org/politics/2020/06/25 /republicans-democrats-move-even-further-apart-in-coronavirus-concerns/.

Pew Research Center. (2021). Voters' Reflections on the 2020 Election. Accessed October 19, 2021. https://www.pewresearch.org/politics/2021/01/15/voters-reflections-on-the-2020 -election/.

Philips, A. (2021). The Filibuster Debate Is (Maybe) Coming to a Head on Voting Rights. Here's What Could Happen. *Washington Post*. Accessed January 7, 2022. https://www .washingtonpost.com/politics/2021/12/14/filibuster-debate-is-maybe-coming-head -voting-rights-heres-what-could-happen/.

Phillips, W. and Milner, R. M. (2021). *You Are Here: A Field Guide for Navigating Polarized Speech, Conspiracy Theories, and Our Polluted Media Landscape*. MIT Press.

Phoenix, D. L. (2019). *The Anger Gap: How Race Shapes Emotion in Politics*. Cambridge University Press.

Piven, F. F. and Cloward, R. A. (2000). *Why Americans Still Don't Vote: And Why Politicians Want It That Way*. Beacon Press.

Popli, N. and Zorthian, J. (2022). What Happened to Jan. 6 Insurrectionists Arrested in the Year Since the Capitol Riot. *Time Magazine*. Accessed April 15, 2022. https://time.com/6133336 /jan-6-capitol-riot-arrests-sentences/.

Pozen, D. and Scheppele, K. M. (2020). Executive Underreach, in Pandemics and Otherwise. *American Journal of International Law*, 114(1), 608–617.

Putnam, R. D. (2000). *Bowling Alone: The Collapse and Revival of American Community*. Simon & Schuster.

Pybus, J. (2019). Trump, the First Facebook President: Why Politicians Need Our Data Too. Pp. 227–240 in *Trump's Media War*. Palgrave Macmillan.

Quinn, S. [@seattlesquinn]. (2021). *The Long 2020* [Tweet]. Twitter. https://twitter.com /seattlesquinn/status/1346934864738570242.

Ray, S. (2021). The Far-Right Is Flocking to These Alternative Social Media Apps—Not All of Them Are Thrilled. *Forbes*. Accessed December 2, 2021. https://www.forbes.com/sites

/siladityaray/2021/01/14/the-far-right-is-flocking-to-these-alternate-social-media-apps--
-not-all-of-them-are-thrilled/?sh=c89cd7655a44.

Reagan, R. (1981). Inaugural Address. Ronald Reagan Presidential Foundation and Institute. Accessed July 13, 2021. https://www.reaganfoundation.org/ronald-reagan/reagan-quotes -speeches/inaugural-address-2/.

Reed, B. (2021). Jan. 6 Rioter Starts Sobbing in Front of FBI Agents When Asked About Trump Calling Him to D.C. *Salon.* Accessed July 28, 2022. https://www.salon.com/2021/12/02/jan -6-rioter-starts-sobbing-in-front-of-fbi-agents-when-asked-about-calling-him-to-dc _partner/

Reny, T. T. and Barreto, M. A. (2020). Xenophobia in the Time of Pandemic: Othering, Anti-Asian Attitudes, and COVID-19. *Politics, Groups, and Identities,* 1–24.

Riehl, F. (2020a). America Burning, We Now Know What to Expect If Trump Wins in November. *Ammoland.* Accessed October 24, 2021. https://www.ammoland.com/2020/05 /america-burning-we-now-know-what-to-expect-if-trump-wins-in-november-video.

Riehl, F. (2020b). Coronavirus Update, Resources and Supplies 3-06-2020. *Ammoland.* Accessed September 20, 2021. https://www.ammoland.com/2020/03/coronavirus-update-resources -supplies.

Riehl, F. (2021). Keep Buying Guns and Ammo, Wherever You Find Them. *Ammoland.* Accessed October 26, 2021. https://www.ammoland.com/2021/01/keep-buying-guns-ammo -wherever-you-find-them.

Riley, D. (2019). *The Civic Foundations of Fascism in Europe.* Verso Books.

Rios, V. M. (2011). *Punished: Policing the Lives of Black and Latino Boys.* New York University Press.

Robinson, B. A. (2020). The Lavender Scare in Homonormative Times: Policing, Hyper-incarceration, and LGBTQ Youth Homelessness. *Gender & Society,* 34(2), 210–232.

Roose, K. (2021). What Is QAnon, the Viral Pro-Trump Conspiracy Theory?. *New York Times.* Accessed August 10, 2021. https://www.nytimes.com/article/what-is-qanon.html.

Roosevelt, K. (2021). I Spent 7 Months Studying Supreme Court Reform. We Need to Pack the Court Now. *Time Magazine.* Accessed January 7, 2022. https://time.com/6127193/supreme -court-reform-expansion/.

Rosenblum, N. L. and Muirhead, R. (2020). *A Lot of People Are Saying: The New Conspiracism and the Assault on Democracy.* Princeton University Press.

Ross, B. (2021). Guns and the Tyranny of American Republicanism. *The Brennan Center for Justice.* Accessed October 27, 2021. https://www.brennancenter.org/sites/default/files/2021 -06/Ross_final.pdf.

Roy, A. (2020). No, Trump Didn't Win "The Largest Share of Non-White Voters of Any Republican in 60 Years." *Forbes.* Accessed April 15, 2021. https://www.forbes.com/sites /theapothecary/2020/11/09/no-trump-didnt-win-the-largest-share-of-non-white-voters -of-any-republican-in-60-years/?sh=754ddc494a09.

Russell-Brown, K. (2009). *The Color of Crime.* NYU Press.

Rust, S. (2019). Report Details How Exxon Mobil and Fossil Fuel Firms Sowed Seeds of Doubt on Climate Change. *Los Angeles Times.* Accessed August 12, 2021. https://www.latimes.com /environment/story/2019-10-21/oil-companies-exxon-climate-change-denial-report.

Salazar, M. (2020). "I Didn't Believe in It": Man Who Thought Virus Was a Hoax Was Days Away from Dying. News 4 San Antonio. Accessed August 10, 2021. https://news4sanantonio.com/news/coronavirus/i-didnt-believe-in-it-man-who-thought-virus-was-a-hoax-was-days-away-from-dying.

Sallaz, J. J. and Wang, C. P. (2016). Sumptuary Labor: How Liberal Market Economies Regulate Consumption. *Politics & Society*, 44(4), 551–572.

Sanders, L., Smith, M., and Ballard, J. (2021). "Most Voters Say the Events at the US Capitol Are a Threat to Democracy." YouGov.com. Accessed April 15, 2022. https://today.yougov.com/topics/politics/articles-reports/2021/01/06/US-capitol-trump-poll.

Saslow, E. (2020). Voices from the Pandemic: "What are we so afraid of?". *Washington Post*. Accessed August 10, 2021. https://www.washingtonpost.com/nation/2020/10/10/coronavirus-denier-sick-spreader/?arc404=true.

Savidge, M. and Cartaya, M. (2021). Americans Bought Guns in Record Numbers in 2020 During a Year of Unrest—and the Surge Is Continuing. CNN. Accessed May 11, 2022. https://www.cnn.com/2021/03/14/us/us-gun-sales-record/index.html.

Schleimer, J. P., McCort, C. D., Shev, A. B., Pear, V. A., Tomsich, E., De Biasi, A., . . . and Wintemute, G. J. (2021). Firearm Purchasing and Firearm Violence During the Coronavirus Pandemic in the United States: A Cross-Sectional Study. *Injury Epidemiology*, 8(1), 1–10.

Schmidt, M. and Broadwater, L. (2021). Officers' Injuries, Including Concussions, Show Scope of Violence at Capitol Riot. *New York Times*. Accessed April 15, 2022. https://www.nytimes.com/2021/02/11/us/politics/capitol-riot-police-officer-injuries.html.

Schradie, J. (2019). *The Revolution That Wasn't*. Harvard University Press.

Schram, S. F. (2018). Neoliberalizing the Welfare State: Marketizing Social Policy/ Disciplining Clients. Pp. 308–322 in *The Sage Handbook of Neoliberalism*. Sage.

Schutten, N. M., Pickett, J. T., Burton, A. L., Jonson, C. L., Cullen, F. T., and Burton, Jr., V. S. (2021). Are Guns the New Dog Whistle? Gun Control, Racial Resentment, and Vote Choice. *Criminology*, 60(1), 90–123.

Schwartz, N. S. (2021). Called to Arms: The NRA, the Gun Culture & Women. *Critical Policy Studies*, 15(1), 74–89.

Seewer, J. (2020). America's Preppers Are Finally Getting a Little Respect. *The Truth About Guns*. Accessed September 17, 2021. https://www.thetruthaboutguns.com/americas-preppers-are-finally-getting-a-little-respect/.

Sefllc. (2020). The Grand Rapids LipDub (NEW WORLD RECORD). YouTube. Accessed August 16, 2021. https://www.youtube.com/watch?v=ZPjjZCO67WI.

Silverstein, J. (2013). I Don't Feel Your Pain. *Slate*. Accessed August 16, 2021. https://slate.com/technology/2013/06/racial-empathy-gap-people-dont-perceive-pain-in-other-races.html.

Silverstein, J. (2019). Why We Published the 1619 Project. *The New York Times Magazine*. Accessed August 12, 2021. https://www.nytimes.com/interactive/2019/12/20/magazine/1619-intro.html.

Simmons-Duffin, S. (2021). Poll Finds Public Health Has a Trust Problem. NPR. Accessed October 22, 2021. https://www.npr.org/2021/05/13/996331692/poll-finds-public-health-has-a-trust-problem.

Simon, J. (2010). Consuming Obsessions: Housing, Homicide, and Mass Incarceration since 1950. *University of Chicago Legal Forum*, 1(7), 165–204.

Simon, R. (2020). State Preemption of Local Gun Regulations: Taking Aim at Barriers to Change in Firearm Policy. *SSRN*, 1–59.

Simpson, M. (2020). For a Prefigurative Pandemic Politics: Disrupting the Racial Colonial Quarantine. *Political Geography*, 84(2021). doi: https://doi.org/10.1016/j.polgeo.2020 .102274.

Sims, J. P., Pirtle, W. L., and Johnson-Arnold, I. (2020). Doing Hair, Doing Race: The Influence of Hairstyle on Racial Perception Across the US. *Ethnic and Racial Studies*, 43(12), 2099–2119.

Singh, R. (2022). Data Shows There's More Diversity at a Gun Range Than a University Faculty Lounge. *Bearing Arms*. Accessed April 18, 2022. https://bearingarms.com/ranjit-singh/2022 /01/24/data-shows-theres-more-diversity-at-a-gun-range-than-a-university-faculty-lounge -n54707.

Skocpol, T. and Williamson, V. (2016). *The Tea Party and the Remaking of Republican Conservatism*. Oxford University Press.

Skolnick, J. (2002). Corruption and the Blue Code of Silence. *Policing Practice and Research*, 3(1), 7–19.

Smallpage, S. M., Enders, A. M., and Uscinski, J. E. (2017). The Partisan Contours of Conspiracy Beliefs. *Research and Politics*, 4(4), 1–7.

Smith, A. (2016). Why Gun Stocks Are Plunging Since Trump Won. CNN. Accessed August 3, 2021. https://money.cnn.com/2016/11/11/news/companies/trump-gun-stocks/.

Sobieraj, S., Berry, J. M., and Connors, A. (2013). Outrageous Political Opinion and Political Anxiety in the US. *Poetics*, 41(5), 407–432.

Sokol, J. (2008). *There Goes My Everything: White Southerners in the Age of Civil Rights, 1945–1975*. Vintage.

Soss, J. and Weaver, V. (2017). Police Are Our Government: Politics, Political Science, and the Policing of Race-Class Subjugated Communities. *Annual Review of Political Science*, 20(1), 565–591.

Spencer, C. (2021). Gun Ownership Among Black Americans Is Soaring. *The Hill*. Accessed April 18, 2022. https://thehill.com/changing-america/respect/diversity-inclusion/546454 -gun-ownership-among-black-americans-is-soaring/.

Spitzer, R. J. (2020). *The Politics of Gun Control*. Routledge.

Spring, M. (2020). Man Who Believed Virus Was Hoax Loses Wife to Covid-19. BBC News. Accessed August 10, 2021. https://www.bbc.com/news/world-us-canada-53892856.

SSRS. (2021). CNN/SSRS PollAccessed October 24, 2021. http://cdn.cnn.com/cnn/2021 /images/09/15/rel5e.-.elections.pdf.

Starbucks. (2022). "Culture and Values." Accessed March 14, 2022. https://www.starbucks.com /careers/working-at-starbucks/culture-and-values/.

Stelter, B. (2021). *Hoax: Donald Trump, Fox News, and the Dangerous Distortion of Truth*. Atria/ One Signal Publishers.

Steuter, E. and Wills, D. (2010). "The Vermin Have Struck Again": Dehumanizing the Enemy in Post 9/11 Media Representations. *Media, War & Conflict*, 3(2), 152–167.

Stolberg, S. G. (2005). Congress Passes New Legal Shield for Gun Industry. *New York Times.* Accessed July 19, 2021. https://www.nytimes.com/2005/10/21/politics/congress-passes -new-legal-shield-for-gun-industry.html.

Stroud, A. (2016). *Good Guys with Guns: The Appeal and Consequences of Concealed Carry.* University of North Carolina Press.

Stroud, A. (2020). Guns Don't Kill People . . . : Good Guys and the Legitimization of Gun Violence. *Humanities and Social Sciences Communications,* 7(1), 1–7.

Suber, H. (1979). Politics and Popular Culture: Hollywood at Bay, 1933–1953. *American Jewish History,* 68(4), 517–533.

Sullivan, B. and Bowman, E. (2021). Garrett Rolfe, Officer Fired in Rayshard Brooks Killing, Reinstated But Put On Leave. NPR. Accessed July 15, 2021. https://www.npr.org/2021/05 /05/993842478/fired-atlanta-officer-who-shot-rayshard-brooks-reinstated-due-to -personnel-rules.

Sulzberger, A. G. (2019). Accusing the New York Times of "Treason," Trump Crosses a Line. *Wall Street Journal.* Accessed August 12, 2021. https://www.wsj.com/articles/accusing-the -new-york-times-of-treason-trump-crosses-a-line-11560985187.

Sun, L. H. and Achenbach, J. (2020). CDC's Credibility Is Eroded by Internal Blunders and External Attacks as Coronavirus Vaccine Campaigns Loom. *Washington Post.* Accessed October 22, 2021. https://www.washingtonpost.com/health/2020/09/28/cdc-under -attack/.

Sunstein, C. R. (2002). The Law of Group Polarization. *Journal of Political Philosophy,* 10(2), 175–195.

Sunstein, C. R. (2009). *Going to Extremes: How Like Minds Unite and Divide.* Oxford University Press.

Swidler, A. (1986). Culture in Action: Symbols and Strategies. *American Sociological Review,* 51(2), 273–286.

Tavernise, S. (2021). An Arms Race in America. *New York Times.* Accessed January 3, 2022. https://www.nytimes.com/2021/05/29/us/gun-purchases-ownership-pandemic.html.

Tavory, I. and Timmermans, S. (2014). *Abductive Analysis: Theorizing Qualitative Research.* University of Chicago Press.

Taylor, C. (2020). Here's Why People Are Panic Buying and Stockpiling Toilet Paper to Cope with Coronavirus Fears. CNBC. Accessed August 3, 2021. https://www.cnbc.com/2020/03 /11/heres-why-people-are-panic-buying-and-stockpiling-toilet-paper.html.

Tchekmedyian, A. (2020). L.A. Supervisors Remove Sheriff Alex Villanueva as Head of Emergency Operations. *Los Angeles Times.* Accessed August 2, 2021. https://www.latimes.com /california/story/2020-03-31/supervisors-vote-remove-sheriff-emergency-operations.

Thebault, R. and Rindler, D. (2021). Shootings Never Stopped During the Pandemic: 2020 Was the Deadliest Gun Violence Year in Decades. *Washington Post.* Accessed October 26, 2021. https://www.washingtonpost.com/nation/2021/03/23/2020-shootings/.

Thomas, D. and Horowitz, J. M. (2020). Support for Black Lives Matter Has Decreased Since June But Remains Strong Among Black Americans. *Pew Research Center.* Accessed July 19, 2021. https://www.pewresearch.org/fact-tank/2020/09/16/support-for-black-lives-matter -has-decreased-since-june-but-remains-strong-among-black-americans/.

Thomas, T., Gabbatt, A., and Barr, C. (2020). Nearly 1,000 Instances of Police Brutality Recorded in US Anti-Racism Protests. *The Guardian*. Accessed July 13, 2021. https://www.theguardian.com/us-news/2020/oct/29/us-police-brutality-protest.

Thompson, L. (2020). A Florida Cop Killed Tony McDade. Now He's Hiding Behind a Law Meant to Protect Victims. *Mother Jones*. Accessed July 15, 2021. https://www.motherjones.com/crime-justice/2020/06/marsys-law-tony-mcdade-florida-police-killing-victim/.

Thornton, C., and Reich, J. (2022). Black Mothers and Vaccine Refusal: Gendered Racism, Healthcare, and the State. *Gender & Society*, 36(4), 525–551.

Torres, M. [@motorresx]. (2021). *"Democracy" is such a weak ideal in the United States that the word is essentially synonymous with the ballot box. Still, it's incredible to see such a crystal clear demonstration of this point lol* [Tweet]. Twitter. https://twitter.com/motorresx/status/1437965123985960962.

Toscano, A. (2020). Last Resorts: Jottings on the Pandemic State. *Crisis & Critique*, 3(7), 387–397.

Trawalter, S., Hoffman, K. M., and Waytz, A. (2012). Racial Bias in Perceptions of Others' Pain. *PloS one*, 7(11), 22–78.

Tripodi, F. (2018). Searching for Alternative Facts: Analyzing Scriptural Inference in Conservative News Practices. *Data and Society*. Accessed August 16, 2021. https://datasociety.net/wp-content/uploads/2018/05/Data_Society_Searching-for-Alternative-Facts.pdf.

Tripodi, F. B. (2021). ReOpen Demands as Public Health Threat: A Sociotechnical Framework for Understanding the Stickiness of Misinformation. *Computational and Mathematical Organization Theory*, 1–14.

TrueJKDAcademy. (2020). The Joker: It's Just a Mask. YouTube. Accessed September 20, 2021. https://www.youtube.com/watch?v=_VCdkNxSda8.

The Truth About Guns. (2020a). National Level Trainers Offering Free Beginning Gun Handling Videos. Accessed September 19, 2021. Accessed September 19, 2021. https://www.thetruthaboutguns.com/national-level-trainers-offering-free-beginning-gun-handling-videos/.

The Truth About Guns. (2020b). NSSF, Firearms Retailers Emphasizing Safety As Gun Sales Soar and Families Stay Home. Accessed September 19, 2021. https://www.thetruthaboutguns.com/nssf-firearms-retailers-emphasizing-safety-as-gun-sales-soar-and-families-stay-home/.

The Truth About Guns. (2020c). Versacarry Shifts Production from Holsters to Masks, Face Shields. Accessed September 20, 2021. https://www.thetruthaboutguns.com/versacarry-shifts-production-from-holsters-to-masks-face-shields/.

Tyson, A. (2020). Republicans Remain Far Less Likely Than Democrats to View COVID-19 as a Major Threat to Public Health. *Pew Research Center*. Accessed August 10, 2021. https://www.pewresearch.org/fact-tank/2020/07/22/republicans-remain-far-less-likely-than-democrats-to-view-covid-19-as-a-major-threat-to-public-health/.

USA Patriot Act, Public Law 107–56. (2001). Accessed August 2, 2021. https://www.congress.gov/107/plaws/publ56/PLAW-107publ56.pdf.

Uscinski, J. E. and Parent, J. M. (2014). *American Conspiracy Theories*. Oxford University Press.

van der Linden, S., Panagopoulos, F. A., and Jost, J. T. (2020). The Paranoid Style in American Politics Revisited: An Ideological Asymmetry in Conspiratorial Thinking. *Political Psychology*, 42(1), 23–51.

van Prooijen, J. W. and Douglas, K. M. (2017). Conspiracy Theories As Part of History: The Role of Societal Crisis Situations. *Memory Studies*, 10(3), 323–333.

Vegter, A. and Haider-Markel, D. (forthcoming). Religion and Gun Purchasing Amid a Pandemic, Civil Unrest, and an Election. In *An Epidemic among My People: Religion, Politics, and COVID-19 in the United States*, ed. P. Djupe and A. Friesen. Temple University Press.

Venkatraman, S. (2021). Anti-Asian Hate Crimes Rose 73% Last Year, Updated FBI Data Says. NBC News. Accessed April 18, 2022. https://www.nbcnews.com/news/asian-america/anti -asian-hate-crimes-rose-73-last-year-updated-fbi-data-says-rcna3741.

Wade, B. (2021). *Grieving While Black*. North Atlantic Books.

Waldron, I. (2020). The Wounds That Do Not Heal: Black Expendability and the Traumatizing Aftereffects of Anti-Black Police Violence. *Equality, Diversity and Inclusion: An International Journal*, 40(1), 29–40.

Walsh, J. (2022). U.S. Gun Sales Plummeted Last Month from Record-Breaking Pandemic Levels. *Forbes Magazine*. Accessed April 18, 2022. https://www.forbes.com/sites/joewalsh/2022 /02/01/us-gun-sales-plummeted-last-month-from-record-breaking-pandemic-levels/?sh =5e5668dd7e67.

Ware, M. (2020). COVID19, Virtue Signaling, and Victimology. *Ammoland*. Accessed September 20, 2021. https://www.ammoland.com/2020/07/covid19-virtue-signaling-and -victimology/#axzz761alXA5q.

Waters, A. M. (1997). Conspiracy Theories as Ethnosociologies: Explanation and Intention in African American Political Culture. *Journal of Black Studies*, 28(1), 112–125.

Waxman, O. B. (2019). Why Did the Manson Family Kill Sharon Tate? Here's the Story Charles Manson Told the Last Man Who Interviewed Him. *TIME*. Accessed August 3, 2021. https:// time.com/5633973/last-manson-interview/.

Weingarten, D. (2020). Breonna Taylor: Another No-Knock Raid Legitimately Resisted by Armed Force. *Ammoland*. Accessed October 24, 2021. https://www.ammoland.com/2020 /06/breonna-taylor-another-no-knock-raid-legitimately-resisted-by-armed-force /#axzz7AF6S7xmY.

Weinstein, A. (2015). The NRA Twisted a Tiny Part of the Katrina Disaster to Fit Its Bigger Agenda. *The Trace*. Accessed August 2, 2021. https://www.thetrace.org/2015/08/nra -hurricane-katrina-gun-confiscation/.

Welch, A. (2021). What Biden's Door-to-Door COVID-19 Vaccine Campaign Is—and Isn't. *Healthline*. Accessed August 2, 2021. https://www.healthline.com/health-news/what-bidens -door-to-door-covid-19-vaccine-campaign-is-and-isnt.

Wertz, J., Azrael, D., Hemenway, D., Sorenson, S., and Miller, M. (2018). Differences Between New and Long-Standing US Gun Owners: Results from a National Survey. *American Journal of Public Health*, 108(7), 871–877.

West, C. and Zimmerman, D. H. (1987). Doing Gender. *Gender & Society*, 1(2), 125–151.

White, K. C. (2018). *The Branding of Right-Wing Activism: The News Media and the Tea Party*. Oxford University Press.

The White House. (2021). Presidents: Woodrow Wilson. WhiteHouse.Gov. Accessed October 26, 2021. https://www.whitehouse.gov/about-the-white-house/presidents/woodrow -wilson/Whitehead, A. L., Schnabel, L., and Perry, S. L. (2018). Gun Control in the Crosshairs: Christian Nationalism and Opposition to Stricter Gun Laws. *Socius*, 4, 1–13.

williams, a., Owens, L., and Syedullah, J. (2016). *Radical Dharma: Talking Race, Love, and Liberation*. North Atlantic Books.

Williams, P. (2021). Kyle Rittenhouse, American Vigilante. *The New Yorker*. Accessed August 16, 2021. https://www.newyorker.com/magazine/2021/07/05/kyle-rittenhouse-american -vigilante.

Williamson, E. (2022). *Sandy Hook: An American Tragedy and the Battle for Truth*. Dutton.

Winfrey, O. and Perry, B. D. (2021). *What Happened to You?: Conversations on Trauma, Resilience, and Healing*. Flatiron Books.

Wingfield, A. H. and Feagin, J. (2012). The Racial Dialectic: President Barack Obama and the White Racial Frame. *Qualitative Sociology*, 35(1), 143–162.

Wintemute, G. J. (2021). Guns, Violence, Politics: The Gyre Widens. *Injury Epidemiology*, 8(1), 1–5.

Wodtke, G. T. (2016). Are Smart People Less Racist? Verbal Ability, Anti-Black Prejudice, and the Principle-Policy Paradox. *Social Problems*, 63(1), 21–45.

Wolfe, J. and Conlin, M. (2021). Landlord Groups Urge U.S. Supreme Court to End Pandemic Eviction Ban. Reuters. Accessed October 22, 2021. https://www.reuters.com/legal /government/landlord-group-urges-us-supreme-court-lift-cdc-eviction-freeze-2021-06-03/.

Wong, B. (2020). The Real, Tragic Story Behind that "Roof Korean" Meme You May Have Seen. *Huffington Post*. Accessed April 18, 2022. https://www.cnn.com/2017/04/28/us/la-riots -korean-americans/index.html.

Wos, D. (2020). The Political Left's Lust for Violence and the Control of Guns. *Ammoland*. Accessed October 24, 2021. https://www.ammoland.com/2020/06/the-political-lefts-lust -for-violence-and-the-control-of-guns/#axzz7AF6S7xmY.

Yam, K. (2022). Anti-Asian Hate Crimes Increased 339 Percent Nationwide Last Year, Report Says. NBC News. Accessed April 18, 2022. https://www.nbcnews.com/news/asian-america /anti-asian-hate-crimes-increased-339-percent-nationwide-last-year-repo-rcna14282.

Yamane, D. (2021). Gun Curious. Accessed July 19, 2021. https://guncurious.wordpress.com.

Yamane, D., DeDeyne, J., and Méndez, A. (2020). Who Are the Liberal Gun Owners? *Sociological Inquiry*, 91(2), 483–498.

Young, I. M. (2003). The Logic of Masculinist Protection: Reflections on the Current Security State. *Signs*, 29(1), 1–25.

Zamudio, M. M. and Rios, F. (2006). From Traditional to Liberal Racism: Living Racism in the Everyday. *Sociological Perspectives*, 49(4), 483–501.

Zengerle, J. (2021). Can the Black Rifle Coffee Company Become the Starbucks of the Right? *New York Times*. Accessed September 16, 2021. https://www.nytimes.com/2021/07/14 /magazine/black-rifle-coffee-company.html.

Zhelnina, A. (2020). The Apathy Syndrome: How We Are Trained Not to Care About Politics. *Social Problems*, 67(2), 358–378.

Zimmerman, D. (2020a). Are You Welcoming All the New Gun Owners or Asking Them Where the Hell They've Been? *The Truth About Guns*. Accessed September 20, 2021. https://www .thetruthaboutguns.com/are-you-welcoming-all-the-new-gun-owners-or-asking-them -where-the-hell-theyve-been/.

Zimmerman, D. (2020b). Karen Isn't Happy About Waiting to Get Her First Gun During an Emergency. *The Truth About Guns.* Accessed August 4, 2021. https://www.thetruthaboutguns .com/karen-isnt-happy-about-waiting-to-get-her-first-gun-in-an-emergency/.

Zimmerman, D. (2020c). Pennsylvania Doctor and School Board Member Threatens to Shoot Anyone Not Wearing a Mask. *The Truth About Guns.* Accessed October 24, 2021. https:// www.thetruthaboutguns.com/pennsylvania-doctor-and-school-board-member-threatens -to-shoot-anyone-not-wearing-a-mask/.

Zimmerman, D. (2020d). Want to See What Real Civil Unrest Looks Like? Try Confiscating Americans' Guns. *The Truth About Guns.* Accessed October 25, 2021. https://www .thetruthaboutguns.com/want-to-see-what-real-civil-unrest-looks-like-try-confiscating -americans-guns/.

Zingher, J. N. (2018). Polarization, Demographic Change, and White Flight from the Democratic Party. *Journal of Politics*, 80(3), 860–872.

INDEX

1619 Project, 89

2020 presidential election: conservative challenges to, 3–4, 27, 165; conspiracy theories about, 72, 147, 159; partisanship and, 101; political and cultural tensions linked to, 24. *See also* January 6th riot

abductive approach, 190, 199–200

Abramowitz, Alan, 109

African Americans: conspiracism among, 216n10; as gun owners, 56–57, 61–62, 145; killings of, in 2020, 37; pathologization of, 10, 54, 61, 213n44; racial empathy gap experienced by, 176, 219n69. *See also* Black Lives Matter; race

Alexander, Michelle, 10

alternative facts, 77, 78

American Rifleman (magazine), 134

Ammoland (news outlet), 31, 43, 109, 124, 126–27, 134, 147, 152, 166

Anderson, Carol, 70

Anestis, Michael, 56

Angeli, Jake, 75–76

anti-elitism, 13, 23, 25, 71–72, 77, 80–82, 84–85, 99, 122. *See also* science: skepticism and mistrust regarding

ANTIFA, 90, 93, 93–94

Arbery, Ahmaud, 145

Aristotle, 130

Arizona, 47–49

armed individualism, 36–69; conspiracism as complement to, 86, 97; freedom associated with, 7, 12, 41–42; history of, 37; January 6th riot as expression of, 6; overview

of, 36–38; Rittenhouse in relation to, 94–95; role of, in conservative worldview, 2–3, 8, 25; security and control associated with, 3, 8, 11, 25, 36–42, 47, 54–55, 57–59, 63, 67–68, 95–97, 102, 112, 115, 137–38, 172–73. *See also* gun culture; gun owners; gun rights; guns; individualism/self-reliance

Asian Americans: as gun owners, 59–60; prejudice and violence against, 59–61, 83, 143

authoritarianism, 26, 27, 67, 98, 151, 190

background checks/waiting periods, 1, 39, 50, 56, 63–64, 210n7

Bailyn, Bernard, 70

Bearing Arms (news outlet), 58

Bellah, Robert, 20–21, 171, 174–75

Belmont, Cynthia, 112

Berry, Jeffrey, 111

Biden, Joe: conservative antipathy toward, 37; and presidential election, 3–4, 24, 26, 27, 72, 147, 159, 165

binary thinking: good-evil as instance of, 78, 83; partisanship and, 48, 101, 104; populism and, 76–77. *See also* partisanship

bipartisanship, 104–5

Bishop, Bill, 106–7

Black Lives Matter (BLM): conspiracy theories and skepticism about, 2, 90–91, 93–94, 149–50; cultural and political significance of, 24, 89, 145, 176; gun sales boosted by, 54, 61–62; partisanship and, 100–101; social unrest attributed to, 54, 61, 90–91, 94–95, 101, 150–51, 213n44. *See also* protests and unrest